TENSIONS IN
THE AMERICAN DREAM

TENSIONS IN THE
AMERICAN DREAM

Rhetoric, Reverie, or Reality

Melanie E. L. Bush and
Roderick D. Bush

TEMPLE UNIVERSITY PRESS
Philadelphia • Rome • Tokyo

TEMPLE UNIVERSITY PRESS
Philadelphia, Pennsylvania 19122
www.temple.edu/tempress

Library of Congress Cataloging-in-Publication Data

Bush, Melanie E. L., 1955–
  Tensions in the American Dream : rhetoric, reverie, or reality / Melanie E. L. Bush and
Roderick Bush.
     pages cm
  Includes bibliographical references and index.
  ISBN 978-1-59213-837-1 (hardback : alk. paper) — ISBN 978-1-59213-838-8 (paperback :
alk. paper) — ISBN 978-1-59213-839-5 (e-book) 1. Social mobility—United States.
2. Marginality, Social—United States. 3. American Dream. I. Bush, Roderick D. II. Title.
  HN90.S65B87 2015
  301.0973—dc23

                                                                                2014017220

♾ The paper used in this publication meets the requirements of the American National
Standard for Information Sciences—Permanence of Paper for Printed Library Materials,
ANSI Z39.48-1992

Printed in the United States of America

9 8 7 6 5 4 3 2 1

To those who gave us so much and who shaped our strength and character:

Margaret Janette Bush (dignity and absolute fearlessness), Stanley Harold Levine (curiosity and unwavering questioning of pretty much everything), Aunt Honey/Margie Whipper (intellectual clarity and wisdom), and the effervescent, always luminous Roslyn Levine

To those to whom we have tried to give our best selves: Malik, Thembi, Sojourner Truth, Sarafina, and Andree

And to those for whom we will always strive to do better: Tajalia, Angelo, Orlando, Isabella, Jedidiah, and Wisdom

With you in mind, heart, and soul, we hope that the Tensions we identify in this book will soon become Celebrations of a more loving world.

This manuscript was submitted just two weeks before we learned that Rod had bile duct cancer and only six weeks before he passed. We had formally worked together on this project since 2006. And so, ultimately, this book is dedicated to him—to his generous and loving spirit; his intellectual breadth, depth, and vision; and his profound beliefs that the people will surely overcome not only Tensions in the American Dream but the inhumane systems that have organized our social world for centuries past and that we indeed build that better world with each loving act of kindness, generosity, fairness, and compassion.

My darling, this one's for you. We will be together again.

Contents

List of Tables   ix
Preface   xi

PART I. INTRODUCTION

1. Key Questions and Concepts   3
2. Citizenship and Nation   7
3. The Shifting Terrain Makes Clear the Tensions
   in the American Dream   15

PART II. STORIES OF MY AMERICA

4. Reflections on the Structural Logic of the System   31
5. Thoughts on the Current Juncture   69
6. Perspectives on the American Dream   91
7. Expressions of Revolt against the Systems   130

PART III. TENSIONS IN THE AMERICAN DREAM: RHETORIC, REVERIE, OR REALITY?

8. Nation: Empire or Liberation   151
9. Racial Nationalism and the Multiple Crises of the U.S. Nation   169
10. Going Forward, with Reflections on the Revolts of the Past Decade   178

Acknowledgments   211
Notes   213
References   219
Index   237

List of Tables

Table 4.1   How Often Do You Think about Your National Identity?   40

Table 4.2   I Consider Myself to Be Patriotic   40

Table 4.3   I Consider Myself to Be American   40

Table 4.4   To What Extent Do These Factors Contribute to the Higher
            Incomes and Wealth of Whites as a Group?   57

Table 4.5   To What Extent Do These Factors Contribute to the Lower
            Incomes and Wealth of Blacks as a Group?   57

Table 4.6   People of Color Are Treated Equally to Whites When Applying
            for Jobs and Housing and When Approached by Police   63

Table 4.7   The United States Is a Land of Equal Opportunity for All   63

Table 5.1   The Election of Barack Obama as President of the
            United States   86

Table 6.1   Questions about the American Dream   122

Table 6.2   To What Extent Have You Already Achieved the
            American Dream?   123

Table 6.3   To What Extent Do You Expect to Ever Achieve the
            American Dream?   123

Table 7.1   Beliefs about Social Supports   145

Table 7.2   Views of "Capitalism" and "Socialism"   145

Preface

Tensions in the American Dream is, in a way, the story of our quest (individually and collectively) to understand the world we were born into, grew up in, and came to live in. It is an expression of our hopes, our dreams, our disappointments, and our rootedness in the struggle for justice. This project was truly one that sought an understanding of the perspectives of those around us and whether, for them, the American Dream is just rhetoric, articulates their visions and reveries of the good life, or has indeed been their reality. We hope that you find yourself somewhere in this journey—in the history, in our analysis of contemporary times, or in our assessment of the future. For us, remembering and being centered by our roots is a matter of principle. We have so often been reminded by our elders never to forget where we came from. It is in this spirit that we share some of that personal history here.

Melanie grew up in the 1960s—a period when the beat of the times conveyed that we were the makers of history and that the poverty, racism, and violence of U.S. society could and would be challenged and overcome. The fury and indignation of rebellions against local, national, and global injustice inspired in her a vision of a better world and a belief in the possibilities for resistance to oppression and the construction of a democratic, just, and egalitarian society.

At the same time, it was apparent that the contradictions of race and class for ordinary white folks struggling to make ends meet collided with the righteous struggles for inclusion and equality of people of color. Most family and friends looked "up" for commonality and community and drew a great divide between themselves and other communities "below" that were struggling for survival, equality, and inclusion. As a child, going door to door with her father to rally against the war in Vietnam, Melanie gained an awareness of the tenuous nature of class consciousness and the way racial identity intersects and undercuts potential connections and community.

Later, shortly after the Québec State of Siege, she studied at McGill University, exploring world-systems theory with Immanuel Wallerstein, researching capital flows from the periphery to the core, and investigating the notion of the United States as a benevolent savior. She learned about the development of underdevelopment and worked with women in Montréal who were organizing around local issues. She was a member of the Women's Collective Press at McGill, examining issues of labor, economy, and gender from academic and community perspectives.

This involvement internationalized her curiosity and initiated an intense simultaneous pursuit of intellectual understanding and grassroots activism. This pursuit, in turn, became the context for the fuller development of her social commitment, ultimately leading her to seek an understanding of the forces that underlay inequality and the means by which people of goodwill could join oppressed people in the fight to destroy the forces of race, class, and gender oppression rooted in a system of capitalism, imperialism, patriarchy, white supremacy, and racism. From the mid-1970s to the mid-1980s, she worked doing full-time community organizing in the San Francisco Bay area. This period was when our paths crossed, as we began working together on issues of social and racial justice. The discussion of this work follows.

Rod, born during the era of Jim Crow, was a son of the southern Black working class whose mother followed the migratory path to northern urban marginality that had been the fate of so many. The circumstances of his birth and his deeply religious upbringing predisposed him toward an abiding interest in the questions of the elimination of poverty and disenfranchisement and the promotion of transformative social change. Since he believed fervently in the biblical injunction that the last shall be first, he was more than skeptical of the condescending visions of the poor that he found in much social science literature when he entered college in the early 1960s. But his close association with the sons and daughters of the Black upper middle class at the historically Black college Howard University undermined his confidence in his own self-worth over time. One of the most frequently invoked declarations about those who were not from an upper-middle-class background was "Some of us just aren't ready," implying that those from the lower classes did not have the sophistication and polish to fit into the Black bourgeoisie, much less white society. These ideas shattered his self-esteem, and for a while he felt totally off-balance among his middle- and upper-class peers at Howard, an experience familiar to many Black and Latino students today in predominantly white university structures with similar class distinctions and the added factor of racial differences.

A dormant social consciousness was complicated by the nationality question mostly unarticulated among African Americans in the South during the 1950s. Grade schools did not teach politics, civics, or history in any meaningful way in the Jim Crow schools that Rod attended; instead, they taught what he came to call "Booker T. Washington–ism," strategies for accommodating oneself to the brutality of white supremacy, ways to impress and avoid antagonizing white people, and demonstrations of studiously subservient and nonthreatening comportment in the presence of whites. This approach was undoubtedly geared toward self-protection, but young minds do not necessarily make the distinction that adult minds can, and internalizing a subservient demeanor can greatly damage a developing personality. Conversely, this instruction fostered very little connection to patriotism or identification with triumphal Americanism. Instead, his community was rooted in churches and in African people's triumphs against great odds, wherever they were evident. In Rochester, New York, the primary destination of migrants from Rod's birthplace in Florida and where he moved at age 14, the idea of questioning the status quo was largely dormant except for the interest sparked by the rise of the Nation of Islam in the early 1960s among inner-city residents.

This period represented historic times at Howard University, whose already incredibly rich history might easily be overlooked by those involved in the everyday struggle to survive and graduate. While studying at Howard between 1963 and 1967, Rod was deeply moved by militants from the Student Nonviolent Coordinating Committee (SNCC) who came to campus to inform students about the struggle in the South and to recruit people to go to Mississippi to join the fight for civil rights and democracy there. He was inspired by their courage but believed that such commitment was entirely outside the realm of what he could do.

Rod was at Howard when the dean of students refused to crown the newly elected homecoming queen, Robin Gregory, because she wore her hair in what was called an Afro or natural hairstyle, and he was there when the university fired Dr. Nathan Hare for proselytizing Black Power among students. He was sympathetic to Hare's plight but primarily from a stance of academic freedom.

He had been quite troubled by the Black bourgeois pretensions of the Howard University scene, both because of his own class position and because of the heightened awareness he gained by reading the works of E. Franklin Frazier, Hare's predecessor in the university's sociology department and the author of *Black Bourgeoisie*. At Howard, Rod was fortunate to be exposed to a rich Black intellectual tradition that included such scholars as Toni Morrison, Owen Dodsen, Frank Snowden, and Hare. After a junior-year class with Sterling Brown, the great Harlem Renaissance poet and literary critic, Rod began the long search for a way to give voice to his skepticism. During the last two years of his studies at Howard University, under Brown's tutelage, Rod undertook a course of study to gain literacy in the great writings of all people. As a child of the working class at a university whose traditions were primarily those of the Black middle class, he was in a confusing position. Although he did not understand class as an analytic construct at that time, he knew the experience intimately. As he sought the tools to understand the context for his racial and class backgrounds, he struggled for clarity. He graduated in 1967, carrying the weight of a great uncertainty about the causes of poverty, inequality, and racism and the possibility that change might never occur.

He continued on to a doctoral program in clinical psychology at the University of Kansas, where two events coincided: (1) When he sought a place to live, he was humiliated and outraged by the racism he confronted in the housing market and (2) the student movement for social change was beginning to gather steam on campuses across the nation. At Howard University (then referred to as the "Dean of Negro Colleges"), insurgents initiated a takeover of the administration building, demanding that Howard become a "Black" university (standing for the experience and concerns of Black people) rather than a "Negro" university (a university with Black students who thought like whites). At Columbia University, Black students took over an administration building to protest the school's expansionist activities in the neighboring Harlem community. White members of Students for a Democratic Society (SDS) entered the strike in support of the Black students and in opposition to the university's role in promoting the war against Vietnam.

Students at the University of Kansas, stirred by the Black Power movement, demanded that the university select a Black student to be on the school's Pom Pom Squad.[1] This action was the impetus for the formation of the Black Student Union on campus; meanwhile, some students (including Rod) also joined members of the community off campus in the Movement for Afro-American Unity (MAAU), which was consciously modeled after Malcolm X's Organization of Afro-American Unity. These were heady times. Rod vividly remembers sitting in Leonard and Alferdteen Harrison's living room during a meeting of MAAU and (at the age of 23) solemnly dedicating his life to the liberation of Black people.[2] At the time, young people often said that they could never trust anyone over 30, because they will change their views and become part of the system. But by the time Rod reached age 30, his convictions were stronger than ever, and there was no turning back. And now, there is *certainly* no turning back.

From MAAU in Lawrence, Kansas, and the Black Student Union at the University of Kansas, Rod went on to join the Congress of African People and then the Student Organization for Black Unity (which later changed its name to the Youth Organization for Black Unity [YOBU]). In the mid-1970s, YOBU joined the Malcolm X Liberation University, the People's College, the Lyn Eusan Institute, and the Marxist-Leninist Collective in San Francisco to form the Revolutionary Workers League (RWL), a Black Marxist organization. RWL merged with an offshoot of the Young Lords Party to form the Revolutionary Wing, but this formation was marked by an extreme form of leftist dogmatism and purged the great majority of its members for their lack of ideological purity. During this period, Rod left the psychology doctoral program at the University of Kansas (ABD) to devote himself more fully to the struggle for justice. He was unaffiliated for a year or so and then moved to the San Francisco Bay area, which was the locus of considerable social ferment and creative organizing.

It was here that our paths came together, as we worked in opposition to the burgeoning attack on the working class and the social compact that had been constituted in the New Deal and in the civil rights and liberation movements in the United States. We were involved with such projects as the Tax the Corporations initiatives and campaigns against U.S. involvement in southern Africa and Central America (U.S. Out of Central America [USOCA] and U.S. Out of Southern Africa [USOSA]). We also worked with people from the women's liberation movement, solidarity networks, and intellectuals involved with Latin America, SDS, the Nation of Islam, and the left wing of the Black Power movement associated with the Institute for the Study of Labor and Economic Justice, the Grass Roots Alliance, the Full Employment Project of Oakland, and the Democratic Workers Party. These organizations recruited thousands of people from the Black, Latino, and older white working classes into mass formations.

We worked with church folk in the Black and Latino communities and with Christians for Socialism, led by the Reverend Jose Luis Lana. There we learned about the vast possibilities of class unity based on opposition to racism and sexism. We ultimately succeeded with the Tax the Corporations initiative in 1980 in San Francisco and took this campaign to cities throughout the United States. The California Supreme Court later declared the initiative unconstitutional, but the effort represented a professional grassroots electoral organization that was more powerful than any other political force in the region.

When Ronald Reagan ran for the presidency in 1980, many asked how anyone could take him seriously—he was just an actor. But the poet Gil Scott-Heron was analytically prescient on this issue when he argued that Reagan was just what America needed in the face of the challenges at that time:

"You go give them liberals hell, Ronny." That was the mandate to the new Captain Bligh on the new Ship of Fools.

Obviously based on chameleon performances of the past: as a liberal Democrat. As the head of the Screen Actor's Guild. When other celluloid saviours were cringing in terror from McCarthyism Ron stood tall!

It goes all the way back from Hollywood to Hillbillies, from liberal to libelous, from Bonzo to Birchite to Born Again.

Civil Rights. Gay Rights. Women's Rights. They're all wrong! Call in the cavalry to disrupt this perception of freedom gone wild. First one of them wants freedom and then the whole damn world wants freedom!

Nostalgia. That's what America wants. The good old days. When we "gave them hell!" When the buck stopped somewhere and you could still buy something with it! To a time when movies were in black and white and so was everything else.

Let us go back to the campaign trail before six-gun Ron shot off his face and developed Hoof in Mouth. Before the free press went down before a full court press and were reluctant to view the menu because they knew that the only meal available was "crow."[3]

These were indeed serious challenges. During the early 1980s, we thought the task was to push beyond the reformism of the 1960s to the elaboration of a genuine revolutionary vision centered on what we called the lower and deeper working class (based among women and communities of color). Then Reagan became president, the air traffic controllers were fired, and the Nicaraguan contras were actively being supported by our tax dollars. We needed new intellectual leadership and activist vision; the organizations of the New Left within which we had come to intellectual and political maturity dissolved one by one. We returned to New York City (having lived there together in 1984) and once again tried to piece together an understanding of the world and a new perspective on local issues.

We were increasingly concerned with the centrality of racial animosity in daily life. Given the frequency of incidences of racial brutality, Eleanor Bumpers, Yusef Hawkins, and Michael Griffith became household names, as did Abner Louima and Amadou Diallo.[4] Most troubling was not the irrational cruelty of the individuals involved but the fact that these incidents appeared justifiable in the eyes of many whites. Why did people, particularly whites, refute the reality of bias? How did a wallet "become" a gun in the mind of the police officers who shot Diallo forty-one times, and how could that level of violence ever be justified?[5] As part of the process of reflecting on how to understand this moment in time and how we could contribute to the struggle for justice in the contemporary context, we returned to school. Melanie initially pursued a master's degree in public health, with a focus on international and community health, at Hunter College of the City University of New York, where she began to consider the relationship between ideology and agency and the maintenance of structures of inequality. She examined how health education was being pursued in the context of socialism and war in Zimbabwe and Tanzania, concluding that the thoughts and actions of ordinary people play a major role in shaping the conditions of everyday life and in turn influence social institutions that organize people's daily experience. Similarly, those structures influence consciousness.

In 1988, Rod entered the doctoral program in sociology at the State University of New York, Binghamton. Coming to adulthood in a period when the capacity for ordinary people to fight for social justice and social change was evident everywhere, Rod embarked on a research program that was infused with a spirit of optimism and possibility. He engaged in an effort to revive and reassess the analytic traditions derived within the Black freedom struggle by such scholars and activists as W.E.B. Du Bois, Paul Robeson, Malcolm X, Martin Luther King Jr., and others who were victims of official retribution and prevented from completing their intellectual agendas. At Binghamton, Rod had the opportunity to work with such world-class scholars as Immanuel Wallerstein, Terence K. Hopkins, and Giovanni Arrighi.

We Are Not What We Seem: Black Nationalism and Class Struggle in the American Century (1999) presents the first stage of this research. In this book, Rod contends that while the appropriate unit of analysis for understanding the modern world is a historical social system larger than the United States, the hegemonic position of the United States enormously magnifies the antisystemic potential of African American social movements. Because the evolution of the racial order after the abolition of slavery has been inextricably intertwined with processes of class formation in the United States and globally, Black activists and scholarly activists are able to speak clearly to the logic of a struggle for human rights over civil rights, a clearly universalistic position (though often in nationalist clothing) that transcends boundaries of race, class, and nation.

His 2009 book *The End of White World Supremacy* (as Malcolm X deemed somewhat prematurely) moves this analysis a step further by emphasizing changes in the global and domestic relations of force between the Euro-American world and the Dark World[6] and the role of African American agency in this ongoing transformation of the twenty-first century.

In 1994, Melanie entered the doctoral program in anthropology at the Graduate School and University Center of the City University of New York, where she worked with leading scholar Leith Mullings. There she formulated the research project that was published as *Breaking the Code of Good Intentions: Everyday Forms of Whiteness* (2004) and later as a second edition with updated primary data, *Everyday Forms of Whiteness: Understanding Race in a "Post-Racial" World* (2011). She sought to investigate the relationship between the thinking of everyday people (particularly whites) in the United States and patterns of racial inequality and injustice—how consciousness affects action and thus shapes how we might challenge historical social patterns that promote privileges for few and agony for many. A significant component of this investigation involved inquiry into the origins of white supremacy and how in national terms it translates into beliefs about "American" identity, the American Dream, and notions of equality, democracy, citizenship, and belonging.

Through the convergence of our fields of study, questions about nation, empire, race, capitalism, and democracy have arisen. In this book, we bring together these inquiries to suggest new ways of looking at the past, the present, and the future by focusing on what King meant when he argued, "We are caught in an inescapable network of mutuality, tied in a single garment of destiny. Whatever affects one directly, affects all indirectly."[7] King emerges in this period as a world leader, a drum major for justice, who "tried to love somebody," sought to redeem the soul of America, and called for a revolution of conscience wherein all people of goodwill should side with the shirtless and barefoot people of the world. It is in this spirit that this book is dedicated.

I

Introduction

1

Key Questions and Concepts

This is a book about belonging and nationalism in the United States of America, referred to simply as "America"[1] by most of its citizens, and many others around the world. It is also a story about the meaning of "America," what is unique about its character and possibilities, and its claim to being special in the history of nations on this planet. These intertwined issues are widely conceptualized in both lay and scholarly discourse as the spirit of American exceptionalism.

A little more than one century after its creation, the U.S. nation-state expanded to become a global power, including a pattern of territorial expansion deemed by many to be imperial. By the mid–twentieth century, the United States was the number-one world power. As the hegemonic power within the world-system, the United States was forced to consider how contradictions within its own borders reflected on its position as *the* world leader. Anticolonial struggles that occurred throughout the globe were often viewed as aligned with movements for social change among marginalized populations within its borders.[2] The nation struggled with the question of how it would be positioned and perceived in this new era of imperialism. How could the rhetoric of democracy and justice be rationalized as interventions around the globe intensified? In the 1980s, the Reagan era provided narratives of benevolence and leadership that justified military actions in the eyes of many people in the United States. By the time of George W. Bush's presidency, nationalism and patriotism expressed through military might were generally assumed to be virtues that trumped all else. After September 11, 2001, Bush told the public, "Either you are with us, or you are with the terrorists."[3]

However, various events simultaneously led to heightened contestation about the meaning and parameters of U.S. nationalism, patriotism, and loyalty. The oft-heard phrase "Support the Troops" began to signify interpretations simultaneously of sending more soldiers to war and of bringing home those already in combat; questioning and dissent were viewed as seditious by some and as matters of social responsibility among other public officials. This "nation of immigrants" spawned a new generation of minutemen to defend national borders from "outsiders," many of whom could claim that we stole their land rather than that they are stealing our resources.[4] We can easily say that "notions of nation" and who "belongs" have been in transition; the tensions of nation and belonging have never been more acute. With a growing foreign-born population,[5] the issue has been raised about whether the United States as a nation ever was or can truly ever be a veritable multicultural union or whether it is a nation guided by a hegemonic (white) Anglo-Protestant culture into which others are asked to assimilate, as Samuel Huntington (2004a, 2004b) asserts. Does claiming national allegiance provide a vantage point from which to stand for peace, justice, and equality (Nussbaum 1996, 136), or does it divide those within the U.S. nation (providing the rhetoric of "unity" despite radically disparate social and economic stations) and separate the U.S. population from peoples of other nations? Indeed, what functions do nationalism, patriotism, and citizenship serve in today's interconnected world in a nation founded and built on the presumption of empire?[6] What is the function of nation? What are the relationships between the political, economic, and social structures and ideologies of capitalism, white world supremacy/Euro dominance, the U.S. nation, and the idea of an American Dream?

With these questions in mind, in this book, we seek to address the origins and development of the U.S. nation and empire, the founding principles and their lived reality, the belief in exceptionalism, the issue of "belonging," the American Dream and the corresponding portrait of a "nation of immigrants," and the relevancy of nation to empire within the historical world capitalist system. We explore these topics historically as well as through the lens of contemporary respondents.

The eminent political scientist Rogers M. Smith tells us that since the inception of the United States, scholars have described the nation as the preeminent example of modern liberal democracy, a country in which governance is determined by popular consent, with respect for the equal rights of all people. Most assert that if this image has not been entirely true, then the history of U.S. political development has been a matter of working out these democratic principles over time. Illiberal and antidemocratic themes in U.S. history are mostly deemed exceptional, irrational, and destined for the dustbin of history, since these expressions are not part of the nation's creed (Smith 1993, 549).

Smith traces this affirming tradition to Alexis de Tocqueville's 1835 classic *Democracy in America*. While he accepts that this analysis of the United States contains some truths, he believes that Tocqueville does not properly recognize and proportion the inegalitarian and antidemocratic ideas that have shaped and undergirded U.S. political culture. For example, for two-thirds of U.S. history, the majority of the domestic population was not eligible for full U.S. citizenship because of their race, original nationality, lack of property, or gender. The subjects of Tocqueville's narrative are white men of northern European ancestry (Smith 1993, 549).

Joel Olsen shares Smith's reservation, pointing out that the early nineteenth century heralded the rise of the first mass democracy in the world yet was also one of the most turbulent and violent periods in U.S. history, marked by riots, lynch mobs, and insurrections, mostly in defense of slavery and the subordination of Africans. Olsen tells us that the mobs attacked "Black people, abolitionists, 'amalgamators' and anyone whose actions or mere existence not only challenged white supremacy, but systematically raised the specter of social equality" (2001, 164). These were not simply the actions of a few drunken mechanics but were organized and led by some of the nation's most prominent gentlemen: mayors, congressmen, attorneys general, physicians, lawyers, and newspaper editors. These riots were not seen by the perpetrators as antidemocratic but as defenses of democracy itself (Olsen 2001, 164). Race and racism were used to frame the very idea of democratic citizenship as a right of only those with no African blood.

Immanuel Wallerstein's (2003a) reflections on citizenship as a historically constructed concept provide a clearer understanding of its role in the modern world-system. While in theory, the concept of "the citizen" as articulated in the French Revolution was intended to be inclusive, in practice, citizenship has always been defined such that some are excluded. The reason for this disjuncture between rhetoric and reality is simple: Historical capitalism requires social inequality, though social stability is best served by public perception of equality of opportunity *and* the existence of real opportunity for upward mobility, at least for *some*. But upward opportunity for *all* would place a great deal of pressure on employers to pay higher wages. In a competitive economic system, employers of wage labor seek to impose some restraints on the pressure to pay higher wages. Wallerstein and others argue that inequality is a fundamental reality of the modern world-system, as has been the case for every known historical system. What they see as particular to historical capitalism is that equality and democracy have been proclaimed as its objective, and indeed as its achievement.

As we explore the contours of belonging, nationalism, and the American Dream, we take heed of the cautionary remarks of Smith, Olsen, and Wallerstein about the simultaneous inclusiveness and exclusiveness of citizenship in the United States. While this component of the tension is similar to what exists in all nations, the scale of the phenomenon in the United States requires special comment. We argue that to understand the modern world, we must recognize the inherent connection between capitalism/imperialism, white supremacy/ Euro dominance, the emergence of the U.S. nation as a "city on the hill," and the concept of the American Dream. Each of these has worked in synchrony, simultaneously supporting the development of the historical world-system aimed toward its contemporary crisis. The question is what will come next for each of these social realities.

We examine this history to understand whether an idea that seems so innocent—that of the possibility of a better life—could possibly have a dark side. Do these "tensions" coexist in a bipolar reality? Is it only a dream or reverie? Is it all rhetoric? Is the dream in fact a reality and questioned only by those unwilling or unable to achieve it? These questions form the substance of our inquiry.

2

Citizenship and Nation

Citizenship as a Concept

Cedric Robinson, Elizabeth Martinez, Roxanne Dunbar Ortiz, and others have argued that the formation of nation-states and political regimes always leads to the development and elaboration of "origin myths," which dominant strata use to promote social cohesion, legitimate the social order, and exercise class hegemony. In the United States, a central motif running through these narratives is the destruction and domination of savages (those who are illiterate, ignorant, undeserving poor, illegals, and so forth) in the interests of a higher civilization. In the original formulation, these savages were the indigenous peoples of the Americas and the Africans, though this discourse has been applied throughout the course of U.S. history to such policies as manifest destiny and in imperial conquests throughout the globe. As labor, land, or resources were needed for expansion, the generation of wealth, or the appeasement of a managerial class with some (but not always extreme) privilege and resources, various populations were assigned such labels as savage, unworthy, criminal, or evil to justify their exploitation.

The conquest and decimation of the native peoples was asserted as a *fait accompli*, establishing them as a conquered people, a historical relic necessarily sacrificed for the greater good of the new utopia, the "newly discovered" home of the brave and land of the free. Africans were captured and remain to this day a significant labor force.[1] The ideological attack on these populations was and has been central to the positive conception of the U.S. social order as a "white republic." W.E.B. Du Bois articulates the significance of the reversal of radical reconstruction as a manifestation of this ideological attack on the African American people:

It is not only part [of the] foundation of our present lawlessness and loss
of democratic ideals; it has, more than that, led the world to embrace
and worship the color bar as social salvation and it is helping to range
mankind in ranks of mutual hatred and contempt, at the summons of a
cheap and false myth. ([1935] 1979, 723)

The frontal attack on racism during the course of the Civil War had not
been intended by the dominant social classes. Many enslaved Africans grasped
their strategic and tactical significance on the terrain of the battleground in
the South and encapsulated themselves within the Union Army, thus depriving
the Confederate Army and the slave system of its workforce. In the course of
these events, they transformed the Union Army temporarily into an army of
liberation. In the aftermath of the Civil War, the freedmen were indispensable
allies in the weakening of the old dominant order in the defeated Confederacy.
But once this alliance of whites and Blacks in the Union Army was no longer
needed, the freedmen were abandoned as part of a larger sociopolitical process.
Howard Zinn argues:

In the year 1877, the signals were given for the rest of the century: the
Blacks would be put back; the strikes of the white workers would not be
tolerated; the industrial and political elites of North and South would
take hold of the country and organize the greatest march of economic
growth in human history. They would do it with the aid of, and at the
expense of, Black labor, white labor, Chinese labor, European immigrant
labor, female labor, rewarding them differently by race, sex, national origin, and social class, in such a way as to create separate levels of oppression—skillful terracing to stabilize the pyramid of wealth. (1980, 247)

The terracing described by Zinn is compatible with T. H. Marshall's notion
of social citizenship, which entails a basic equality associated with a concept
of full membership in a political community, yet it is still consistent with the
inequalities that distinguish the various economic levels in society. In the eighteenth and nineteenth centuries, citizenship became the architect of legitimate
social inequality as individuals and groups were assigned different stations in
society. For those who received public benefits, such benefits were provided at
the expense of their citizenship rights. Otherwise, citizenship rights would have
disproportionately distorted the balance of social power in favor of the lower
social strata, thus interfering in the market-based stratification system. Marshall distinguishes between three elements of citizenship: civil rights, political
rights, and social rights. For Marshall, the original source of social rights was
membership in a local community and functional associations. This source was
supplemented and progressively replaced by a Poor Law and a system of wage
regulation that was nationally conceived and locally administered.
The Poor Law was the last remnant of a system that sought to adjust real

income to the social needs and status of the citizen and not solely to the market value of his labor. But a startling reversal occurred in the administration of the Poor Law Amendment Act of 1834, which renounced all claims to interference with operation of the free market and the wage system. Hereafter it offered relief only to those who, because of illness, were incapable of competing in the free market or those who were weak, gave up the competitive struggle, and cried for mercy. By requiring the lower strata to effectively renounce their citizenship rights, the upper strata protected the market-based system of social stratification for those with dominant market-based power.

Marshall explains:

> The Poor Law treated the claims of the poor, not as an integral part of the rights of the citizen, but as an alternative to them—as claims which could be met only if the claimants ceased to be citizens in any true sense of the world. For paupers forfeited in practice the civil rights of personal liberty, by internment in the workhouse, and they forfeited by law any political rights they might possess.... The stigma which clung to the poor relief expressed the deep feelings of a people who understood that those who accepted relief must cross the road that separated the community of citizens from the outcast community of the destitute. (1964, 80–81)

Marshall distinguishes between two conceptions of class: one based on the hierarchy of status, and the other based on the hierarchy of the market. The establishment of citizenship rights was profoundly destructive to status-based class distinctions but had a more gradual effect on market-based class distinctions. Perhaps counterintuitively, it initially strengthened the class system by eliminating its less defensible (status-based) consequences. These more subtle class distinctions putatively rooted in the operations of the market were said to be a natural phenomenon operating outside the control of societies, and therefore attempts to control such market forces would be harmful to the economy.

During the eighteenth and nineteenth centuries, social rights were explicitly separated from the rights of citizenship. As Marshall argues:

> Where they were given officially by the State, this was done by measures which, as I have said, offered alternatives to the rights of citizenship, rather than additions to them. But the major part of the task was left to private charity, and it was the general, though not universal, view of charitable bodies that those who received their help had no personal right to claim it. (1962, 87)

While citizenship rights were based on a principle of equality, they were also necessary for the efficient functioning of the competitive market economy, which was rooted in a principle of inequality. Marshall explains that civil rights gave each person the power to engage as an individual unit in the economic struggle.

This meant that the individual could be denied social protection, because he or she was theoretically fully equipped with the means of self-protection. The modern social contract is therefore an agreement between people who are equal in status but not in power. Thus property rights imply the right to obtain but not to own property; the right to freedom of speech is bestowed on those who have the means to make themselves heard, but not all people have such means, so freedom of speech is not effectively available to all people. Equality before the law applies only if one has the means to seek remedies in cases that are contested. Clearly, under these types of conditions, social equality is quite limited, though the *appearance* of equality is there.

In the later part of the nineteenth century, however, as the social power of the working class increased in the industrializing pan-European world, a growing interest developed in equality as a principle of social justice and thereby rooted in community and the common good. With an increase in the political power of the working class, measures were taken to broaden the scope of citizenship rights. This effort effectively narrowed the magnitude of economic inequality, first through the broadening of civil rights (e.g., the right to collective bargaining) and then through the broadening of social rights (e.g., minimum wage laws, social security).

The diminution of inequality strengthened the bargaining position of the working classes and gave increasing strength to a sentiment that demanded its complete abolition. By and large, this demand was met through incorporating social rights into the status of citizenship and thereby creating a universal right to a real income not tied to the market value of the claimant. In this way, social democracy and notions of social entitlements as basic human rights became hegemonic forces in the advanced industrial societies of the pan-European world.

Marshall does not view the extension of social services as a means of equalizing incomes. What matters for him is that "there is an enrichment of the concrete substance of civilized life, a general reduction of risk and insecurity, and equalization between the more and the less fortunate at all levels. Equality of status (entitlement) is more important than equality of income" (1964, 102–103). However, the compromise entailed in the social compact of the postwar period is especially significant in our discussion because of the limited incorporation of Blacks, Latinos, Asians, and women in what Richard A. Piven and Frances Fox Cloward (1997) refer to as the "American Social Compact" and the public awareness of those limitations. The racialized and gendered nature of the exclusions (from the social solidarity expressed in the social compact) was central to the social reality of the United States from inception. We must acknowledge this history if we are to fully understand the evolution of U.S. society, who is considered to belong (or not), and what the nation is truly about.

Nation as Political Community

"Nation" is the name given to the construction of a political community that is considered to coexist with a state. Converting the structural apparatus of a state into a nation-state provides coherence and creates a kind of glue in which citizens identify themselves with this political entity. Patriotism allows citizens to express their solidarity and loyalty through the defense of this political community and makes the nation one of their highest priorities.

As indicated above, this coherence does not imply equality among citizens, but, as Marshall argues, it provides an articulation of personhood and community and eliminates status distinctions as a basis of inequality. Inequality within such communities is therefore deemed solely to be market-based. Though the long civil rights movement sought to eliminate the status and economic distinctions of race in U.S. society, almost all members of the movement came to recognize the relationship between the status distinctions based on race and the deeply institutionalized structures of racism embedded in all aspects of society. Status as an element of inequality was at first quite explicit but became unmentionable, since it provoked extensive efforts to end racism among a large segment of the population. Such efforts also combined with efforts to transform structural inequality, or what had previously been viewed as market-based inequalities, which were deemed to be a natural result of unequal abilities and not a problem of concern to society.

When some social scientists and activists responding to the struggle for racial equality began to interrogate the relationship between so-called market-based and status-based inequality, they discovered that substantial portions of what had been considered market-based inequalities were rooted in social status and reproduced by the structures and institutions of society. The Black intelligentsia who identified this connection thereby developed the concept of institutional racism. Thus, the question of who belongs to the nation evolved with an increasing demographic and social significance and became a central issue for the twentieth-century development of the U.S. nation.

It is here that the central question of *Tensions in the American Dream* arises: How can the principle of equality in citizenship be reconciled with the principle of inequality in the economic and political structure? The founding myths noted above gave rise to categories of citizenship that fit more neatly into the image of the modern world. Robinson argues that Black history began in the shadow of the national myths about Black people and was their dialectical negation (Robinson 1983, 190).[2] While this effort sought to negate the racist myths, it also encapsulated racial-uplift ideology, which benefited the Black middle class. This strain ran through the sentiments of what Wilson Moses (1978) calls the "golden age of Black nationalism" (1850–1925), what he argues was largely the ideology of the Black middle class. Alexander Crummell and Du Bois's notion of the talented tenth derived essentially from the racial-uplift themes of their era. This concept was essentially an assimilationist ideology closely tied to that of the pan-European group, but it differed in the articulation of who could be assimilated. For whites, Blacks were considered to be beyond the pale of citizenship. For Robinson, this position entailed a price that had to be paid, supporting "integration" but not equality. This disparity is precisely Marshall's point and an extremely important analytic statement: The pairing of the antiracist and anti-sexist struggle with the overall struggle for social equality is anathema for those who wish to continue operating on the principle of inequality. Though the radicals in the New Negro Movement of the early twentieth century emphasized the issue of Black Pride and self-respect, they also argued that racial oppression was part of the essentially and inherently oppressive nature of the capitalist world.

The definitions of race and racism, then, were important elements in the evolution of the identity of not only African American people but also those who would be constituted as members of the white nation. Du Bois's radicalism emerged in the context of debates with elements of New Negro radicalism (especially Hubert Harrison, the Messenger Group, Marcus Garvey and the Universal Negro Improvement Association [UNIA], Cyril Briggs and the African Blood Brotherhood); with the Communist Party USA (CPUSA) and, in turn, its criticism of the centrist liberalism of the National Association for the Advancement of Colored People (NAACP); and in the multiple splits within the NAACP. Du Bois did the most to develop the scaffolding on which a new identity would emerge, but he was far from alone. While Du Bois is widely acknowledged today as a giant in the intellectual life of the modern world, he was a marginal figure in academia for most of the twentieth century. Despite the positive contributions of sociology to the study of race, Du Bois's marginal position within sociology is consistent as well with the shortcomings on the study of race and racism among sociologists. Sociology, too, was a site of the hegemony of centrist liberalism *and* the colonial ontology that so dominated pan-European world views.

While social scientists have played an exemplary role in changing the tenor of the scholarly and public discourse on race, in this book we focus on the issues of structure and agency in the formation of racial, ethnic, and national categories and identity. While oppressed groups have been and continue to be categorized in an invidious manner by the more privileged, for the more privileged, such distinctions are central in reinforcing the identity formation that they view as the basis for their dominance in society.

We examine several dimensions of this dynamic, including how oppressed groups form a sense of racial or ethnic identity and reflect on and act on racial oppression or ethnic stratification in their national identifications and affiliations. We also question how privileged groups align around practices and ideas with a legitimating notion that their ideas and practices are universal, objective, and civilizing in who they consider to be members of their own national community. Subsumed within this question is the issue of how race, racialization, racism, and liberation are viewed, particularly in the way that the concept of "nation" articulates a cohesive force for both groups but with very different meanings.

At times in this book, we particularly focus on white versus Black polarity, not because of a belief in the essentialism of such a binary but because of the central role that this opposition has played in defining the "race first" ideology of the pan-European world both on an international scale and within the borders of Euro-dominated states. The creation and elaboration of the concept and structures of race first took place within British North America and later throughout the capitalist world economy under European hegemony in relationship to Africa.

The central role of racialization in the creation of the U.S. nation and the New World accounts for the centrality of the fight against racism and for the rights of "communities of color" who have been so central to U.S. history. Thus we must examine the emergence and development of the concept of the American Dream in U.S. history in various temporalities that provide the context for the struggle for equality and U.S. history more generally. The development of the nation as Benedict Anderson's (2000) "imagined community" helps us understand this social-political-economic construct.

The nation is the name given to the construction of a political community that is considered to coexist with a state. It should be clear, however, that though we tend to believe that the construction of peoplehood gives rise to nations and subsequently to the demand for a sovereign state, in reality the political structuring of the world-system gives rise to the nation. As Etienne Balibar and Immanuel Wallerstein argue, "The states that are today members of the United Nations are all creations of the modern world-system. Most of them did not exist either as names or as administrative units more than a century or two ago" (1991, 80–81). However, once the interstate system was constructed within the modern world-system, nationalist movements emerged and demanded the "right to self-determination," which amounted to the creation of new sovereign states.

The creation of new states reflected again the inherently polarizing logic of the social system, which led those excluded to organize in an effort to protect themselves against those who would subordinate and marginalize them in the social order. Counterintuitively, the creation of new states was a part of a liberal program, an idea that is clear if we briefly review the revolutionary movement that emerged in the European arena of world capitalism during the 1840s.

The nineteenth-century workers movement included members who were implacable foes of a capitalist system that they believed would increasingly undermine the very foundations of social life as it ground workers beneath the wheel of a heartless profit-making juggernaut; other players within the movement hoped that the social struggles of workers would result in humanizing the capitalist system. During the 1840s, workers rebelled against this system, culminating in what has been called the revolution of 1848. When this revolution was defeated and order was restored, the upper strata pursued a policy not of reaction but of liberal reform to co-opt the danger of popular revolt. The package extended to workers included an extension of suffrage, the protection of the weak in the workplace, the beginning of redistributive welfare, and the building of educational and health infrastructure for citizens. This liberal reform program combined with the propagation and legitimization of the notion of the white man's burden in the wider world, the civilizing mission, the "Yellow peril," and a new anti-Semitism that Wallerstein (1999) argues served to incrustate the pan-European lower strata within a national identity that was right wing and nonliberatory.

Nationalism organized within the liberal states of the pan-European world received even greater cohesion from their hostility to enemies from the extra-European world whom they dominated politically and economically. This domination was for the benefit of the dominated, because they were being offered the gift of civilization. Wallerstein thus argues that the pan-European world "defined itself as the heart, the culmination, of a civilizational process which is traced back to Europe's presumed roots in Africa. Given the state of its civilization and its technology in the nineteenth century, the pan-European world claimed the duty to impose itself, culturally as well as politically, on everyone else—Kipling's 'White man's burden,' the 'manifest destiny' of the United States, France's 'mission civilisatrice'" (2004, 66).

This nationalistic worldview was not merely the action of the state, which the masses simply passively observed; "it was the passion of the nation, the duty of the citizens" (Wallerstein 2004, 66). Here, the liberals and the conservatives converged in their common interest of ensuring internal order within the state. But for Wallerstein, the effectiveness of nationalism as internal pacification is highlighted by the fact that despite their ideological adherence to the notion of proletarian internationalism, the radicals also bought into this liberal program, such that "when virtually all European socialist parties opted in 1914 to support their national side in the war, it was clear that the conservative belief about the effect of nationalism on the erstwhile dangerous classes had been correct" (2004, 67).

Samir Amin argues that the concept of the nation has deep mythological roots that present it as a "natural" phenomenon, something of a biological perception, which he argues leads to racism. The concept of a universal humanity did not exist during the time when ethnic groups, tribes, and clans were the predominant forms of societal organization that led these groups to feel distinct from one another; even deities were thought of as being specific to individual groups. But the first big wave of what Amin refers to as the cultural revolutions that inaugurated the tributary age (500 B.C.E. to 700 C.E.) saw the birth of the concept of universality, with the birth of the great religions (Zoroaster, Buddha, Christianity, and Islam) and of the great philosophies (Confucian, Hellenistic; 1997, 8).

For Amin, the concept of nation as a political community evolved during the rise of capitalism in Europe and the conquest of the New World, which was also the period in which the Enlightenment, or the Age of Reason, took hold in politics, philosophy, science, and communications. The Enlightenment defined the nation not on the basis of a biological myth but on the basis of a social analysis of society. Thus the nation was said to be based on a social contract between free men who wanted to live according to the nation's laws (Amin 1997, 9–10).

3

The Shifting Terrain Makes Clear
the Tensions in the American Dream

In this book, we focus on a time period when citizenship, belonging, and questions of community are in flux. In doing so, Melanie's previous work *Everyday Forms of Whiteness: Understanding Race in a "Post-Racial" World* insists that we frame our understanding of contemporary white racism and racial animosity as evidence of a transition from a period from the 1930s to the 1970s (centered in the 1960s), when public opinion was weighted toward a collective responsibility for the common good, toward a time emphasizing a belief in the social survival of the fittest (M. Bush 2011, 1). During the 1960s and 1970s, the working-class Americanism of the 1930s and 1940s came to maturity. This period is often treated *only* as a break from the past sparked by the immaturity of youthful rebels who, because of the upward mobility of their parents, did not appreciate the historical trajectory of the United States toward "a more perfect union." However, the intersection of these two historical strands is crucial to our understanding of the evolution of the concept of the American Dream.

The accumulation of social power that was sparked by the coalescence of working-class Americanism with excluded populations did indeed provoke a break from the liberal geoculture.[1] This newfound power incited a segment of the white population to move away from a commitment to the common good, partially involving a redefinition of who was included in the collective "we." This transformation was related to tectonic shifts in the social structures of the United States and the larger world-system that altered the social psychology of everyone within the United States. However, this change was not simply a matter of individual psychology; the redefinition of "we" was a profoundly social phenomenon. This period was an important marker in the social history of the U.S. nation.

The brief narrative presented here suggests that substantive support for a commitment to the common good has emerged in many "societies" as well as in global movements that wanted a transnational organization of society devoted in principle to the common good rather than the benefits of the propertied few. In the twentieth-century United States, this sentiment came increasingly to be identified as the "American creed," a liberal civic nationalism that viewed the United States as exceptional due in part to its lack of a feudal past and thus a natural source of the development of democratic and egalitarian institutional structures. Such historians as David Hollinger have distinguished between the civic nationalism of the United States and the ethnic nationalism of other countries.

Those who uphold the United States as a model of a potentially democratic civic nationalism should be mindful of Stephen Steinberg's (1989) cautionary epilogue in the second edition of *The Ethnic Myth*, entitled, "Ethnic Heroes and Racial Villains in American Social Science." Here, he argues that the dominant thesis of U.S. social science and popular culture is that those who have successfully assimilated into U.S. society and moved up the economic ladder have been able to do so because of their ethnic values. This myth also states that for those who have not done so, it is due to shortcomings in their cultural values. In the most extreme cases of Blacks and Latinos, it is attributed to their cultural pathologies or their adherence to a culture of poverty. Steinberg's class analysis applies to groups who have been racialized, so he posits that U.S. society could be divided into ethnic heroes and racial villains.

The real possibilities for democracy within the United States and within the world-system are most evident when communities of color are involved in the creation of democratic publics. Nothing is clearer to those who have historically been excluded from the benefits of the American Dream than the fact that the United States is a deeply divided society in which inequalities are justified by the supposedly different cultures of some groups, which, in turn, isolate them from the economic mainstream and its values. This U.S. civic nationalism has been the glue of U.S. civil society, serving as not only the basis for the idea of U.S. exceptionalism but also the focus of a set of counterhegemonic discourses and practices from those at the margins of U.S. society and for those in the periphery of the U.S.-dominated world-system, whose strengths have varied over time. They not only have articulated values that were much more faithful to the putative U.S. ideal but also have seen that ideal as intimately linked to the values and ideals of all humankind struggling for liberation from political domination and economic exploitation.

Is the United States a meritocracy? How frequently does hard work lead to success? Do those who work at the hardest jobs with the longest hours reap the greatest rewards? We pose these questions as the grounding for our exploration of what we feel to be a fundamental contradiction between the vision of the United States as a "shining city on a hill" and the vision of the United States as an imperial nation, with a manifest destiny to extend human elevation and human happiness.[2] Thomas Jefferson identified the United States as the "Empire of Liberty" (Foner [1990] 1998, 50). The belief was established that the United States had been chosen by God for the greatest experiment in human history—the achievement of liberty—and its expansion was part and parcel of this nation's providential design. Eric Foner quotes the French historian Michel Chevalier, who argues that the idea of liberty in the United States was a practical idea as well as a mystical one that meant a "liberty of action and motion which the American uses to expand over the vast territory that Providence had given him and to subdue it to his uses" ([1990] 1998, 50).

Foner, however, points out that the land was not empty. For centuries, the West had been a meeting ground of peoples whose relationships were shaped as much by conquest as free choice, and thus these relationships were characterized by clashing concepts of liberty. Native Americans wished to preserve their cultural and political autonomy and to retain control of their ancestral lands, but this desire was incompatible with the Western settlers' notion of liberty as the right to expand across the continent and establish farms, ranches, and mines on land that the Native Americans considered their own. Indian removal by fraud, intimidation, and violence was therefore the order of the day throughout this period (Foner [1990] 1998, 51).

According to Carl Degler, one journalist of the era described the American people as "the most independent, intelligent, moral, and happy people on the face of the earth" (1984, 119). Within that framework, Caleb Cushing, a member of the Massachusetts legislature and an army officer, justified the annexation of Mexican land by the United States after the Mexican War by asking, "Is not the occupation of any portion of the earth by those competent to hold and till it, a providential law of national life?" (Degler 1984, 119). This idea of design from above was thus an important element of the self-perception of the United States, but that idea was also connected to practical designs. In the summer of 1845, John O'Sullivan, editor of the *Democratic Review*, argued that it was "our manifest destiny to overspread the continent allotted by Providence for the free development of our multiplying millions" (Zinn 2003, 151).

The idea that the United States is a living manifestation of a meritocracy is at the very heart of what some refer to as American exceptionalism. In this chapter, we evaluate the rather contradictory social reality in which the United States has been described by some as a perfect democracy, the "city on a hill," and by others as an imperial nation. Here, we explore the origin and development myths of this nation and empire.[3] Bacon's Rebellion (1676), the institution of slavery (1619 onward), the Declaration of Independence (1776), the Constitution (1787), Black Codes (1800–1866), the Treaty of Guadeloupe Hidalgo (1848), and such legislation as *the People v. Hall* (1854), the *Dred Scott* decision (1857), Jim Crow laws (1876–1965), and the ruling in *Brown v. Board Education* (1954) are some of the many markers in U.S. history of how nation, empire, and white supremacy have been intrinsically linked in the development of the U.S. nation. The story of "America" is entrenched with and built on the presumption of exceptionalism and superiority. From the early years of European conquest, enslavement, and expansion, "nation" was equated with a white European racial portrait, contradicting notions of enlightenment, common unity, and belonging. Did "all" ever truly mean *all*, did "men" ever truly mean "human," and did "equal" ever truly mean equal access, opportunity, outcome, or treatment?[4]

The relationship between the construct of nation, the political and economic structures of capitalism, and the presumption of white supremacy have together provided the foundational justification for trespass, genocide, domination, exploitation, and presumed entitlements of land, labor, and wealth. As the colonies were established and then the nation was created, struggles occurred regarding whose interests would be served and who could claim which rights. Ideas about who would be valued and protected were embedded in the nation's documents and its laws. Subsequently, in the nineteenth century, the demand was made of European immigrants to become like "us," like it or not, but peoples from other parts of the globe were told that they would never be like "us" (Smedley 1993, 32). The case was built for who belonged and who did not; who was "same" and who was "different," "civil," or "savage"; who could own land; who could be educated and literate; who could assemble; who could be in charge of and exploit other people's labor; and who could not. These questions were resolved into naturalized hierarchies of race, language, culture, and gender and through thinly disguised notions about national belonging. Such core values as "democracy," "equality," "freedom," and "justice" were evoked on behalf of "all" yet implemented only on behalf of "some."

Patriotism in this context demanded unquestioning loyalty and presumed European superiority and the equation of might and right. This ideological framing of nation disallowed discussion about the structure of society and asserted an elusive notion of national identity evoked as needed to enlist complicity with the whims of those in power. The question of who belongs (and which entitlements their belonging implies) has vacillated between tangible notions of naturalization and citizenship, unambiguous birthrights, and an ambiguous notion that being "American" corresponds to a particular belief system.[5]

Ideas about belonging and inclusion were embedded in the Declaration of Independence and the early years of the U.S. nation, as described by William J. Wilson in 1860: "They the white people and they alone, find its boundaries too circumscribed for their greedy grasp. Possessing acres by the millions, yet they would elbow us and all others off of what we possess, to give them room for what they cannot occupy" (qtd. in Roediger 1998, 65). In his famous speech "What to the Slave Is Your Fourth of July?" Frederick Douglass puts the spotlight on the issue of whose perspective is assumed and whose does not matter ([1855] 1970, 349). In her discussion of the annual practice of "muster" (a time when armed whites terrorized the enslaved population in anticipation of revolts), Harriet Jacobs (1861) suggests that this institution served to unite whites across class lines (Roediger 1998, 336); the practice also defined the parameters of citizenship.

These examples of the centering and privileging of the European experience have been endemic, "not just a by-product of white supremacy but also an imperative of racial domination" (Roediger 1998, 6). The new nation of the United States was built by using the labor of Africans, Chinese, and new immigrants and exploiting the land and natural resources of indigenous peoples and Mexican territories, simultaneously excluding most of these groups from citizenship and the benefits of "belonging." Immigrants from Europe in the nineteenth century were initially excluded but ultimately integrated into the expanding industrial economy where there was opportunity for upward mobility. Through this economic assignment, and the policies and programs of the early twentieth century that provided further opportunities and supports for upward mobility, such as the G.I. bill and Federal Housing Administration (FHA) loans, European immigrants and their descendants were enlisted in a pan-ethnic racial "club" and "became party to strategies of social closure that maintained others' exclusion" (Waldinger 2001, 20). National identification in the United States has always been inherently tied to racial status.

The initial emergence of the notion of European racial superiority corresponded to the appearance of capitalism more than six hundred years ago (Cox 1948, 322). While contact and interaction across geographically distinct populations occurred during earlier times, no evidence of racial prejudice exists even in the Hellenistic empire, which had extended farther into Africa than any other European empire (Cox 1948, 322). St. Clair Drake describes the sixteenth century as "a historic watershed in global relations between Black and white people" and states that neither racial slavery nor systemic white racism existed prior to this time, although color prejudice was present in some places (1987, xxiii). While interethnic interactions have a long history, in the past they did not necessarily reflect inevitable conflict, competition, or struggle (Smedley 1998, 690). Identities were constructed by a wide range of characteristics, including, but not limited to, place of birth, language, kinship, religion, or occupation. They were generally context-specific and malleable up to the seventeenth century (Smedley 1998, 691–692). Drake has found that until the seventeenth century, Blackness was not a stigma, nor was race essentialized in the way that it later came to be (Harrison 1998, 620–621).

With the emergence of capitalism, the colonial exploration of the globe, and the beginning of the slave trade between Africa and parts of the "new" world, racial notions were used to justify the subordination and exploitation of large numbers of people who formed a labor pool for building settlements and cultivating agriculture. During the earliest period in the development of capitalism, "the white man had no conception of himself as being capable of developing the superior culture of the world—the concept 'white man' had not yet its significant social definition—the Anglo-Saxon, the modern master race, was then not even in the picture" (Cox 1948, 327). Racial dynamics, however, quickly developed within the context of the expansion of capitalism and colonial settlements. This process initially took the form of a European center with Euro-dominated colonies. The link between national development under capitalism and white supremacy was forged at this time.

Ultimately, the British settler colony of North America evolved into the United States, which then became the new center of the economic and political world-system (Drake 1987). A vivid example of this process of racial development was the fateful Bacon's Rebellion in 1676 in Virginia, which established early boundaries distinguishing Africans, Europeans, and native peoples (Zinn 1995, 37–59). This event is generally portrayed solely as a response to common exploitation and oppression, as African and European bond-laborers rebelled to demand an end to servitude. However, another key component of this struggle was an orchestrated attempt by the dominant elites to drive a wedge between these groups and the native population. Any combination of these forces was a tremendous threat to the white planters, whose wealth was great compared to that of the general white population. Poor Europeans had much more in common with enslaved Africans, and a potential alliance could have been disastrous for those in power: "In the early years of slavery, especially, before racism as a way of thinking was firmly ingrained, while white indentured servants were often treated as badly as Black slaves, there was a possibility of cooperation" (Zinn 1995, 37). The plantation bourgeoisie responded to the threat of coalition by offering European laborers a variety of previously denied benefits, such as amnesty for those who rebelled; corn, cash, and muskets for those finishing their servitude; the right to bear arms; and the opportunity to join slave patrol militias and receive monetary awards: "They constituted the police patrol who could ride with planters, and now and then exercise unlimited force upon recalcitrant or runaway slaves; and then, too there was always a chance that they themselves might also become planters by saving money, by investment, by the power of good luck; the only heaven that attracted them was the life of the great Southern planter" (Du Bois [1936] 1979, 27). This may be viewed as the nation's first "affirmative action" policy (Harrison 1998, 621).

These actions were taken to quell this potentially dangerous alliance and as a means for control. Racism on the part of poor whites became a practical matter (Zinn 1995, 56). The explicit use of race and white supremacy was implemented as a tool to divide and conquer and framed the development of nation from the very beginning. Prior to this period, there was little advantage and therefore little motivation for poor whites to ally themselves with the ruling powers. At this time, though, they were accorded "social, psychological and political advantages" calculated to alienate them from their fellow African bondsmen (Du Bois [1936] 1979, 700; Morgan 1975, 331–333, 344).

Racism was implemented as a means of control to establish and then maintain the structure of social organization in the "new" world. Racial domination became encoded in the process of nation-state building for the United States, as "Blacks were sold out to encourage white unity and nationalist loyalty to the state" (Marx 1998, 267). Slavery, therefore, played a critical role in providing a justification for the unification of whites racially as a nation (Marx 1998, 267), a pattern that continues to influence national identity, notions of whiteness, and formulations of race in society today. Whites were told that their whiteness rendered them "superior" and that to maintain this status they needed to place their allegiances with those in power who controlled the resources and could divvy up benefits.

"During America's colonial era the ideal of white identity was male, English, Protestant, and privileged. Over time this ideal evolved into free, white, male, Christian, propertied and franchised. These characteristics developed into a norm that subsequently became synonymous with American" (Davis 2005, 155, citing Babb 1998). This identity was also intertwined with notions of freedom, thereby reinforcing the relationship between whiteness and Americanness: "There were perfectly strategic reasons to allow the identity of American to evolve in opposition to Blackness—exploitation, appropriation, and subordination of Blacks and Black labor" (155).

While it particularly applied as a Black-white polarization, this ideological formulation of race was also flexible. A stigma of racial inferiority could be invoked as needed to maintain divisions and enforce a social hierarchy. For example, during the mid–nineteenth century, Chinese workers were used as the primary labor force in building California's railroads. Their subsequent brutalization, subjugation, and exclusion were framed overwhelmingly in racial terms (Smedley 1993, 268). This stigma was similarly applied to native and Mexican peoples who were characterized as savages unfit to own and govern their land "coincidentally" at the time that those lands were desired by the wealthy elite. The "Trail of Tears" and the annexation of one-third of Mexican land are brutal testaments to this history of internal colonization, land appropriation, and genocide.

Throughout the eighteenth and the early nineteenth centuries, the formation and consolidation of working-class whiteness (Roediger [1991] 1999, 14) and "American" identity were founded not just on economic exploitation but also on racial folklore (Du Bois 1970). Du Bois describes this dynamic eloquently:

> It must be remembered that the white group of laborers, while they received a low wage, were compensated in part by a sort of public and psychological wage. They were given public deference and titles of courtesy because they were white. They were admitted freely with all classes of white people to public functions, public parks, and the best schools. The police were drawn from their ranks, and the courts, dependent upon their votes, treated them with such leniency as to encourage lawlessness. Their vote selected public officials and while this had small effect upon the economic situation, it had great effect upon their personal treatment and the deference shown them. (1979, 700–701)

Throughout the eighteenth and nineteenth centuries, various theoretical trends emerged in the social and biological sciences to further justify this ordering of the world: "These models created a new form of social identity as the concept of 'race' developed as a way to rationalize the conquest and brutal treatment of native populations and the institution of slavery" (Smedley 1998, 697). Another dimension was the emergence of "American English" during the early part of the nineteenth century: "When the new nation formed, British culture was still dominant, and it was not yet clear what it meant to be American. [Noah] Webster thought it was vital to shake off 'foreign manners' and build an independent national culture. . . . Webster's political purpose in writing his dictionaries was promoting national unity. . . . He believed that a 'federal language' could be a 'band of national union'" (A. Cohen 2006). Certainly, this viewpoint played a significant role in the much later emergence of the "English-only" movement and the depiction of those speaking languages other than English as less "American" and therefore unworthy.

By the mid–nineteenth century, this arbitrary ranking of peoples and racial ideology had spread around much of the world (Smedley 1998, 695), translating directly into emerging notions of who was "American." A vivid example of this phenomenon was the 1903 World's Fair, where being "American" and being "white" were explicitly viewed as superior to coming from the colonized world of those considered lesser beings, such as Filipinos and Africans.[6]

The end of the nineteenth century and first half of the twentieth century were marked by two significant U.S. Supreme Court decisions concerning the Fourteenth Amendment,[7] signifying important shifts in the racial order within the United States (Baker 1998, 2). In 1896, *Plessey v. Ferguson* codified the practice of "separate but equal," and in 1954, the *Brown v. Board of Education* ruling overturned it: "The social context from which turn-of-the-century constructs of race emerged—industrialization, poll taxes, public lynching, unsafe working conditions, and Jim Crow segregation—at the same time gave rise to a professional anthropology that espoused racial inferiority and, as a consequence, supported and validated the status quo" (Baker 1998, 3). Much of this framing rooted in white-supremacist terms also applied to other scholarly disciplines and state policy as well. The legitimacy of the racial order was thereby validated and inscribed in "science" and social practices that reinforced the concepts of race, hierarchy, and nation.

The turn of the twentieth century marked a period of contestation about who was to be designated "white," as a huge influx of immigrants from Europe and other parts of the globe tested the boundaries of citizenry and racial identity. Paralleling the pace of immigration at the end of the nineteenth century, the first decade of the twentieth century witnessed the largest number of immigrants (8.8 million) admitted into the United States (Kraly and Miyares 2001, 47). The vast majority (92 percent) of these people originated from Europe.[8] At issue was the question of how they would be integrated and racially designated in U.S. society. The nation's expanding industries needed labor; mass immigration made cheap labor easily available.

Immigrants were exploited but also "used as an instrument for more effective exploitation of others, whether native or immigrant. For this reason, immigrant workers were sometimes compelled to put aside their ethnic loyalties" (Steinberg 2001, 38). African, Asian, and Mexican workers were used as low-paid labor for the least skilled jobs and sectors and established the infrastructure for industrialization and modernization. European immigrants worked primarily within the modern industrial sector, which strategically provided them with opportunities for upward mobility (Blauner 1972, 62). This reality challenges the popular notion that "all Americans 'start at the bottom'" and work their way up the ladder, because the racial labor principle designated a different bottom for different groups (62–63). The slogan "nation of immigrants" therefore describes most predominantly the European experience, despite the fact that Jews, Italians, and Irish were not fully accepted as whites.

During this period, Du Bois significantly contributed to a paradigm shift in the social sciences toward recognition of the connection between race and the concept of culture, united in an understanding of economics and politics (Baker 1998, 107–110). He describes race as a social relationship, integral to capitalism, and the ultimate paradox of democracy constructed to reinforce and reproduce patterns of systemic inequality (Du Bois [1903] 1986, 372): "Back of the problem of race and color, lies a greater problem which both obscures and implements it: and that is the fact that so many civilized persons are willing to live in comfort even if the price of this is poverty, ignorance and disease of the majority of their fellowmen: That to maintain this privilege men have waged war until today" (Du Bois [1953] 1961, xiv). In this way, race and nation have been intrinsically linked.

During the first half of the twentieth century, an ethnicity-based paradigm was often used to understand the social relations in the United States emerging as an extension of challenges made to biologistic and social Darwinist conceptions of race (Omi and Winant 1994, 12). Ethnicity was offered as a description of group formation that focused on culture and descent rather than biology and on the process of migration and the adaptation of immigrants in the United States. In 1913, Robert Park of the University of Chicago, a leading theorist within this group, asserted that by their second generation, Poles, Lithuanians, and Norwegians were indistinguishable from native-born Americans (Schaefer 1995, 111). Park projected that ethnicity would dissolve as immigrants integrated into society, and he identified a pattern of integration into U.S. society that he labeled the "race relations cycle," which involved stages of contact, accommodation, assimilation, and amalgamation achieved through intermarriage (Steinberg 2001, 47). Park considered all modern nationalities to be a mixture of several groups. According to this idea, ethnicity was expected to disappear into a new American culture.

This period marked a new stage in the consolidation of whiteness as a racialized category such that European Americans were transformed into a pan-ethnicity that represented the distancing of individuals from their national origins, heritages, and languages and labeled them as "white" (Alba 1990, 312). Hence, too, white classification was always clearly linked to national identity.

Americanity[9]

The founding principles asserted in much of the mainstream historiography about the United States conform to neither the actual beliefs of the settlers (who were not immigrants) nor to their practices, which were based on very clear principles of inclusion of some and exclusion of others. These practices were not exceptions to the rule, as is often (mostly) argued. Rather, exclusion *was* the rule; it was *systemic and systematic, structurally and institutionally embedded.* The expression a "nation of nations" is more than a just a metaphor, and it is a much more precise depiction of U.S. social reality than the expression "a nation of immigrants." The notion of "America the Beautiful" as a nation of immigrants who consciously forged a New Eldorado, "a city on a hill," a beacon to the world, a magical land like no other that offered opportunity to all those willing to work, is now and has indeed always been a myth.

"Nations" exist in a worldwide system of inequality, ordered around the ideology of pan-European racism, which derived precisely from the European colonization of the Americas.[10] During this period, the idea of race was invented to naturalize the power of the Americas, the enslavement of Africans as a labor force in "new world," and the subsequent generalization of pan-European supremacy to the rest of the world as European conquest spread to the far corners of the globe. This concept involved the construction of a hierarchical social-economic-political system that elevated Europeans above all other people in the world. What we refer to as "white world supremacy" is the structural and ideological bedrock of the modern world-system, a capitalist world economy. The "nation of immigrants" story of the United States masks the reality that this fabled liberal utopia, the "shining city on a hill," is part of the European conquest of the non-European world and the very creation of race to naturalize the conquest of the so-called inferior peoples, so that it is viewed as simply a fact of life, an example of survival of the fittest. We contend that the United States of America was a settler colony, born of the conquest of the land of the indigenous people, the capture and enslavement of Africans to use as labor, the conquest of Mexican territory in the U.S. American Southwest, and imperial intervention in Cuba and the Philippines and throughout what is arrogantly referred to (with all too little self-reflection) as the U.S. backyard. The geopolitical and geocultural elements of our social world are fundamental and not ancillary to the stratification order. Some have sought to understand racial domination as a form of internal colonialism or internally colonized "third world within." This is *not* some "colonial analogy" but part of the reality of the modern/colonial/capitalist world-system. Though the U.S. American trajectory from settler colony to global hegemon fits well into the narrative of U.S. American exceptionalism, we argue that the very concept of the American Dream has come to imply that the dream of human possibility is not the dream of all humanity and *does not* (coincidentally) consider how our practices in the global arena restrict the possibilities of others.

The contradictions between the vision of the nation as a "shining city on a hill" and the vision of the nation as an imperial nation have led ultimately to tensions in the American Dream. A sector of the population sought to replace the American Dream of opportunity for all with a vision of a nation that focused on the survival of the fittest.

The long social struggle for racial justice that has been so central to the story of the United States, which then-presidential candidate Barack Obama described as America's "original sin," combined with the interlocking struggle for justice for the working class and for women to ultimately pose a potentially revolutionary challenge to the nationalism of empire and other forms of conservatism that high-ranking "public-safety" official J. Edgar Hoover took great pains to spell out starting in 1964. The very idea of the American Dream in a society where the racialized, gendered, and classed lower orders believed they were all entitled to such a dream became a destabilizing force. The revolutions of conscience and getting on the right side of history, as Martin Luther King Jr. demanded of us, were incompatible with the nationalism of empire and with the capitalist economic and social order and its inherently polarizing social dynamic. Though the demand for social equality had become the legitimate demand of the overwhelming majority of the population and was supported by President Lyndon Johnson as completing the great American revolution, it was not compatible with the maintenance of an inherently polarizing social system.

The ensuing conservative backlash taking form in the neoliberal counterrevolution and the neoconservative justification of inequality were sustained efforts to stem the tide of the surging social power of the social strata and the people of goodwill who supported their rise within American society.

Introduction to "Stories of My America"

A central theme of this project is that the construct of nation is ensconced in legal and political frameworks that constrain our ability to understand the real structure of the social world. The idea that the modern world consists of interacting nations, each with its own sovereign power and its own private citizens to whom these states are mainly obligated and to whom the private citizens are *only* obligated, is widespread. However, this perception does not reflect the reality of the world-system in which we have lived since the establishment of a capitalist world economy in the long sixteenth century.[11] This world economy consists of a set of interrelated production processes bound within an axial division of labor that spans the entire world economy from core zones to the peripheral zones. The core zones are locations of high-profit, high-technology, high-skilled production; the peripheral zones are locations of low-profit, low-technology, low-skilled production; and the semi-peripheral zones contain a mix of corelike processes and peripheral processes. The class structure of the capitalist world economy was skewed by the creation of race to naturalize the conquest of the non-European world and to degrade its inhabitants to subhuman levels below those of the so-called civilized races with full personhood.

The political structure of the modern world-system is an interstate system that consists of a system of strong and weak states as well as states of intermediate strength. The evolution of the modern world-system in Europe meant that historically the strong states were concentrated where capitalism was "most developed." The domination of weak states by strong states within the system was routine, and thus the violation of the so-called sovereignty of the weak states belied the notion of sovereignty itself.

Despite the rhetoric of humanism adopted by the strong states of Europe and the European settler colonies, the reality of the world-system is that "might makes right." The modern world-system is not simply a capitalist world economy; it is a colonial/capitalist world-system. The creation of the state structures was the consequence of historical political action in which national identities were constructed. Such national identities are not natural or God-given, but created by human actors. But once the state structures were created, they became part of an interstate system that involves a process of mutual recognition.

Neither nations nor citizens are truly separate. Falsely constructed borders and boundaries obfuscate the inherent interconnectedness of all humanity. While the concept of nationhood emerged in Europe, the founding and development of the U.S. nation embedded the idea that this way of organizing society makes sense. This is an essential *Tension* in the American Dream. We are led to believe that these constructs reflect a "natural" rather than human-created arrangement and that they are to be assumed, protected, and defended at all costs.

As we discuss in previous chapters, the structure of the world-system in the past five hundred years presumes capitalist, white-supremacist, and patriarchal forms of organization and discourse. With the emergence of the "new" world, U.S. exceptionalism was (and is) articulated in origin narratives that shaped (and shape) the psyche of the nation's peoples in hegemonic terms. The story of "America" provided a framework for justifying the national and global racial hierarchy and explaining why some people and groups have been (and are) particularly poor or rich, powerful or less so. This tale explains the U.S. hegemonic and material rise in the twentieth century as an extension of past centuries' establishment of Euro dominance and justifies imperialist practices while rationalizing both increased impoverishment of nearly all peripheral regions of the globe and the increasing peripheralization of some segments of the core. This follows the logic of an inherently polarizing social system that operates on the basis of the endless accumulation of capital, which is not socially possible. This system, like all historical social systems, will come to an end at some time in the future.

In Part II, "Stories of My America," we explore how individuals think about these narratives, drawing from discussions with more than one hundred people interviewed for this study.[12] Along the lines of a multiplicity of themes, Part II is organized into four chapters: Chapter 4, "Reflections on the Structural Logic of the System"; Chapter 5, "Thoughts on the Current Juncture"; Chapter 6, "Perspectives on the American Dream"; and Chapter 7, "Expressions of Revolt against the Systems." Participant comments and stories are thoughtful, though often contradictory. These passages provide evidence of deep internal struggles about how the ideological narratives that people ascribe to sometimes explain but more often disregard the challenges they face in everyday life. These "Stories of My America" provide insight into the everyday struggles engaged to reconcile the rhetoric, reverie, and realities embodied in the notion of an American Dream. Participants' reflections demonstrate the simultaneous contradictions evident in the ideology and lived experiences of inclusion and exclusion embodied in the history and present-day realities of the U.S. nation, thus forming the Tensions that we speak of in this book.

II

Stories of My America

4

Reflections on the Structural
Logic of the System

This chapter explores the ways that structural location within the system is understood and internalized in the consciousness of the people we spoke with. Nation, race, ethnicity, class, and gender organize society but also frame the ways that individuals think about the social world and groups within it, including how nationalism and patriotism are viewed by people within the United States. Are the espoused principles of the U.S. nation considered self-evident truths? How do we benefit from questioning them? To what extent do social characteristics play a role in an individual's or group's attainment of the material success of the American Dream? To what extent do they play a role in how people think about their own achievement? How does the assumption of a capitalist world-system as the only viable option shape and/or constrict individual and group possibilities? Participants reflect on these questions and offer deep insight about the complexity of the social world and the narratives that explain social realities. It is apparent, however, that they feel significant uncertainty regarding whether better options exist and fear that the privileges they presently have could be lost.

Nation as Identity

Nationalism, or an individual's or group's identification with a nation, establishes a vantage point for thinking about one's position in society (Cohen and Nussbaum 1996). It situates one within a "team" and provides a narrative about the character of the people with whom one is allied. This identity can be a source of strength and offer a sense of belonging. However, by definition, it can also be

self-centered and limited, especially when we consider that nations are not entities unto themselves but part of a vast network of interconnected people. Martin
Luther King Jr. expressed that sentiment well, saying that all mankind is tied
together, all life is interrelated, and we are all caught in an inescapable network
of mutuality, tied in a single garment of destiny. Whatever affects one directly
affects all indirectly. I can never be what I ought to be until you are what you
ought to be, and you can never be what you ought to be until I am what I ought
to be—this is the interrelated structure of reality.[1]

For rich and powerful nations, nationalism has served to justify imperial
conquest and colonization. Rudyard Kipling's poem "The White Man's Burden" is rooted in this way of thinking, articulating this mind-set as a rationale for European global expansion. The narrative of nationalism in the United
States is also one of exceptionalism, of being the "city on a hill." This perception
makes it difficult for people in the United States to understand the history of
their own country and the role that it has played and continues to play in the
world. Nationalist discourse presents the United States as unique in its provision
of opportunities for upward mobility and its care for the downtrodden of the
world. To many, the United States is known as the land of possibility, of milk
and honey, and the benevolent savior of the globally dispossessed. The nation
has been known as one that stands for democracy, equality, and justice—yet in
the twentieth century alone, it was involved in more than a hundred military
interventions around the world. Furthermore, internal racial and gender inequalities persist, and class divisions continue to intensify. Nationalist rhetoric
is primarily articulated in a vision that equates freedom with economic and material options (such as what kind of cereal one can "choose" to eat from among
the many varieties presented to us) and political choice—usually between two
well-funded (wealthy) candidates, representing similar interests. For those with
resources who are considered worthy of privileges, the system appears to make
sense. Those who do not have such luck are considered undeserving. The system appears puzzling, because there is tension in the narrative about material
rewards being guaranteed to those who work hard. If the United States is the
locus of endless opportunity, then why not for me? If it is not, then what is the
United States in reality?

What is the true character of "America"? What function does nationalism
serve? Who belongs? How is community constructed? The following comments
speak to how people think about these questions:

We think the world is our oyster. America is Mecca in the same way
that everything led to Mecca. (Patrice, Black, female, born outside the
United States, 46–65)

That's why so many people, immigrants have always come here. They
think the streets are paved with gold. But it's all hype! (Ina, white, female, U.S.-born, 46–65)

When I came to this country, everybody was saying that the U.S. was the superpower, blah blah blah. I never thought of the U.S. like that and never heard that term outside the U.S. The U.S. meddles in foreign affairs a lot, and I didn't think it is fair to exert themselves. (Alice, Asian, female, born outside the U.S., 18–25)

Others reflect a similar sentiment:

I am constantly critical [of] American exceptionalism. Aren't other people in the world affected by our decisions? How could we operate with our blinders on—not really seeing the impact of what we do on the rest of the world? (Dan, white, male, U.S.-born, 18–25)

My dream would be to live in a community that doesn't do the things that we do as a nation as far as foreign policy goes. Everyone thinks that it has only been Iraq, but if you review the last fifty to sixty years, you notice that we've been in and out of constant war. I so strongly disagree with the choices that this country [makes]. It makes [choices that] really destroy my perception of who I am as an American and my idea of being an American. (Carl, white, male, U.S.-born, 18–25)

Thomas (white, male, U.S.-born, 26–45) suggests that nationalism is problematic everywhere (not just in the United States), because it generates patriotism and encourages an "us" versus "them" dynamic. He says that if one perceives someone to be a problem, one seeks to annihilate that person rather than talk. Thomas adds that in the United States, a combination of religion (Christianity), ideology (individualism), and economics (capitalism) form the foundation of U.S. nationalism. The diminution of the power of the United States has worried "patriotic" Americans who want to preserve its place in the global hierarchy. He suggests that it does not bode well for the future if a majority of the people are willing to fight to maintain U.S. hegemony. The following comments offer additional reflections on these issues from different points of view:

You don't feel the claws of the monster inside the monster. Europe dominated Africa, India; all the crown jewels of Europe were stolen. Our natural resources were taken from other countries. When you watch things like *The Jungle Book,* it talks about the history of Europe dominating India and that whole mentality that the Europeans are better. I'm not sure of exactly what forces it was, but there were things that went Europe's way. If it happened to be somewhere else, another people might have been the dominant one. (Joseph, Black, male, U.S.-born, 46–65)

Other countries have this view that America is the land of no crime, no poverty, where money grows on trees. It's almost unbelievable how many people think that, especially [those] who live in the third world. A friend visited me from Brazil when I was living in the border between Bed-Stuy and Bushwick. They said, "I had no idea that I would see something like this in the United States." People come here with this view of what the United States is like and then get mugged or end up living in neighborhoods that have homicide rates similar to the urban centers of developing countries. There is a big myth really behind that. (Gringo_b, white/Latino, male, born outside the U.S., 26–45)

In Poland, everyone knew that what you see on the news is a lie. Here, everyone takes for granted what the news said. I remember being really surprised that people just believe things that they hear. (Andrew, white, male, born outside the U.S., 26–45)

In this exchange, participants reflect on the positionality of the Europeans in the social hierarchy and consider different reasons for their privileges:

Tim (white, male, U.S.-born, over 65): The economic engine and education brings opportunity here. I don't know which is the horse and which is the cart. They both go hand in hand. As people get more education, you literally can solve problems better than the third world.
Michael (white, male, U.S.-born, over 65): Is there any industry in El Salvador other than maybe tourism? All the Europeans came over here. The Italians came over. The Polish came over. You know? And they didn't go to El Salvador. They came here. The people who made all the major inventions were all Europeans who came over here. They didn't go to El Salvador. They didn't go to Cuba. You know?
Tim: You hit something—the Europeans that came over here brought systems with them. They already had education systems. They already knew about school. Even though they brought a lot of prejudice with them, they already brought over economic systems. That just puts a white civilization way up there, and the third world is still, still struggling. There still is a huge contribution from Mexicans. First of all, people are willing to work hard as hell. My God, you look at services around this town, and you see the guys that are really doing the grunt work—it's the Latinos doing everybody's lawn, number one.
Michael: But they're still not the leaders here. There's not a lot of leadership from them. Europeans brought the structure, institutions, and technology.

Reflections on Patriotism

These discussions of nationalism frequently generate reflections on patriotism and national loyalty. Participants speak frankly about their questions related to the role these ideas play in maintaining a social order and the qualities that constitute responsible citizenship:

> For me, to be patriotic is to contribute to change where you see change needed. Here, if you are patriotic, you've got stars or a ribbon on your SUV. (Joe J., white, male, U.S.-born, 26–45)

For others, patriotism is a matter of principle based on their understanding of the difference between the United States and other nations:

> I like being in the United States. I wouldn't want to live nowhere else. I have my freedom. There's so many countries that you can live in and be dictated on what you have to do. I don't have to follow nobody's dictatorship. I do what I want to do as a woman, as an American citizen. In a lot of them countries that's run by dictatorship, you know, you can't do what you want to do. Everything is dictated and delegated what I must do, what I can do, and what I cannot do. So yeah, I'm patriotic. (Spankey, Black, female, U.S.-born, 26–45)

> People in power want you to believe that compliance and not asking questions is patriotism. I don't think it has to be, but it's deliberate. (Carmella, white, female, U.S.-born, 26–45)

> Patriotism is not confined to waving the flag and staring at fireworks. It's not confined to going to a protest, because that's exercising your right to dissent. Patriotism is doing whatever you think benefits the country. What can you do to help your country by yourself? You're one person out of three hundred some odd million. If you view helping your community as helping your country, that's a perfectly valid viewpoint. If everybody helps his or her community, then every community is helped, and the entire country is helped. Serving the country in the military is certainly patriotic. If you honestly believe a war is unjust and you [refuse to] fight, that could be considered a form of patriotism, even if others disagree. Even just boosting the general morale—there's something to be said for a certain level of flag waving; as long as you don't blind yourself with it, it's fine. (Jon, white, male, U.S.-born, 18–25)

> Here it seems that the most honorable thing you can do for your community is always in terms of military service. In other countries, being associated with the army is a negative thing—well, not negative, but not seen like it is here. (Gringo_b, white/Latino, male, born outside the U.S., 26–45)

> The problem with this country [is that] if you disagree, they say you are unpatriotic. Why can't I disagree? Why [do] I have to agree with every-

thing that you're doing and everything that [you're] saying? I'm talking about freedom of speech. If you start saying things about America, even on the news, they start hating you. You start getting hate mail. They want to throw a brick through your glass. Why do you have to agree with what's going on? Why when you disagree with what America is doing are you unpatriotic? (Cee East, Black, female, U.S.-born, 26–45)

Many participants struggle with how to balance their desire for allegiance to their nation with their ambivalences about national practices. They express significant uncertainty about whether it is appropriate and acceptable to be critical of the government's actions. To negotiate this conflict, some make statements that appear to demonstrate a show of allegiance while stating the downside of *blind* allegiance:

I love my country but don't agree with everything that they do. I'm partially patriotic. I don't want to seem like I hate where I was born. I would never tell nobody I don't like America. I keep it to myself. I'm not going to talk bad about the place. (Cee East, Black, female, U.S.-born, 26–45)

The following comment reflects ambivalence about the notion of allegiance to one nation:

I don't have any attachments to the U.S. If I had to go fight a war, it's because they forced me. I wouldn't go because I want to defend my country, whether the U.S. or the Dominican Republic. I don't know if that's horrible to say. A lot of people say it's the best country in the world, but we're in a lot of the issues that we are today because of that idea. We all live on this globe. We're part of this bigger world, and the same way we need them, they need us. (Damaris, Latina, female, U.S.-born, 18–25)

Others are clear regarding where they stand:

My son told me he was going to enlist in the service, and I wanted to get a pot and bust him upside the head. I'm saying, "Why? Why are you going? I don't feel like this country did that much for you that you need to go. I don't know if you're going to get sent over in the war. I don't know how long this war is going to keep going and going and going." I said, "I'm going to kill you first before I let you go up and go into somebody's war." He said, "Ma, this is the country. You're supposed to love it." I don't love nothing about this country. I can't respect the higher authority of the country because there's so much scandal, and you know the rich getting rich and they doing everything not to give to the people. (Redd, Black, female, U.S.-born, 26–45)

Deidra (white, female, U.S.-born, over 65) expresses even more certainty:

Patriotism has nothing to do with what's happening in the U.S. The people who were supposed to be doing their jobs as watchdogs of the economy are not doing their jobs. Congress was not doing their jobs. They were hired to do certain things. Nobody wants to be a whistle-blower, because whistleblowers are not highly regarded, so people see bad things and most people don't say anything. It just gets more and more into problems until it blows up and has nowhere to go. It's like steam building up and then all of a sudden—bingo. That's what you had with this situation. There's a lot of rotten eggs. Even our bridges and highways are not being watched.

Some participants indicate that their thinking has changed over time:

When I was a kid, being patriotic meant buying T-shirts that said U.S.A. I was so proud. I'm not saying I lost that, but I don't see the patriotism this country has for itself. I just don't see it like when I was a kid I used to see it. (Chino, Latino, male, U.S.-born, 46–65)

I remember those times with them T-shirts. I used to love wearing them, especially on the Fourth of July: red, white, and blue. I'm going to say I'm patriotic, because I lost a lot of family in World War II and the Vietnam War, so whenever I'm somewhere and they raise that flag, I do my pledge of allegiance with not a problem. I have two kids in the service. That was, you know, by their choice. They got my blessings, and my prayers are always with them. (Spankey, Black, female, U.S.-born, 26–45)

I love this country, because it has helped so many other countries and because it has so much to offer to me. I wish there wasn't an age limit that you can go to participate in the United States Army or in the Ma-rines. I'm not a young man—51 years old—and I would go not to fight, [because] I had my opportunity to join the Army and I didn't want to go. I would like to give back to the United States, maybe assist with supplies or anything that they may need out there. There's a certain age that they won't take you. They should extend that, because you have a lot of Black men out there that don't have nothing to do or maybe some that want to give back to this county but because of their age bracket, that age limit is held against you. But I would like to go. (Chino, Latino, male, U.S.-born, 46–65)

Some write-in comments on the survey provide insight into thoughts about patriotism:

I am patriotic in the unconventional sense that I uphold people's right to challenge government leaders and policies to improve the lives of those who live and work in this country, because it would result in a more responsible and humanistic nation.

I don't believe in patriotism in terms of broad abstract national boundaries. Depending on the issue, multistate regions may feel more appropriate, or even subnational state[s]/cities.

Race and country are imaginary things, social constraints, and while I realize they "exist" to the extent they have very real repercussions on people's lives, I reject them personally and define myself as a human and that is it. Further, I am a patriot in that I criticize the government and the country in the hopes that it may progress. If what constitutes being a patriot is blind allegiance, then a patriot I am not.

That I don't consider myself to be patriotic should not be construed as being anti-American. I'm just too much of a humanist to be a patriot.

I strongly disagree with actions approved by the U.S. government, but I am patriotic in upholding the Constitution, not the people presently in the White House.

Some participants consider whether nationalism and patriotism could be reconciled with an understanding of the interconnectedness of all humanity:

I am patriotic, too. I am from Trinidad, and I love my country. Everybody's country is the best, but we are always all integrated in some way or the other. (Singing Dianne, Black, female, born outside the U.S., 46–65)

This includes thoughts about the tension between national and other identities that are conveyed in written comments on the survey:

I strongly consider myself an American because this is my birthplace, my home, but being an American is not a blanket that suppresses other fires. It is a fire too, just as being a father does not dim the fact that you are a brother, a son, a professional, a baseball coach. However, just as a parent knows [that] without critically watching and being willing to discipline, a child can run wild possibly doing destructive things, the same is true also for a society. Without being willing to critically watch our government and speak up when something is wrong, we are not patriots. We are absent parents.

For others, national identity is not primary, and questioning ideas about social categories makes sense:

> Look at how people react to certain types of people *and* how they react to other people's reactions. They usually go along because they know and trust this person, so they feel that anything they say is viable. There's a lot of people thinking so much in the box that you don't even consider that there's an outside to it. (Andy, white, male, U.S.-born, 18–25)

> My first identity isn't American. It's probably woman. (Justine, white, female, U.S.-born, 18–25)

On Being American

Many people express ambivalence specifically about being American:

> I consider myself American because I lived here most of my life from 19, and I'm almost 60. This country gave me the opportunity that I wanted. I have a good family. I have a good living here, and I contribute to this country. I'm a citizen now. I consider myself more American than Italian. I have Italy in my heart because I was born there and have good memories. I have family there, and we keep in touch all the time. This is something in me. My kids are born here. My husband is American and served in the war. I live a good life in the United States. If I have to choose, it would be a terrible choice, a terrible position for me to choose, but I love this country and I hate to see what's happening now. (Louise, Italian, female, born outside the U.S., 46–65)

> If you're Hispanic, you can tell the difference between who's Puerto Rican or Dominican, but in front of everybody else you're just Hispanic. I guess it's the same thing with being white or Korean. They know how to distinguish each other, so I guess it doesn't really make any difference. I identify as Dominican and get the questions because I was born over here. They ask me, "So why don't you say you're American?" I don't feel that saying I'm American means much. America was built on immigrants, and to me there's not a strong culture like saying I'm Italian or I'm Jewish or I'm Jamaican. In my house, we cook Dominican food, and I was raised on the music, and my grandmother was here a lot. (Damaris, Latina, female, U.S.-born, 18–25)

> I don't even know what an American is. There is no American. The only Americans are people like the Bushes and Cheneys and the Kerrys. There's not really an identity there. It's very kind of generalized. There is no real American except when you go to people who are descended from

the first people who colonized the country. Everyone else is hyphenated Americans. That's what it is . . . Jewish American, African American, etc. I can't relate on that level at all, because it doesn't really even make sense to me. (Andy, white, male, U.S.-born, 18–25)

Survey respondents ages 26 to 45 indicate that they think about their national identity more frequently but are less likely to consider themselves patriotic than those ages 46 to 64. Whites are more likely than Blacks to consider themselves to be American. (See Tables 4.1 to 4.3.)

The following comments written in the survey further explain these responses:

The dominant conceptualization is one that requires whiteness, maleness, and heterosexuality. Individuals who do not meet these criteria will never be considered true or "full" Americans (hence the plethora of dash-Americans—e.g., "African American").

I despise the term "American." I consider myself a sometimes-proud citizen of the United States.

Even though I was born here, I don't always identify with being American. I have ancestors that go back a zillion years here! This may be because I grew up with my mother, who is an immigrant and never identified with being American. But Obama helps me to identify with being an American again to a certain extent.

The concept of America as a nation (i.e., the United States) is imperialist. America is a continent, therefore I am American, but I'm not from nor do I carry a U.S. identity.

TABLE 4.1. HOW OFTEN DO YOU THINK ABOUT YOUR NATIONAL IDENTITY?

Never	Occasionally	Once a month	Once a week	Daily
7.8%	39.4%	10.2%	18.1%	23.4%

TABLE 4.2. I CONSIDER MYSELF TO BE PATRIOTIC

Strongly disagree	Disagree	Agree	Strongly agree	Don't know
6.1%	15.4%	47.5%	22.5%	8.5%

TABLE 4.3. I CONSIDER MYSELF TO BE AMERICAN

Strongly disagree	Disagree	Agree	Strongly agree	Don't know
4.0%	6.1%	45.1%	42.7%	2.0%

As indicated in the opening of Part II, nation as identity is complicated by political implications as well as questions of belonging. "Stories of My America" includes a sense of pride as well as deep reflections and critical views about nation, patriotism, and the particularities of those concepts for people living in the United States.

Identity, Community, and Belonging

Sociologists contend that culture is the knowledge that members of a social organization or a "society" share. This knowledge includes (1) ideas about what is right, (2) ideas of how one is to behave in various situations, (3) religious beliefs, and (4) patterns of communication (Eitzen and Baca Zinn 2001, 78). Culture constrains not only behavior but also how people think about and interpret their world (107). For many social scientists, however, culture is not a given but emerges as individuals interact and exchange ideas that develop into common beliefs and ways of doing things. Furthermore, once culture emerges, it is always undergoing change. Social science has long carried an evaluative component that ranked cultures in a hierarchical fashion, from civilized to primitive. Hundreds of years ago, the world was made up of countless small, tight-knitted, and more local cultures, but modern communication and industry have greatly narrowed the distance between these local groups, leading to some forms of global identification (Eitzen and Baca Zinn 2001). It is important to keep this framework in mind when reading the following discussions, as they complicate our understanding of the relationship between culture, society, and individuals.

Nationalism in this context can be viewed as an expression of a particular society's culture or identity. In the following section, we share reflections on the complex forces that influence identity formation and ways that the experiences of belonging and of exclusion can foster community, though in different ways.

"Nation of Immigrants?"

A central component of the discourse about the United States is the idea of the nation as a melting pot, drawing on people from around the globe, all receiving an opportunity to work hard and get rich. This narrative affirms the specialness of the United States and promotes the idea that all groups have equal access to the American Dream and upward mobility. Here are some of the thoughts that study participants have about these ideas:

> Europe has a lot of immigrants, too, so the idea that everybody is banging down the doors of America is not true. France has a lot of immigrants. England has a lot of immigrants. It's sort of self-centered. Like, there's the American Dream that everybody wants to come here. No, people in poor places, oppressed places want to come to wealthier, slightly freer places. Canada has a lot of immigrants, too. It's not an American thing.

That's our self-centeredness, thinking that people just want to come to America. Wealthier countries have jobs. It's not about just love of country. It's like navel-gazing. Just oblivious. This is a bigger demographic structural issue that's not we just love America to death. We want to get out of poverty and go to a country where there's jobs. Europe has immigration issues, too. (Carmella, white, female, U.S.-born, 26–45)

Groups of color have trouble, especially immigrants, because even though the country was built on immigrants, they're almost hated. The country is built on immigrants, so there shouldn't be this attitude or this attack on immigration. Like the Chinese being interned in camps—meanwhile, they're responsible for building some of the most magnificently engineered railroads' right of ways through mountains. Not to mention the slaves from Africa that got this country started, after they [the Europeans] stole it from the Indians. We were kidnapped and brought here to work the land. A war was fought because some people thought it was wrong, yet some people thought slavery was necessary. Jim Crow laws were written to hinder certain people. A lot of groups have struggled to achieve upward mobility. (Joseph, Black, male, U.S.-born, 46–65)

People want the law to be obeyed because of illegal immigration. We have to separate the two, because the idea that Americans hate immigrants is uninformed, because we're a nation of immigrants. Most people or at least some people have friends who are from other countries, are Americans now, or live here through the legal means. The issue of illegal immigration is difficult, because you don't want people to be mistreated, but you don't want the law broken. You don't like to look [at] images of families being broken up with mothers being torn away from their babies, but at the same time how do you deal with people who may have broken a law? How do you deal with the fairness of people who came here legally? (Jon, white, male, U.S.-born, 18–25)

And, then, there are the voices of people who have taken great risks to find the means for livelihood:

My sister came to the U.S. to follow her husband. They were married when she was 14, and then she had a child. She said, "Come to New York." I was thinking to go to Madrid, as it was easier. I could go as a tourist and borrow money but return it as soon as I got there. My sister said, "Don't go there; you have no family there."

So I found someone who was bringing people to the U.S. and they wanted $13,000, but now it is more. I took a plane to Mexico and then walked for two days and two nights. We were one hundred people. Some were from my town, so we talked as we walked. I heard that the women were being pulled into the bushes by the paleros,[2] but we just walked. I didn't know if I would live or die. I was very nervous. I had one gallon of water, bread, tuna, snacks. I was very sad and thinking about what did I do and prayed to God about the big danger I was in. I asked God to take me safely. (Marisol, Latina, female, born outside the U.S., 26–45)

What does this story indicate about our image of a nation of immigrants? Those sacrifices are real. The benefits of those challenges can be real, even if the individuals involved do not find streets paved with gold. There are greater opportunities in the United States. It is true that so many, particularly in Latin America, have been stripped of their means of farming. How do we reconcile local and global allegiance to community? The answer for the United States has to do with understanding the logic of the system that underlies the inequalities and provides the historical framework for why wealth is concentrated in some areas (and communities) and not in others. Once we understand that, we must reckon with a broader responsibility to those who resist their subordinate positioning in the global hierarchy.

The experiences of groups in the United States currently vary dramatically: from Africans brought and maintained in bondage to provide the labor with which the great wealth was produced to the Irish, Italian, and Eastern European immigrants who entered the United States poor and were then positioned in the political economy of the rising nation as a middle strata with significant (though not the greatest) wealth. At the top of the economic ladder were the white Anglo-Saxon elites whose experience was of colonizer, and at the bottom were the native peoples whose land was stolen and whose way of life was destroyed. Yet the rhetoric of the United States as a nation of immigrants provides a narrative that reinforces the image of the U.S. nation as exceptional in its practice of democracy and in its provision of opportunity for all. Many study participants share their thoughts about this idea.

Ties That Bind and Divide

As discussed above, political identity is complicated, because it often reflects how an individual understands power relationships and also reflects one's personal and group location. These factors are often influenced by the dominant narratives about different group characteristics, which tend to provide a rationale for inequality based on individual or group deficit or superiority and rarely reveal the structural logic of the system itself.

Participants evidence ambivalence and uncertainty about the significance of how they identify. Forging a unity based on an incomplete and inaccurate history complicates the social solidarity that we might feel for one another, because we do not understand the nature of the social relationships between us. How, for example, do we explain social inequality? Is it based on merit or structural relations that sort groups into winners and losers within particular economic-class positions (e.g., upper working class, lower working class, professional-managerial class, new petty bourgeoisie)? What is the impact of racialization on class position? Some question whether identities are determinative or whether people can choose how to understand their own places in society (both globally and locally). Implicit in this conversation is the question of how "real" is race. These comments illuminate the complexity of the conversations on these topics:

> I identify as biracial, specifically "Euro Asian." It has always been something pretty straightforward growing up in Hong Kong, because there is a lot of us. When I came to the U.S., everyone thought I was making it up, like I was trying to be special or something. Everyone should be able to self-identify, and I can't really do that here. People are always going to argue with me as to what I am, which is very irritating. Everyone always tries to guess your race. (Alice, Asian, female, born outside the U.S., 18–25)

> My name is Jung, but everyone calls me "Joe." I was born in Brooklyn and grew up in a predominately Italian American neighborhood. I never saw myself as Chinese until I saw a picture of myself in grade school. I was the only Asian kid, and that is when I knew I was different. The teacher would tell my parents not to speak to us in Chinese because it would impact us learning English and we could get confused. Not that I am not loyal or proud to be a Chinese person, but I think I am American first and then I am a Chinese person. (Joe, Chinese, male, U.S.-born, 26–45)

> Mostly people think that I am only Chinese because of my looks. I am Chinese *and* Puerto Rican, because I am proud of both aspects. My last name is Ramirez, so when they call my name, people don't think that it would be me. (Tara, Chinese/Latina, female, U.S.-born, 18–25)

> When I came to this country, after entering high school and then finishing, I had these questions: "Who are you?" "What is your ethnicity?" "Why do you have dreadlocks?" I was like, "Okay, I am Polish." Then immediately there are another set of characteristics that apply to you. Well you know Polish people—pretty stupid, drinks a lot, is very closed-minded, and the list goes on. Maybe there are some good characteristics as well, but the main point is that you identify yourself as something, and all of a sudden I found myself having to say I am Polish. In Poland, everyone looks the same. There aren't really a lot of people from other countries. It was this communist and socialist country, and everything was about this idea of internationalism. By identifying myself, I was doing something against my beliefs. I went to high school and I go to the

cafeteria, and everyone is sitting separately. I remember reaching out to people that spoke English, but then when they realized that I don't speak English, they never talk to you again. It was a very alienating experience. I was between these two worlds. (Stefan, white, male, born outside the U.S., 26–45)

What is interesting about my coming about—each grandparent left a stamp. One of them watched very difficult times—1920s—born in Georgia, worked in New York. The work ethic he developed out of the Depression made him a really strong individual. My other grandparents—born on a Caribbean island in English control—did not see themselves like everybody else. I got a taste of what people would call "the distancing"— we look alike, but we do not think alike. It fascinated me that I can be a part of a family with different roots. I had someone born on a reservation—brings to mind that they were born in a concentration camp. America is somewhat like a dysfunctional family—you claim it because you love it, but you know there are problems. (John, white, male, U.S.- born, 46–65)

My father is mixed; my mother is mixed. It's like somebody put puree on me. When I was younger, black kids wouldn't believe that I was black, and white kids wouldn't believe that I was white. It kind of turned into not fully being accepted by anybody. What's funny about it is my brother introduced me to Japanese pop-culture stuff when I was younger. I got interested in that and didn't even really hang out with anybody who was even Asian much, let alone Japanese, until I got to college and met a Japanese group of friends. Funny thing is even though I am black and white and I've been surrounded with people who are black or white or mixed all my life, I never felt as accepted as I did when I met those people and I went on a vacation with them to Japan. It felt more at home than even what I've already gone through or like logically you should feel. It's just kind of ridiculous—the boxes and clichés that they make for people. They try to size you up and can't understand or accept when something doesn't go the way or look the way they think it should. (Pike, Black/ white, male, U.S.-born, 18–25)

Citizenship

In many conversations, individuals talk about what citizenship means to them. They speak of it as a means for belonging and a way to be entitled to certain rights. They frequently refer to gaps between one's ideas about what citizenship should mean and what it really means in practice. Several respondents describe feeling alienated from the idea of citizenship because of just how hard surviving has become for them. They believe that if they truly belong and are valued as members of society, life will not be so difficult. One reflects on the role of government and the American Dream:

> After the hurricane, I immediately thought about this powerful earthquake in China, how people suffered from the disaster, and how the Chinese government moved quickly to help people, to help the country, and devoted a lot of effort to save people's lives. When I saw the TV, I cried every day. The earthquake killed so many people. The Chinese government saved people, and then the people helped each other. That's great. It's very emotional. Why can the Chinese government do that? But what did the American government do to help its people? So many people died, and then the government came to help, but not before. When the earthquake happened in China, the Chinese leaders immediately went to the province to contribute food and material. The people in power and the [ordinary] people helped to save the people. I make a comparison. I never see why people say the U.S. is a democracy. (Edward, Chinese, male, born outside the U.S., 26–45)

Individuals expressed that there are many ways to feel like an outsider:

> I always had the feeling that it was that community feeling to stay together and be safe in your own group, but that point of view has a negative effect on trying to achieve an American Dream. The American Dream is to achieve peace between everybody. If that can happen, then there would be no more fighting, no more war. My grandmother telling me marry Jewish [or] don't trust anybody else because they're not like you is kind of saying that I should have no trust in other people. I might be scared of other people and unwilling to even associate myself with anyone else. It makes a boundary there. (Jana, white, female, U.S.-born, 18–25)

> I got this attitude from my grandparents that you have to be very careful. The outside world is out to get you. It was this feeling of being very wary and very always having to keep to yourself. There was so much prejudice and hatred against Jews, so that feeling got transmitted through generations. You can't trust anyone outside our family. They're going to do you harm. (Ellen, white, female, U.S.-born, 46–65)

> The way you live your lives, the way you believe or the way you dress, the way you talk, the way you have some education, that is not mine, [it] is freedom. If my family wants to speak Spanish and they want to do all kinds of rice and beans, please, amen to that. If you want to do all spicy food, and I'll try it too. Learn a new language, Chinese, Japanese, whatever, it's all good. That's how it makes the American Dream. You bring

your culture with you; if all of a sudden you can't bring your culture with you, then this is not America. America should be free for people to come, but they have to follow rules and regulations. You have to protect your country. We do need restrictions [to] protect America. I'm against prejudice. I'm not against protecting America. (Genesis Ruth, Latina, female, U.S.-born, 46–65)

If I have to make a reservation in a restaurant and I have to give my last name, what kind of table am I going to get? So I give them a name like Murphy or Smith to ensure that when I get there, I'm going to get a nice table. (Joe, Chinese, male, U.S.-born, 26–45)

I never got a sense that there is someone else so ethnic as me. It was embarrassing as a kid (even how we ate different food). My friends were very American; I always felt really ethnic. I do not know whether they noticed it or I noticed it. Everyone wore Nike; we could not afford it. Once when I got it, one person pointed [it] out; then, I realized that people *are* noticing it. We were not rich, relative to those people, but were, relative to the rest of the country. I felt a sense of community when visiting my grandparents in Brooklyn—she [my grandmother] lived in a very bad neighborhood. Everyone there felt as part of each other. It felt so alive. People knew who my grandmother was; they cared about her. People had her back; no one had our back in our community.

I had a job at the age of 14; my friends did not. I identify as an Italian American. I do identify with Italy, but I have lived my whole life here. I have an uneasy relationship with the U.S., but I am pretty aware it shaped my views. I am not that close with my family in the U.S.—I do not see them. But my family in Italy—I can show up tomorrow and it will be okay. My cousins here—we do not keep in touch, but I keep in touch with the people in Italy, Australia, and Belgium. If I move to Italy, I would be happier. I am very privileged here—I am extremely aware what comfortable existence I have. It is not that I do not feel welcome, but I feel as a second-class citizen—it mostly has to do with my sexuality. Here it is either you are in or out; I feel I am out. Here it is either black or white—this country does not handle well with gray. This country does not exist on middle ground. It takes a lot more energy to be on middle ground. It is challenging for people to bump up into something which they cannot put into a category. (Lisa, white, female, U.S.-born, 26–45)

My father was a postal worker. . . . I remember this day my father was just practically spitting at the television at Ronald Reagan for firing the air traffic controllers and how that was the beginning of the end of America. I asked my father why he didn't love Reagan, and he said, "He's for the rich." Republicans are for the rich . . . and people don't see it. This country is being destroyed by the Republicans; people are so stupid. They've had it too good for too long. Roosevelt put all these programs in place, and we've got unions and things. People have gotten soft and they don't see. . . . (Carmella, white, female, U.S.-born, 26–45)

I'm torn with regard to birthright citizenship. It isn't the fact that I don't really like the idea of simply being born here making you a citizen. It's hypocritical. A good compromise might be the people who came here as resident aliens, people who came on visas and green cards and say they expired. I would give them preference over people who just crossed the border. People say, "Well you can't deport X million people at once." We can try. What if we try and we still don't do so? Well, you make murder, rape, and theft illegal, and it still happens. (Jon, white, male, U.S.-born, 18–25)

The Logic of Location

In this section of the chapter, we share comments by respondents about their understanding of opportunity differentials provided depending on a range of characteristics, including, but not limited, to race, class, gender, and geography. For example, several participants note that people in the United States as a whole have greater access to educational and economic options than those in poorer countries. One's experiences are shaped by one's environment, and both influence one's perspective about society.

Joseph (Black, male, U.S.-born, 46–65) offers his reflections:

Growing up, my friends included Black and Latino people. It wasn't because I didn't like white people—it's just because I didn't come in contact with them until high school. I wanted to travel outside of Harlem, and I'm glad I did. I heard folks in Harlem say, "I've never been south of 110th Street," and I wanted to make sure that was not the case for me. I wanted to experience as many things as I could, so I went to high school in Brooklyn. I didn't show outward pride, but I love East Harlem. It did mean a lot to me when eventually I ended up back in East Harlem doing environmental work.

Bessie was born in the West Indies in a mixed family. Though she did not think of it much while growing up, she says that she clung to the "Black side," since she did not feel as good as those with straight hair and lighter skin, who were clannish and cliquish. She always dreamed that she would move to the United States, where she believed that there were no clans or cliques. When she moved to the United States and into a building with mostly white residents, where she now lives, she felt welcomed by them, much more so than when at home. During this discussion, the following exchange takes place:

The New York view of Mexicans and Russians, it's almost the same. They start in almost the same place, except all the Mexicans you see seem to be in very low-paying jobs—extremely hard-working but they get nowhere, while the Russians aren't here for very long, learn enough English that they need to get by, and become really successful in their own neighborhood. (Andy, white, male, U.S.-born, 18–25)

In this neighborhood, there's lots of Asians, Russians, and Mexicans. Mexican people work so hard, but it's much more fractured for them. It's often just the young guys here and living ten in a small apartment, sending money home to family. They're trying to improve their situation for themselves and their family. They work together. Often they don't have legal status, so they don't get the decent paying jobs, so they're really struggling. In Brighton, growing up in the mid-seventies, there was this whole influx of Russian Jews. Our country had made this agreement with Russia that they would let the Jews come here, because they had been very oppressed. Jewish groups would sponsor them, so it was this mass exodus of Russians that came. Within an extremely short time, they were opening up these huge businesses, and we just couldn't understand how they were doing so well so quickly. It probably was a lot of illegal things, but there was this kind of cooperative, organized system where they worked well together. They pooled all their resources as a group and managed to beat the system. (Ellen, white, female, U.S.-born, 46–65)

The Russians—not all are illegal, but they're shrewder. Under the Soviet Union—and a lot of them are Jewish—they had to be clever and wheeler dealers just to survive under communism. They're just used to doing things, whatever it might be—paying people off or whatever it is—so they manage to get here and quickly get a lot of advantages. (Tony, white, male, U.S.-born, 46–65)

What determines success seems to be culture. It's the major variable in who you are. They're both very hard-working, but the difference is the mentality. There's a lot of stereotypes for everybody, but it's how you look at those stereotypes and where they come from. There's a lot of open stereotypes about Mexicans, about Jews, about Russians, about Blacks, about everyone. It's not just like somebody spouting out, because it comes from somewhere. It comes from somebody seeing something more than once, a certain trend, and those trends lead to stereotypes. It comes from a lot of—it comes from just a lot of truth. (Andy, white, male, U.S.-born, 18–25)

Mexicans are illegal because there's a lot of them. Some of them are legal, but there's so many of them that it's just a poor country. They really are desperate, so they come over and take whatever work. A food stand might hire them because they can get them to work thirteen hours a day at under minimum wage. (Tony, white, male, U.S.-born, 46–65)

The power of Russia itself is [such that] we might want to have better relations with them. It's in our interest, so we are willing to accept more legal Russians in than Mexicans. What would Mexico particularly do for us as a country? (Ellen, white, female, U.S.-born, 46–65)

Participants are ambivalent about the roles that group culture and social context play in improving or decreasing the chances for any one group. Is the Russian community in a stronger position than the Mexican community due to illegal activity? Culture? Political interests of the United States? It is well documented that members of this community have been provided supports inaccessible to other immigrants. Many believe that this situation has occurred because it is to the United States' advantage to provide refuge from the "evils" of communism. However, the dominant explanation speaks to cultural differences as the reason for differential success in upward mobility.

The Role of Social Characteristics

Racialization repeatedly emerges as a key factor that people note as affecting an individual and group's location. Participants speak to the impact of this experience in their own lives:

"Discriminate" is not a word that I use often, but one time I applied for a job that I [was] overqualified for and never got a call. I changed my name in my résumé (so it wouldn't appear Haitian), and they called me. They asked, "Why did you apply for this job? Why do you have this name?" I felt discrimination. For my name, my country—in New York, there is great discrimination. (Bobole, Haitian, female, born outside the U.S., 46–65)

People would ask me, "What are you?" and I would answer, "I'm Jamaican," and it wasn't enough. It was, "No, but what *are* you? You have that hair and that skin. What *are* you?" I would go back to my mother, who understood the dynamic better. I would ask her, "What is it that they're asking me?" That's how I learned that I had to have an identity based on the color of my skin, because up until that time it was not a facet of my life. (Patrice, Black, female, born outside the U.S., 46–65)

Anna (female, U.S.-born, 18–25) identifies as Puerto Rican, Dominican, and Danish:

People can never tell what nationality I am, and they are shocked when I tell them. They are surprised that I speak well—at times, it is a little bit insulting. Because I come from Latina background does not mean I speak in a certain way. I am Spanish, but I also am educated. People are closed-minded.

After a while you can tell the difference between how someone is going to perceive you. You can feel the vibe and read it. People will treat you in a certain way because of who they think you are. They have certain expectations, regardless of how valid they are. When it comes to the race thing, all people see is skin color. (Jay, Black/Latino/Native American, male, U.S.-born, 18–25)

In high school I would come home on weekends and was allowed to bring home a friend from El Salvador, but when I asked to bring home a Haitian, my parents refused. That bothered me, because I saw my parents as religious. Coupled with that, I went for the first time into a neighborhood that was entirely Black, and I was the only white. I noted this is how it must feel to be on the other side of the fence. My awareness began then, and it's progressed ever since. (Carmella, white, female, U.S.-born, 26–45)

I have a brother who's [been] married to a white woman for over fifty years. When their baby was born, she was arrested, because there was a law on the books that says any white woman who has a baby by a Negro or a mulatto, it's against the law. It took them almost two years to get our nephew back. (Mandy, Black, female, U.S.-born, over 65)

Having a child and wife of color makes me much more sensitive to the very many difficulties. I'll tell you honestly that I hoped that our child would be a girl, because I knew that life would be a lot easier for a black female than for a black male. We were not revolutionaries. We weren't hippies. I didn't want to prove anything. You know? I didn't go looking for minority girls to date. We worked together. We had similar interests. We fell in love, and we got married. Forty years later, I'd say it's fine. (Stan, white, male, U.S.-born, over 65)

My mom is Scottish. My dad is German. Middle-class Caucasian. American. People say, "I'm this American, that American." I go, "Are you from Scotland? Are you from Germany? No. You know what? You're not. You're American. Sorry." (John, white, male, U.S.-born, 46–65)

I still cry, because I know what my ancestors went through. I know what the people and the generations behind me went through. I've seen a lot.

I've seen cops beat up guys for no reason. I've seen guys getting stopped talking on the corner to their grandparents, just because [they] fit the "description" of a Black male. There are fifty million black males running the streets of Brooklyn, so are you going to stop every black male? It still hurts to know that my people are getting treated a way just because of their skin tone. I lived in Montréal for five years, from 2000 to 2005. They treat everybody as one. There's no color barrier. If anything, they're more strict on their language, if you don't speak their French language, but as far as color barrier, it's all one. To live in a country that's right on the same continent as mine and know that you can just cross a line and people treat you so different—it's kind of strange. They're living different rules then we are here in the United States. They're run by two different governments. In the United States, we've been brainwashed for thousands of years, and they continue to still try to brainwash us now with the stuff that they put on TV and in newspapers. All that stuff is brainwash. My grandmother likes to say, "If you don't want a black person to know something, you put it in a book, because they won't read it." But that's not true. The people that you think don't read is the people who read the most. (S. Westmoreland, Black, female, born outside the U.S., 18–25)

I'm 23 years old, born and raised in Brooklyn. My father was Puerto Rican, and my mother was Italian. My family is fractured in class, not only race. I've grown up with an outsider's view of race. People try to box me into one or the other race but not so much class, as there wasn't any ambiguity to which I was boxed into. I don't really view my nationality. . . . [I]t isn't forefront in my mind. (Dennis, white/Latino/Puerto Rican/ Italian male, U.S.-born, 18–25)

I'm Black. You're white. This is what it is. You know? Keep the little folks focused on little things that aren't a big deal, so you miss the big stuff that is a big deal. You keep them fighting amongst themselves. Racism and prejudice is a learned act. (Harold, Black, male, U.S.-born, 26–45)

Prejudice certainly plays a role. The fact is, how did Blacks come here? They came in chains. Whites came of their own volition with the intent of a better life. They consistently fought for it, and that's how they lived. Blacks came here against their will and eventually got their freedom, but there were people who didn't want them to have those rights, so to deny that discrimination plays a role is ludicrous. At the same time, there is a separatism. My bus to school took some of the children from the northern part of my town, so I had a mostly Black bus. They were almost always talking about race. Whenever I was with my white friends, they talk about race much less. When you are part of a group which has been oppressed or maybe just not as well off, that frames your reference and how you live. (Jon, white, male, U.S.-born, 18–25)

I'm very sheltered, because I grew up in an all-white town, and there's no culture. Honestly, I've never been around so many Black people in my life. They're just people, but growing up, people don't go to certain areas, basically just because it's a black neighborhood and it's dangerous. It's really not fair. A lot of that is what you're taught. I don't really like the whole idea of race, because it's just a social construction anyway. (Justine, white, female, U.S.-born, 18–25)

I have [a] personal example. If you cannot speak good English because you're born outside, you have a different accent. When you speak with Americans, they look down on you. They don't give you the interview, or they interview for 15 minutes and then let you go. You have no equal opportunity to get the job even though you have the same ability. My experiences tell me I have to work harder, get more skills, and learn three times more than others, and then you get a job. (Edward, Chinese, male, born outside the U.S., 26–45)

Women are entering the workforce. How many of them are actually CEOs? How many own Fortune 500 companies? How many of them personally own businesses rather than simply working for them out-side of the home? You have Blacks achieving equality, but how many of them are actually in government? Barack Obama was the only black man in the Senate when he got elected. That says something. Everybody else in the Senate was white or Asian, but 12 percent of the population is Black—you'd think that twelve senators would be Black. Remember, most white people voted for McCain. The demographic shift made a dif-ference. We still have a country where a Black man lives five years less than a white man. Infant mortality is twice for Blacks that it is for whites. It's money. It's not your skin. Your skin color doesn't automatically put you at a disadvantage. (Jon, white, male, U.S.-born, 18–25)

In these varied reflections, participants speak to the ways that race, lan-guage, nation, and class influence one's life experience and chances. The individ-uals interviewed indicate that the location of different groups depends on how they are viewed by society and that such societal judgments become interwoven in the consciousness of individuals. Through this lens, tensions in the American Dream become apparent.

Not separate from race but with its own particular ways of shaping individu-al and group experience, gender positioning plays a role in how one is perceived, treated, and located in the social structure. This participant speaks directly to this point:

I have an older brother who completed his engineering degree. That was a big thing in my mother's life. One of my cousins made a comment to my mother that I'm one of those overeducated black women. So he's not an overeducated black man, but I'm an overeducated black woman, which just goes to show you not only are you dealing with color but you're dealing with gender and all of that stuff that goes with it. The potential is the beacon, but it is also the pitfall. (Patrice, Black, female, born outside the U.S., 46–65)

Unlike the mythical representations of people that we see in so many portrayals, people are generally more discerning when they speak in their own voices. Here, many participants convey a strong sense of class identity and awareness of the ways that their socioeconomic positions play important roles in shaping their life experiences and chances:

I started seeing the difference. I work at a PR firm, and everybody that works there lives such a different life. It's the way you speak, who you like, what you read, the type of shows you watch. My boss knows Broadway plays and goes to performances every other night. Those are things that we didn't do, so I feel like an outsider. After you go to college, you start being taught that you have creativity. Don't go to work just because it pays you, go to work because you like it and because you want to really do something. In my community, the main goal is to make money, but not just to have more money—it's to be able to pay the bills. (Damaris, Dominican, female, U.S.-born, 18–25)

We always had books in the house, but my parents didn't have college degrees. Going to college was a different world just because there was a class difference, even though I was white and I fit in. Like having a roommate talking about her father's union problems. I was thinking, "Oh, my parents are part of the union, too," and then I found out he didn't want his shop unionized. I felt sort of like, "Whoa, okay, different world here." (Carmella, white, female, U.S.-born, 26–45)

Some reflect on the ways that class plays a role in political debates. Isabelle suggests that we need to "figure out what 'middle class' really means" to understand the American Dream. Other participants agree:[3]

It's just mind-blowing that a huge deal was made that Obama said "spreading the wealth." I can't comprehend $250,000 a year. . . . [I]t is not something I understand. If a person were making $250,000 a year, if they were to pay $100,000 in taxes on top of what they pay now, that's so much more than I earn. What does that say about the American Dream? (Dennis, white/Latino/Puerto Rican/Italian, male, U.S.-born, 18–25)

A lot of the American Dream is really bound up with wanting to be the quintessential consumer of everything, consuming houses, consuming cars, just wanting to have . . . why one house, [have] two; why one car, have three. There [is] something to be said about . . . American vanity, as everyone wants to self-identify as closer to the wealthy than they are to the poor. (Dan, white, male, U.S.-born, 18–25)

But money and happiness are not always equated in people's minds:

It is also good to be poor, as we were happy. The rich had their problems, as they don't know what to do with themselves and don't know how to be happy. I was happy but just needed money. Starting at age 10, I began to work to help my family. I took care of the rich people's horses. We went to school together, but the poor children were not treated right. (Marisol, Latina, female, born outside the U.S., 26–45)

Being high class in an Eastern European country shaped my views. Things have been automatically provided for me. I do not need to work to obtain these things—my parents will do it. It will be provided for me, because I deserve it. Some people have $50,000 in their checking account at the age of 4. This is not a bad thing, since their parents worked for it. Their parents deserve to have this money, [so] why not give it to their children, why not use it? In Bulgaria, everyone had a house in the nineties; the government provided you with housing. The communist ideology was that everyone who works should have a house. We had food, we ate, but we were poor in the sense—no shopping, I had to wear my sister's clothes, no new furniture—everything was marginal. (Victoria, white, female, born outside the U.S., 18–25)

This country is set up to keep people where they are. It gets passed down from generation to generation. The working class stays in the working class, and the middle class stays in the middle class. The rich stay where they are by sending their kids to the best schools and to events where CEOs of Fortune 500 companies go. The majority of people probably do stay in their status. (Damaris, Dominican, female, U.S.-born, 18–25)

There's rich because there's poor. That's the way I'd put it. (Carmella, white, female, U.S.-born, 26–45)

There's one because of the other. One can't be there without the other. The only way you're able to make profit or to increase your profit is by decreasing your labor cost. I never thought about that. To me, you have your supplies and the time that people put in and the labor and all that. You add it up and then whatever is left over is profit. It is true. That's the only place they decrease in order to make a profit. (Damaris, Dominican American, female, U.S.-born, 18–25)

Think about, like, where all this stuff comes from. Half of it is made in China now. People are living in poverty in China and working their butts off so we can buy things for cheap. Our gain is somebody else's labor. You've gotta take somebody else's labor to be wealthy. You can have a division of labor and do that in a flatter society where some people are a little more wealthy than other people. America is in a different stage of development than China. If you were born in America at this point in the century, you were born [in]to a wealthy country. If you were born into China, you were born into a poor country. Also it depends on where you were born in America, as poverty and wealth tend to be inherited. There are exceptions. People can switch. A very wealthy person could wind up poor. A very poor person can push and get ahead and slowly move up. But there's not unlimited mobility. People love to tell stories about how this person worked hard and got ahead. Well you know what? Maybe they did work hard to get ahead, but a lot of other people worked hard and didn't get ahead, because there was only one scholarship. I grew up with somebody whose mother was a second-generation Polish immigrant and couldn't read or write, and his father was Italian American, like second-generation. He was never very good at school. We were both ethnic white people. I was smart and got straight As and got recommended for every-thing and got ahead. Did I work hard? Sure, but I didn't have a learning disability. My parents were literate. His mom was illiterate. I got lucky. Did I work harder in school than him? Maybe, but school was easy for me. His father was in Vietnam and has psychological problems and beat the kids. That probably had something to do with it too. My father was in World War II and didn't have as bad an experience as people did in Vietnam. It's not because I worked so much harder. He works hard as a janitor. I got born with more stuff. When people say, "Why do people make it?" I look at me and my next-door neighbor. We used to play to-gether as kids, the same neighborhood, same schools. He's a janitor. I'm a grad student. You know? (Carmella, white, female, U.S.-born, 26–45)

The G.I. bill is garbage. It's a lie. It's a fraud. It's a setup. The G.I. bill is a hustle. We're going to take some of the money that you earned, and then we're going to give it back to you and tell you it's the G.I. bill so you can think we gave you something. (Harold, Black, male, U.S.-born, 26–45)

A conservative believes a cotton-candy nanny-fanny dream that any-body can achieve anything. It's contradictory, because when we talk about the American Dream, we do speak about how America enables anybody to do anything. However, conservatives also believe that some

TABLE 4.4. TO WHAT EXTENT DO THESE FACTORS CONTRIBUTE
TO THE HIGHER INCOMES AND WEALTH OF WHITES AS A GROUP?

	Not at all	A little	Somewhat	Quite a bit	A lot
Strong work ethic	48.1%	17.6%	20.6%	7.8%	5.8%
Greater intelligence	81.9%	4.4%	8.0%	3.4%	2.2%
Institutional privileges	3.8%	5.2%	13.5%	25.0%	52.5%
Preferencing by individuals	3.2%	8.6%	15.2%	33.0%	40.0%

TABLE 4.5. TO WHAT EXTENT DO THESE FACTORS CONTRIBUTE
TO THE LOWER INCOMES AND WEALTH OF BLACKS AS A GROUP?

	Not at all	A little	Somewhat	Quite a bit	A lot
Lack of motivation	39.6%	24.3%	17.7%	11.5%	7.0%
Less intelligence	80.8%	7.4%	5.4%	4.6%	1.8%
Institutional disadvantages	3.8%	7.3%	14.3%	27.4%	47.2%
Discrimination by individuals	2.6%	6.5%	28.9%	34.2%	27.9%

people are just not naturally able to do certain things. It's painfully obvious that some people have a certain inherent quality, and I'm not speaking in any kind of eugenics context. Some people have certain qualities that others don't. I do not believe that somebody who has muscular dystrophy would be able to win a gold medal in swimming.

There is kind of a romanticizing of the American Dream, which in my opinion is hippy-dippy, that anybody can do anything. That's not true. You can't be anything you want to. Some people can do some things. Some people can't. That doesn't mean that you should take one of those awful preordained tests which says the job you're best for, because that's awful and crushes your creativity, but some people have better skills than others. I like to draw and write and sing, but, I mean, I can't do math to save my life. I could get better at it, but I'll never be a great mathematician, no matter how hard I try. We're all people, but we're all different.

There's also a certain degree that opportunity brings. If you have a set of identical twins who are 99.6 or so percent the same, and you raise one in a rich household and one in a poor household, they probably will have very different futures, even though they may have the same or very similar abilities. It's very hard to find experiments like that, because that would be a gross abuse of people. Poverty stifles people's abilities, because you probably won't get certain educational opportunities which would foster your innate skills. (Jon, white, male, U.S.-born, 18–25).

In the survey responses shown in Tables 4.4 and 4.5, systemic and institutional factors (institutional privileges/advantages or preferencing/discrimination) in explaining racial inequality receive greater support than those that point to individual or group deficits (work ethic, intelligence, motivation).

Regionality

To some, New York City is a nation in its own right, with particular characteristics distinct from other parts of the United States. As focus groups were held in the metropolitan area, participants reflect on how this environment influences their experiences and perspectives:

> I have been all over the country; they do not see New Yorkers as being American. In the South, you are not a real American, you are a New Yorker. Not one of Sarah Palin's "real Americans." (Ron, white, male, U.S.-born, 46–65)

> In New York City, you're exposed to people of different backgrounds, so to me, that's normal. (Dennis, white/Latino/Puerto Rican/Italian, male, U.S.-born, 18–25)

> Everyone always says that New York is this melting pot and that all the cultures stick together. But New York City is really segregated. They segregate themselves according to their religion, or their race/ethnicity, or their neighborhoods, or the boroughs they live in. I was disappointed. (Audrey, Black, female, U.S.-born, 26–45)

> New York is its own little country. It's almost like everyone was bad-mouthing New York. Maybe [we] should consider some kind of New York City secession from the rest of the country. It would make a lot of sense, because the views are so varied about everything, and anything goes. (Andy, white, male, U.S.-born, 18–25)

A related component of the identity of the metropolitan area is that of the suburbs. The creation of Levittown and establishment of segregated towns on Long Island was part of the post–World War II period of supported upward mobility for whites and a corresponding new era of marginalization for Blacks. Despite the rhetoric of opportunity, homeownership and educational access were in practice provided for only the Europeans who immigrated at the turn of the twentieth century.[4] This period marked the firm creation of a middle class that would enact and then defend the Horatio Alger narrative, using themselves as the example and denying the reality of systemic and institutional barriers to mobility that were firmly entrenched. Such scholars as Stephen Steinberg (*The Ethnic Myth*) and Karen Brodkin Sacks (*How the Jews Became White*) have written extensively about the way that these openings for a particular segment of the white community provided just the imagery of the actualization of the

American Dream, as if it were accessible to all. This situation also created a constituency firmly committed to its defense.

Ideology and the U.S. Nation

The U.S. nation developed along ideological lines, with notions of equality, democracy, and freedom built into the narratives that assert the character of both the nation and the people. This section examines how these ideas are viewed now, at this period of economic and political challenges both domestically and globally, by exploring participants' reflections about this question. Most people express the idea that freedom and opportunity are the most outstanding characteristics of U.S. society, and there is a strong belief that people come to the United States from around the globe because they value democracy. However, some respondents challenge these ideas:

The American Dream goes back to the folklore this country turns to. If you go all the way back—it was not the same, there was a lot of disparity between how the country was set up and how it is actually run. Our government system has a fundamental mistrust of people yet calls itself [a] democracy. The system is different from the story. (Lisa, Italian American, female, U.S.-born, 26–45)

We are told that we're free, and we're really not. We're just allowed to *think* that we're free, so it's a question of about what freedom really is. We're free until you start stepping on the wrong people's toes. (Damaris, Dominican American, female, U.S.-born, 18–25)

Freedom is very constrained within the system in a lot of ways. You're free to get a job or shop at Walmart or Target, but you're not free to start a labor union there. If you try that, they have vast amounts of money and resources to wipe out your union and blackball you. You have this illusion of freedom. It's like, if you don't like working at Walmart, get a job somewhere else. We're not as oppressed as the workers in China, but workers in Walmart still have their freedom very much constricted. It's less brutal, it's less extreme, but we're kidding ourselves if we think that there aren't certain lines drawn around just how free you can be. If you cross them, you'll find out pretty quickly what happens to you. It seems free and happy and little yellow smiley faces until you cross the wrong line, and then the resources crack down. Drugs are another perfect example, as they are a great way of keeping people in line, too. (Carmella, white, female, U.S.-born, 26–45)

From what you hear on, like, the news about other countries, I'm glad I'm not there with them, saying you have to be inside at a certain time or you've got to do this. To be free is not to be told how you have to do things, how you have to dress, what time you have to be in your house, and where you can go. My thinking about freedom and democracy is having to work, and that you get to vote. That's being democratic, because it's your choice of what you want to do and how things go for you. Just to be able to say if I want to be Christian, if I want to switch to be Catholic. It's my choice, and people can say what they want, but I still can do that. (Geneva Diva, Black, female, U.S.-born, 18–25)

People come here because of capitalism and the idea of having money here. The whole idea was that you can be self-made. Most people start with a big plan, and as you become experienced, your dream falls to the picket fence and 2.5 kids. I always felt as if I was trying to get somewhere, to hurry up to some place. (Barry, white, male, U.S.-born, 26–45)

Because the government has written the Constitution that tells us we are endowed with inalienable rights, the government gives us these rights. People forget that those rights and the pursuit of those things go beyond any government. We lose sight that the pursuit of happiness existed outside of America long before America came to be. (Yusef, Black/Native American, male, U.S.-born, 26–45)

Democracy was equal rights [and] freedom of speech that our ancestors fought for, but today, do we really have truly a democracy? You have to be careful what you say today. Freedom, it comes with [a] penalty, so where is the democracy at? (Chino, Latino, male, U.S.-born, 46–65)

They tell you it's free, but certain things you cannot say. They [are] ready to lock you up. You should be able to joke. If I'm among so-called Americans, what's the problem, what's the big deal? (Cee East, Black, female, U.S.-born, 26–45)

To me, freedom is when you're able to do what you want to do to become successful. There's a lot of different kinds of freedom. You can be an entrepreneur, own your own company. That's one freedom. You can actually work for a company, where you have to go up the stepping ladder, and that's another kind of freedom. Say you have a criminal record; it's going to be harder for you to get a job. I'm not saying impossible. It's going to be harder, because they, you put yourself at a default. (Rome, Black, male, U.S.-born, 18–25)

What democracy means and freedom means is not the same [as] how it was two hundred years ago. When Abraham Lincoln said that the slaves were free, they wasn't free to go vote. People that vote was just the middle-class and the high-class people. I'm not going to say that lower-class people wasn't voting, though, but if you check statistics, that's all a part of democracy. You know, the people run the government, not the government itself. It's kind of hard when you've got people in higher classes with different agendas on their mind already. America hasn't fallen yet, so the things that the government has done has kept us here at the top. We're not a second-world country. We're not a third-world country. We run the show. When you look at it from a media perspective and you see how they live, it's kind of crazy. Democracy really doesn't mean anything, but the way I look at it, I've gotta look at it from both perspectives, and that's probably what makes me stay alive. (Paul, Black/Latino, male, U.S.-born, 18–25)

Many of the discussions include robust exchanges about the role of environment, culture, and individual effort in determining one's economic position:

Not everybody can be successful. There are hundreds of people that are not. Do they have the same opportunity? The mind-set is not the key—it's the environment makes the difference. It is nice wanting to be successful while living in a box over a heating grate. At the end of the day, this does not give you success. In this circumstance, mind-set doesn't mean anything. (Yusef, Black/Native American, male, U.S.-born, 26–45)

If you take socialized medicine, like the National Health Service in England, there are people who have benefited from it. If you don't have enough to provide for everybody, if you have a system where everybody is guaranteed health care, and, as a result, you have long lines waiting at the doctor, a shortage of doctors, etcetera, then there is a problem with that. We already have a redistributive system with large government programs like Medicare and Medicaid, which are obviously not quite the same scale as in other countries, such as Canada. I would never want to see people suffer, and if we can provide for that person, then fine. Charity plays an important role as well. Sometimes capital can be better invested in the private sector than in the public sector. You're doing the exact same thing, but some of it can be more efficient when you have less tape and less bureaucracy. You've always got to explore every option. (Jon, white, male, U.S.-born, 18–25)

Some people are blessed and can rise above anything. Most people are products of what they come from. The values of the culture that you grow up in makes a difference. Some groups have a little more opportunity. People who become successful were bent on becoming successful. If you are from a culturally starved background, you have to be very talented to be successful. If you come from three generations of drug dealers, it is going to be pretty hard to pull that off—in the second case, you do not have the tools, but it does not mean you cannot do it. (Ron, white, male, U.S.-born, 46–65)

If I were younger, I would define the American Dream in terms of having a job and just to have a comfortable life. I am very Christian-hearted, so I like friendship, church-going, and these are the things that are the American Dream to me. Not the modernistic things—they don't attract me that much. Like that kind of music that is going on now. I really hate it. All this kind of hip-hop just blows my mind. I wouldn't call it the American Dream, but for most people, this is what is going on with them now. (Madge, Black/Native American, female, U.S.-born, over 65)

The American Dream is possible, but not for everybody. Some of it is hard work, but most of it is a lot of luck. We grew up on the idea [that] if you study hard and don't hang out on the street or with bad people, you'll be okay. But everything is about the boys. And anyway, there's still the impact of slavery. And class plays a big role. My brother is a model minority, but my husband and I are moving toward poverty. (Layla, Chinese American, female, U.S.-born, 46–65)

Some reflect on whether competition is a positive social value or detrimental to the common good. Many people express the opinion that in an unequal society where opportunities and access are provided differentially to different groups, those with wealth, power, and status have an unfair advantage:

Companies try to control people in this country. People are not bold, they are afraid. They do not challenge their government. They are terrified. (Frizzy, male, self-describes as "Other," U.S.-born, 46–65)

I have [spent] three months fighting with my job because they wouldn't let me have my days off to take the test, and if I couldn't take the test, I couldn't get into school. Three months, and then in the end my boss says, "Well, it's not like you're going to be a doctor." Like it wasn't important enough for me to get my GED. He's Caucasian, and I don't have nothing against Caucasian people. I love all of them. But it's the way he treated me. He doesn't like Spanish people. So you're saying just because I'm 40 years old, I can't get my GED. It's not important for me to get it? I have struggled all my life. I raised my sisters. I raised my kids. I raised my sister's kids, and I'm taking care of my father. (Genesis Ruth, Latina, female, U.S.-born, 46–65)

While some in this group display a clear understanding of the role of individual agency in achievement, they are not wedded to the notion of the Protestant work ethic as a meaningful goal in and of itself. Hard work is viewed as a means to an end and not an end itself. Take note of the following exchange:

If you don't have a good education, you get the worse [sic] jobs ever. You have to work on your feet. You gotta do all the heavy lifting. You have to deal with people that are going to be mean to you. They're going to talk down to you because you don't have an education, or because you are Latino or an African American or an Indian. You have to swallow so much just to try to get a paycheck. There were lots of times that my boss was very prejudiced against me. He even cursed me out, and I had to swallow it and say [to myself], "Man, my rent is due, and I have to pay fifteen hundred dollars. I can't leave this job." Once I worked sixty-five hours in one week. I got sick, but I had to do it, because I owed the rent and I owed the light and I owed the gas, and I had no food in my house. I had to do it. (Genesis Ruth, Latina, female, U.S.-born, 46–65)

It's troublesome. You go to college to go into debt. You go to jail to get out of debt. It confuses me. (Niecey, Black, female, U.S.-born, 26–45)

The American Dream is supposed to be perfect, so there should be no rule of hard work. Once you achieve what you need to achieve, there shouldn't be anything more hard to do, because getting there to me is the hardest. (Ziana Zania, Black, female, U.S.-born, 18–25)

Not surprisingly, survey respondents with family incomes of more than $200,000 are more likely than those with family incomes under $50,000 to believe that all people are treated equally and that the United States is a land of equal opportunity. (See Tables 4.6 and 4.7.)

TABLE 4.6. PEOPLE OF COLOR ARE TREATED EQUALLY TO WHITES WHEN APPLYING FOR JOBS AND HOUSING AND WHEN APPROACHED BY POLICE

	Income less than $50,000	Income $50,000–$100,000	Income $101,000–$200,000	Income more than $200,000
Strongly disagree	63.9%	54.7%	51.4%	44.0%
Disagree	31.6%	37.4%	44.1%	40.0%
Agree	2.6%	4.2%	2.7%	4.0%
Strongly agree	0.0%	2.6%	0.0%	12.0%
Don't know	1.9%	1.1%	1.8%	0.0%

TABLE 4.7. THE UNITED STATES IS A LAND OF EQUAL OPPORTUNITY FOR ALL

	Income less than $50,000	Income $50,000–$100,000	Income $101,000–$200,000	Income more than $200,000
Strongly disagree	47.1%	33.9%	37.8%	24.0%
Disagree	36.8%	41.8%	36.0%	44.0%
Agree	13.5%	17.5%	19.8%	12.0%
Strongly agree	2.6%	5.8%	4.5%	20.0%
Don't know	0.0%	1.1%	1.8%	0.0%

Capitalism and U.S. National Interests

In what ways do nationalist and capitalist ideology converge? How do they diverge? Are the national interests of the people of the United States the same as capitalists' interests? A significant part of U.S. national identity is our feeling of unique entitlement to capitalist patterns of consumption that prevail in the richest states of the world-system:

> All you have to do is go to an inner city and see the American Dream is a myth. Whose dream is it anyway? Who came up with the term? The American Dream is almost something we have to look up on Wikipedia to know what the heck we are talking about. It is the whole white-picket fence or house in the suburbs, that "land of opportunity" kind of thing. For generations and generations, certain groups have not benefited from the supposed opportunities that are here. We have to ask why that is. If you are born in a slum in Brazil or other developing countries, your chances of reaching middle class or wealth or elite are almost none. There are no rags-to-riches stories . . . maybe not even riches, maybe just rags to middle class. . . . [H]ow much of that comes at the expense of other parts of the world? Is the supposed American Dream or the European Dream possible because of some form of exploitation? You don't have Bangladesh and Bolivia getting huge [numbers of] immigrants from France and Germany or the United States and Canada. It's people moving from the third-world countries to the wealthier country to follow the so-called American or Western European Dream. You can have theories that these countries aren't as advanced or as sophisticated, but you have to break it down. Why is it still like that? All these former colonies are still poor. (Gringo_b, white/Latino, male, born outside the U.S., 26–45)

> With the American Dream, there is no concern for what goes on outside the immediate community in which people live. There is no critical reflection on why I can do this and others cannot. In what ways does this affect other people inside the country or community that I live in and outside it? It's not a reflective experience. It is self-centered and individualistic. There's no balance between concern for yourself and the immediate others and then the broader community. (Thomas D., white, male, U.S.-born, 26–45)

> Here, getting involved in other people's lives in a social movement or civil society, some kind of NGO, or just trying to make a difference is considered individualistic. In other countries, being associated with the army is not negative, but not seen like it is here. Modern capitalism in itself is an ideology that has its own values. It values capital, and that

values money. The developed world exploits the third world, and within the developed world the upper-class elite exploits the working class, and they have a comfortable life. It's about exploitation . . . beliefs, values, and philosophies of life. (Gringo_b, white/Latino, male, born outside the U.S., 26–45)

How far can our government really pull up the poverty issue if we follow capitalism? It requires a certain level. (Michael, white, male, U.S.-born, over 65)

There is a sense of entitlement . . . what I make, what I do, what I buy. It gets to the mentality of "I'm entitled to that" and "I'm going to use the system the way I can to get those things." There is a lot of structural factors in terms of the way society is organized. It goes back historically, perpetuating what has been in existence for a long time in terms of class inequality, racial inequality, and gender inequality. It's ingrained in the system that certain groups will do better. The legal system favors certain groups. When we look at the way taxes are organized, the percentage of working- or middle-class salaries that go to taxes compared to the percentage of upper-class salaries are just not comparable. Their $40,000 or whatever they might pay in taxes doesn't hurt as much as the $10,000 or $15,000 or $20,000 that the middle class has to pay. (Thomas D., white, male, U.S.-born, 26–45)

When I first got here from Poland, I remember looking at the airport, and it was dirty and had cracks and stuff. I didn't expect to see that here. I saw all these homeless people, and that affected me. This country has a lot of wealth, but there are still so many poor people. When people see poor people, they just say they are lazy, they don't work. It's an easy explanation—if you [are] poor, then it is your own fault. If you are poor, that means that you don't work. Many people who work hard are still poor—they aren't poor by choice. I always thought of the American Dream as materialism, obsessing over things and wanting to succeed. In Poland, we wanted to build a society where everybody was included and everyone had a chance to make it. I didn't believe [in] race and ethnicity. But I saw that all of those things played a role [in] the chances that you received in America. People had reactions to me because I identified myself as Polish. These all play a role in the decisions of your life in America. (Stefan, white, male, born outside the U.S., 26–45)

Society has raised us to just worry about myself and not care about anyone else, anywhere, going on in the world. But then . . . also it pushes other people out of the way. I'll have my mansion and my perfect life, and then there will be homeless people. (Jana, white, female, U.S.-born, 18–25)

Some families are actually born with the silver spoon in their mouth, and some have to work. Some families got it made. Like Paris Hilton, or imagine if your last name was Heinz—you never need to lift a finger for the rest of your life. As long as people are eating ketchup, you're good. Last name Macintosh. I'd take any of them right now. I'd be a Macintosh for one day. (Rome, Black, male, U.S.-born, 18–25)

Opportunity is not equal, because the rich always make their money off the middle class and the poor. Economics and society are like that. Monopoly is one of the first games you play—take others' money to destroy them at every turn around the board. (Barry, white, male, U.S.-born, 26–45)

Colonial Legacies

Some participants draw a connection between capitalism, colonialism, and global hierarchies of wealth. They call on historical examples to explain current realities though often express ambivalence about the reasons that groups have ended up being positioned as they are in the world-system and in U.S. society. Several point out the contradictions between ideological explanations for location and actual practice:

Maybe the Europeans taught Africans things they didn't know, like how to wash a dish or how to use soap. But I disagree with how they brought us over in bondage, like animals. Shackled at our feet and our hands, they wasn't giving us no soap and water to wash. [We] were sweating and stinking. They was working us. Get up. Come on. That's it. They wasn't showing us how to wash. Soap? They lying. You have to shackle me up to show me how to use some soap? You was using me from the beginning. If I want to show you something, why I got to chain you? You just done snatched us up and did what you wanted to do. You didn't do nothing but use me, work me to the bone until I didn't have no more strength. (Redd, Black, female, U.S.-born, 26–45)

We helped build civilization. They slaughtered the indigenous people. They stole the land from them. (Cee East, Black, female, U.S.-born, 26–45)

The majority of the rich people that are rich these days are because of old money. That's generations of generations of generations of other generations of money. We're talking about these people who helped build the United States. They keep it—from the Africans that they herded and the Indians who built this country from their blood and sweat. Anybody got their forty acres and a mule? "We're entitled to it," so they say. The reason that our culture is not where we [are] supposed to be is because every time we have come up somewhere, they take it from us. While Obama is in office, anything that we want and we feel like we need to get, me personally, I'm going for it. I'm grabbing it while I can, because I don't know how long this freedom is going to last. (S. Westmoreland, Black, female, born outside the U.S., 18–25)

The history of this country is how far it has gotten because of imperialism. All people see is that the U.S. has gotten ahead. People are not looking at the fact that it was able to get so far because it destroyed other countries to get ahead. (Pat, Black, female, U.S.-born, 26–45)

When the Europeans did come here, there was no civilization. They taught a lot of people how to live. To some places in Africa, it's not a place where people in America would live. They make their houses with manure. They pack their houses with dirt to make huts. The Europeans taught them how to hunt and kill in order to eat. Even though back then everybody didn't have rights, it wasn't right, because they wasn't doing it to everybody. They wasn't doing it to their fellow Europeans. They was using the people that they was trying to teach to do things for them. It was nice to try to teach them civilization, but it was not right to make somebody a slave. You just really start thinking, like, wow, like, how would you have felt during that time? But they taught them how to live. I think it was good. It was right, because you have to get somewhere in order to get somewhere else. (Ziana Zania, Black, female, U.S.-born, 18–25)

The Logic of Location

In these thoughtful comments, it is apparent that the narratives that explain logic of location are useful in upholding the structure in place by providing explanations for inequalities of all sorts, yet it is also evident that most respondents question these rationales. They express a significant degree of cynicism about upward mobility and true equality.

In their answers to the survey, many respondents write passionately about these issues:

The concept of America as a nation (i.e., the United States) is imperialist in itself. America is a continent, therefore I am American, but I'm not from nor do I carry a U.S. identity.

"Inequality exists because some people want something for nothing." I strongly agree. The "some people" in question are called the "ruling class," who want to make money off of the rest of us in exchange for nothing—or, more correctly, in exchange for the political contributions they use to buy the government.

I have encountered unmotivated, unintelligent, and institutionally disadvantaged people of all groups! These characteristics would effect and contribute to each and every one of their income levels. However, the color of their skin or ethnic background would not be the deciding factor. The discrimination by *other* individuals, for instance, the hiring personnel, could play a huge part in the success or failure to acquire the job and attain said income.

I would not say that most workplaces are inherent[ly] bigoted, but there are definite institutional restrictions against minorities, such as housing discrimination.

The problem is structural, not personal.

In my opinion, our society is set up in a way for the white-upper[-class] members to be successful. Minorities are still discriminated against.

Our world is not going to be about skin color, it's going to be about the size of your bank balance or credit access. The greener someone is, the more advantages they will be able to use and will be able to get.

We now move to an examination of participants' thoughts about contemporary society.

5

Thoughts on the Current Juncture

This chapter focuses on participants' reflections on the current moment in political-economic-social history. How do people understand the decline of U.S. power? To what extent has the election of President Barack Obama reshaped thinking about the U.S. nation, race, politics, and inequality? How have changing demographics reshaped the public's views about groups, positionality, inequality, and the racial and national order? Respondents' comments provide insight into current thinking about these important questions.

The United States in Decline

By all indicators, the United States is in a weaker position economically and politically than it was in earlier decades. As we have argued throughout, from 1945 to 1975 was the period of U.S. hegemony within the world-system. One might call it the "short American Century." It also witnessed the most dramatic expansion of the world economy in history. During the years 1967 to 1973, that period of easy expansion of the world economy came to an end, and concurrently the configuration of political power underwent a dramatic shift, threatening the stability of the world-system from the perspective of its most powerful actors. A key element in this instability is what some refer to as the unruliness of the Global South (also known as the third world, the extra-European world, or the Dark World); India, China, Korea, Bandung, Ghana, the Belgian Congo, Cuba, Algeria, Vietnam, Guinea-Bissau, Angola, and Mozambique were all sites of dramatic alterations in the balance of world political power after 1945. But we should also be mindful of the accumulating pushback of the extra-European world prior to 1945, including the Japanese defeat of Russia in 1905, the Chinese

Revolution of 1911, the Ethiopian defeat of Italy in 1896, the Mexican Revolution in 1910, and the formation of the Indian National Congress in 1910.

Public recognition of the magnitude of the alteration in the world balance of power is uneven among people born in the United States after 1980. Many trace the alteration in the balance of power to the dramatic attack on the U.S. homeland on September 11, 2001, followed by the fumbling incoherence of President George W. Bush, who was given a clear message to convey by a team of neoconservative intellectuals. Despite what seems to be over-the-top language by Al Franken (2003), who has referred to them as "lying liars," this group is notable for its recognition of the crisis of U.S. hegemony and its aim to establish a "New American Century" by armed intimidation of any of the weak states that posed a serious challenge to this U.S. geopolitical strategy. Members of this group have since reconstituted to form the American Legislative Exchange Council (ALEC), which is responsible for much of the reactionary legislation aimed at dismantling the public sector, disbanding unions, supporting pro-corporate tax law and anti-immigrant legislation, and so forth. The September 11, 2001, attack on the U.S. homeland provided just the license needed for the United States to step up its efforts to reassert U.S. geopolitical power.

The developmentalist strategy that had been central to U.S. hegemony tended to contribute to world opposition to the colonial powers. Indeed, the United States had argued that it was the first national liberation movement. But the global liberalism of the U.S. hegemony was a double-edged sword that functioned as a mechanism to constrain opposition to the new global power. However, it also contributed to the overall unruliness of the third world between 1945 and 1975. The search for a solution to the restive populations within the core states and within the Global South was replaced by neoliberalism, formalized by the Ronald Reagan–Margaret Thatcher tandem and articulated as "There Is No Alternative" (TINA).[1] During the 1990s, the signature achievement of neoliberalism was the North American Free Trade Agreement (NAFTA), which went into effect on January 1, 1994:

> The immediate result in a large number of countries was to worsen economic conditions, with the disappearance of social safety nets, increasing rates of unemployment, and declining currencies—all occurring side by side with the spectacular rise of new wealthy strata. Internal inequalities in the less developed countries of the world greatly increased. When the one area of the South that had been doing rather well economically— East and Southeast Asia—suffered a severe financial crisis in 1997, followed by similar setbacks in Russia and Brazil, the neoliberal option lost much of its credibility as a solution to the world's economic problems. (Wallerstein 2006, 13)

The eruption of the Zapatistas in Chiapas, Mexico, on the day NAFTA came into effect provided a powerful image for the entire world of indigenous populations calling for control over their own lives and a global refusal of neoliberal options. A movement for global democracy, deemed the antiglobalization movement by the popular media, became a prominent feature of the landscape after 1994, leading to a global opposition to the world economic elite that had not been seen in the decades following the decline of the American Century.

The challenge of U.S. decline continued in the wake of the failure of neoliberalism. As noted above, Bush installed a group of neoconservatives in high positions in his administration who had constituted themselves in the 1990s around the project for a New American Century. Immanuel Wallerstein argues that this group rejected the whole thrust of U.S. foreign policy that had tried to slow down the decline of U.S. hegemony after 1970. They attributed the U.S. decline "to the lack of tough resolve of successive U.S. presidents. They did not exempt Reagan from this critique, although they did not say that too loudly" (Wallerstein 2006a, 14). They called for a radical revision of U.S. foreign policy to replace what Wallerstein calls soft multilateralism based on partnership with allies "with unilateral decisions, to be offered its allies on a take-it-or-leave-it basis. Those countries that seemed to be resisting nuclear non-proliferation were to be forced toward immediate adherence" (14). This could hardly be rationalized to an attentive public, whose eyes were sharpened by the call to arms of its government, using the September 11, 2001, attack as a rationale for going to war with those who were obviously not involved. In this chapter, study participants share their thoughts about what this means, demonstrating a keen sense of appreciation of the social psychology of decline.

Political Standing

> At one point, we were the most powerful country in the world, and a lot of other nations looked up to us. But presently you wonder how people are looking at us. Russia was once called a . . . the . . . what was the term . . . a world power. Now it's the U.S. (Scorpio, Black, male, born outside the U.S., 46–65)

> Ever since the attack on the World Trade Center, everything started going down. You know that expression that says money talks? They are noticing that the money is not there, so they lost respect. The government loses; everybody loses respect from the other countries. They're [saying], "Oh, look at you now. Look at how you're struggling. Look at your country now. You're telling me how to run my country? You can't even run your own country!" (Genesis Ruth, Latina, female, U.S.-born, 46–65)

> Young people are so ignorant to what's really going on. They are totally snowed. They are taught that there's no more racial divide, that there's no more segregation, and that you can do anything you want to do. I wouldn't tell no Black boy that you can be anything, because that ain't

true. There is a glass ceiling. You could look through, but you're going to
hit your head on it. (Harold, Black, male, U.S.-born, 26–45)

This country started declining right after the Bush administration.
That's when it started going down. (Scorpio, Black, male, born outside
the U.S., 46–65)

People have lost faith. I don't know if anyone is actually proud to be an
American. (Jana, white, female, U.S.-born, 18–25)

The money that the government is spending on the war, that's a lot of
money. Once the countries and all the world see that you're losing money, they're not going to treat you the same. If you used to be a millionaire
and then a couple of months later you come back and you [are] so poor
you need food stamps, people ain't going to treat you the way they used
to treat you. If the countries lose respect for America, America is going
to have a hard time, because they need to socialize, go over to other
people so they can get help. If they turn their backs to us, how [are] we
going to survive? How America is going to survive? It's how you represent yourself. If you represent yourself really nice, if you come with a hat
or a T-shirt and baggy pants down there, we ain't going to listen to you.
We're going to think you're a nut. A lot of things handicap us right now.
Section 8 is [under a] freeze; there's a lot of help that the poor people
need. It's [under a] freeze because of all the stuff that Bush has done. If
you can't help the community, you can't help your country, because then
they can't get good jobs. They can't teach their kids right if they don't
have the right education. If they don't educate young minds, how are
we going to have other Einsteins? Why do you think Japan is so smart?
They give 100 percent to the education of their people. Over here, the
first thing they knock out is housing and education, and you can't live
without that. You have to help the community so the community can
help the country. That's how it goes. United, we don't fall. (Genesis Ruth,
Latina, female, U.S.-born, 46–65)

United we stand—divided we fall, so we don't want to be so divided.
We'll stand united as a people, as a nation. (Scorpio, Black, male, born
outside the U.S., 46–65)

Aaron McGruder's satirical attacks on the "United We Stand" motto in *The
Boondocks*[2] have a satirical echo here, though there is also a seeming nostalgia
for America's glory period based on solidarity among the people, not the elites:

American money is losing value, too. Ain't nothing cost a dollar. I was
so mad when I went to the corner store the other day for this little, tiny

fifty-cent Little Debbie cake. They don't even have ten-cent lollipops no more, five-cent candies no more. Like Jamaica, Africa, Guyana, the West Indian countries, and all them places over there—their values are low, and our value is losing, too. The American Dream could be for anybody that comes here, but it really can't translate to other countries, because they are not developed as much as we are. (Cinnfox Pebbles, Black, female, U.S.-born, 26–45)

Other countries are not even listening to the United States. They do what they want to do. They don't even care about America. To this day, you hear them say America is weak. (Cee East, Black, female, U.S.-born, 26–45)

Other countries are finding our weak points. If they want to come and bomb us again, they can do it. That's why we act like bullies—to try to scare other nations—but it's not working anymore. They've wised up. (Redd, Black, female, U.S.-born, 26–45)

Some participants articulate an analysis of entrenched power and what is needed to challenge it:

The American government's policies did us dirty in the eight years of Bush. You have to have the people's faith and belief in you. Once you lose that, then you start the foreground for a revolution. If people don't believe in the government anymore, there has to be a[n] uprising. There has to be a change, something that we believe strongly in. In tragedy or crisis, we as Americans form that universal bond of patriotism or nationalism. What gets us through the night is the bond that we have amongst each other, with the people that we deal with day to day. Not the Supreme Court and all those people that sit up there and just pass laws or veto them. We believe in the freedom of speech, but does that freedom really mean much to that higher power, aka the government? Even though they're hearing us out, they'll sit there and laugh. People want to throw shoes at us and do the little crazy at the end of the day. It's a sign of disrespect. It's to say that you're less than the dirt I walk on. That's their traditional way of disrespecting. Even when they knocked down the statue of Saddam, you see these people beating up a former statue with their shoes, as [if] to say, "You're beneath me." But we feed into it. We're going to either float or drown together. When you look at big business and the economy right now, they are deciding whether we will bail out General Motors and Ford, while they are stead[il]y firing people. Yet in the turnaround, you're biting the same hand that's putting that money back into your pocket. When those people that's behind the scenes that has their hand in every pot that's draining our economy, what happens then when they are affected? The problem is they haven't been affected. We've been there when they need us, but we're not needed. This person that doesn't have that real patriotism in him standing behind a podium preaching to a bunch of people who are supposed to be patriotic. They're pulling up the blinds over our eyes, and we're going with it. Those that wake up rebel. If it wasn't for previous revolutions and uprisings, we wouldn't be halfway where we're at right now to even have a black president. (Rome, Black, male, U.S.-born, 18–25)

It declined in power, because now a lot of people are getting caught for fraud. Taking people's money. They're giving people power that's not supposed to have it, and the economy is going down. (Ziana Zania, Black, female, U.S.-born, 18–25)

We're like a balloon that's about to pop. We used to be liked everywhere. It used to be that America actually cared about the rest of the world. We're like the big bullies of the world. A lot of poor judgment was based on the views and ideologies of people who should not be in power. (Andy, white, male, U.S.-born, 18–25)

It's unfair to call us the bullies of the world, because it's obvious there are terrorist groups. Nobody has forgotten 9/11, so it's too black and white to say we're the bad guys. The world is in general just not in great shape. There are threats of all kinds, climate change, and the economy. (Tony, white, male, U.S.-born, 46–65)

This exchange demonstrates the weakening of the triumphalism of right-wing ideology that had so intimidated the Center and the Left into a defensive posture. Prior to this time, some people contested the mainstream narratives about capitalism, imperialism, and the U.S. role in global affairs, but insufficient contention between the competing currents did not allow space for debate in the public realm. The Center and the Left were being silenced. Therefore, this kind of debate is long past due in public discourse:

We were making a lot of progress in this country leading up to the civil rights movement. In the sixties, there was an attempt to get equality. Some of it was misplaced, because equality comes from attitudes as opposed to mandates. Then you have quotas as opposed to people being exposed to people of different backgrounds and learning how we're all the same. That has to come from people themselves. You can't tell people what to do, so we actually had some big steps back as a result of good-intentioned attempts at equality toward the end of the middle and the end of the twentieth century. We needed to have laws overturned that were for discrimination, but certain laws were misguided. When laws are believed to be unfair or so-called reverse discrimination, it just makes people mad. Then people get bitter, and we've just been in this lingering state since then. (Jon, white, male, U.S.-born, 18–25)

If the main draw to our shores and the primary source of contentment of our citizens and residents is the open structure of opportunity, then the ideological counterpart is the stress on individual effort, will, and resources to make one competitive in U.S. society. In other words, if we are a meritocracy, the only explanation for being poor is individual failure. This outlook emphasizes the role of the individual in economic success. But it simply ignores the practices of New Deal Liberalism and the dramatic expansion of the life chances of working people; though the benefits were not evenly spread to the racialized strata, they did receive some benefits. We now examine participant reflections on the current economic situation.

The Economic Crisis

As we have argued, the period of easy accumulation that characterized the post-1945 world economy ended circa 1967 to 1973, dramatically reshuffling the social landscape. Some sectors of the labor movement theorized that in an attempt to change the relations of force between capital and labor that had prevailed during the post-1945 expansion of the world economy, the employing classes launched what they called an "attack on labor," which over the course of the next decades became formalized in the political-economic strategy of neoliberalism, manifested in the policies of Reagan in the United States and Thatcher in the United Kingdom.

Overall, this neoliberalism involved moving production to lower-wage areas, shifting the locus of employment to lower-wage service and clerical employment but dismantling the mass-production, heavy-industry system that had been the site of working-class employment during the post-1945 period. The corporate sector then embarked on a strategy of financialization that involved organizing profitability by blowing up economic bubbles, using financial wheeling and dealing to generate huge profits for the corporate sector, but not creating living-wage jobs for the working class. The neoliberal economic strategy (also referred to as neoliberal globalization) sought to conceptualize the playing field as having moved for the first time into a global arena that favored the "natural laws" of economic organization against which local social groups were powerless.

Many participants speak to the decline of opportunities in the United States, increasing unemployment, and foreclosures. They are uncertain about what these financial issues mean for the status of the United States in the world and the future of the American Dream. What do these crises signify about the narrative of the United States as the land of opportunity? What is the relationship between the domestic and global economic crisis, and what role does politics play?

I experienced a neighborhood being a village. This idea dwindled: My generation was the last one that experienced it. It died in the city as the drug epidemic in the eighties disassembled the family connection. I was a teenager and watched a lot of families come unhinged—we are still rebounding from that. (Yusef, Black/Native American, male, U.S.-born, 26–45)

Things are getting tighter. There's more competition for less and less resources. American wealth and Western European wealth is built on nonrenewable resources and cheap energy and oil. You can't go on using up the soil and the oil forever to get wealthy. Sooner or later, you're going to run out of stuff, globally speaking. We're sort of maybe on the cusp of that big picture. I don't know if it's going to happen next year or in the next century. The world is getting smaller. There's more people needing to eat, and we're even depleting water. We're using up our oil and the soil by growing stuff in ways that deplete it. Who is going to feed and water and run everything as there's more and more people and less and less resources? (Carmella, white, female, U.S.-born, 26–45)

Is it people using too much or more than what they're supposed to? There is this idea that there's not enough food for the people on Earth when there actually is. (Damaris, Dominican, female, U.S.-born, 18–25)

People are trying to buy houses who now can't. My brother works for a bank, and he says, "I can't get people loans, the bank doesn't want to lend any money." This home thing, the quintessential part of the American Dream, is now out of reach, not to just people who don't have money but even for the people who do, because the banks are reluctant to lend unless you can give them [a] 50 percent down payment. You['re] talking about a lot of money you need to front to get a loan. (Dan, white, male, U.S.-born, 18–25)

Some speak to the congressional debates about redistributing wealth:

The whole debate about the redistributed wealth is the opposite of Reaganomics. I was like, why not? We've been cutting taxes for the top, wealthiest people and letting it, you know, trickle-down kind of thing, but it wasn't really working. (Justine, white, female, U.S.-born, 18–25)

I've been going to a food pantry for about a year now, and the number of people has tripled. More of the people coming to pantries are families and working people. That tells me that all the money is concentrated to fewer and fewer people. It's greed. Changes have made the dream more difficult to obtain. All the corruption and dishonesty in the corporate sector and even in the faith sector is rampant. It's a lot harder for honest people to just get what they need.

All the J. P. Morgans and the Vanderbilts and those guys have gone home. Now their kids are looking for the quick fix, and they're ravaging the country. The older generation was more upstanding, more honest. Maybe they were cutthroat, but I don't think they stole or lied to do the business. Even the quality of goods is not what it used to be. Everything is fast. A lot [of] people get their meals from the Chinese restaurant instead of cooking themselves. The cars, a larger portion of the car is made from plastic instead of metal, just the quality of goods and foods. Things fall apart. Things are not made the way they used to be. (Joseph, Black, male, U.S.-born, 46–65)

The economy has been taken over by the corporate, and we get less re-sults for our community. Big business gets millions of dollars to spend at their own leisure while we're in a deficit and recession. They're taking money that we're bailing them out with and they're going on vacations to these nice little private estates and stuff like that. The middle class has been dissolved into low class or high class. The middle class had more leverage as far as persuasion, as far as what was in the interest for the people. I know people that don't have a great job, but they still find time to do charities. They know what it's like to be there. I don't want to be judgmental and say that a person who has a ten times bigger bank account doesn't do the same thing. I'm just saying the responsibility is larger because you have more. (Eddie C., Latino, male, U.S.-born, 18–25)

It's one thing to identify entrenched power, yet another to address it. It's all political. They're not going to put out where they're not going to gain. When they put up public housing, it's for displaced people, so most of them, they're not working, so what are they gaining? Why can't you take from these people that have these seven, eight, nine figures. Take something from them and use it to [do] whatever you have to do. Why are you hitting the people that don't have anything? You don't give them anything, because you're not going to gain nothing. It's sad. I'm in that bracket. If you take away Medicaid, you can't go the doctor, so we've got to sit around and be sick and just wait to die. They don't even care. That's the thing. They don't care. It's like not even thinking about how it's going to affect the people. (Redd, Black, female, U.S.-born, 26–45)

Somebody was saying the definition of patriotism is supporting your country and being willing to change things when they're going wrong. Not just standing up for your country right or wrong, but if things aren't going well, to do something different to change the course. That's what people were feeling—that we've gotten way off course. We've lost a lot of prestige in terms of other countries and what they think of us. Economically, we're not doing very well. (Ellen, white, female, U.S.-born, 46–65)

It's like the millions of dollars in Iraq for this senseless war. Wall Street fell, seven hundred to bail them out—what was it million, billion? It's ridiculous. Who is going to bail out Medicaid? The subway system, the working poor work, so they have to take it. They're talking about raising the fare to $3. It's ridiculous. Who is going to bail all these things out? Food stamps—people are scared to apply. They sit them down there eight hours. They give up their leave. They've got to go back to work. Everything is hard for the poor. I don't care what anybody says. It's really hard, and it's getting harder. Especially if you don't have the time to get to school because you've got five kids. They're working minimum-wage jobs. They want to do better, but they can't. Who is going to mind the kids? If you leave the kids by themselves, they grow up running wild. They get in trouble, and it's just another system. Everything starts from the bottom again, jail, prison, and dropping out. It's a cycle. (Cee East, Black, female, U.S.-born, 26–45)

What's happening now? All these changes that are going on are bad. People are losing houses. This country is not flourishing like all these years when everything was possible. When I hear of people losing a home, I feel like crying. I watch the news and I say, "God forbid, this could be my son; this could be me," because it can happen. They lose a job—my kids, they work, but they both have a big mortgage. God forbid they lose their job, they will lose their home. We didn't need this war. This was a stupid war. All the factories, all the work is being exported out of this country; there's no work. If they bring back all of those automotive factories, the clothing, made in China, made in Korea. You don't see "made in the U.S.A." anymore. My cousin owned his own factory, and he lost it. He couldn't afford to keep it open anymore. Now my sister is out of work for a year. Little by little, it became about two hundred people, until they downsize[d] it to fifty. The reason she stayed after the last day when they closed completely was because she was doing a little of everything, and they were paying only for one thing. They had a good deal with her. She says, "I need the job, I can't open my mouth because I will lose my job." They pay cheaper labor. Very, very cheap in India. What they pay one person to work as a diamond setter, they pay one month in India what's paying the guy for one day here. The U.S. is on the decline if we don't wake up and bring it back. We're really due for a big, rude wake-up. It's scary. (Louise, Italian, female, born outside the U.S., 46–65)

They want to raise the train fares, and now they want to raise the gasoline. They want to raise the rents. Any more rent, I'm going to have to be in the park. I'll have no place to go. We're struggling, and if I have anything left after my bills, let's say $40, I feel rich because I have $40 in my pocket. If they raise the carfare, what am I going to do? It's so much already, and then the food is getting higher now. We do have sales monthly, but it's not even enough anymore. I get food stamps, but every time they want to lower it, I have to go there and fight. This is my bills, and this is what I'm supporting. Help me out. It's always a struggle. So the economy is getting worse. The companies are also suffering, because they need people. Like right now, they used to hire a lot of people in my job, now they can't. They put a freeze over it, and they need people. They can't afford it anymore. They are even cutting everybody's hours. This is illegal. They say they're not going to give nobody a raise. They work hard for it. It's really hard. (Genesis Ruth, Latina, female, U.S.-born, 46–65)

Think about why the majority of the Black men is in jail. It's so hard to even get a job, and sometimes they're not going to hire you because you're Black or your age or whatever. The young guys want a job, and nobody will hire them. You've got to have money. The next thing you know, you're either trying to hustle and sell weed, or you're going to snatch somebody's bag, thinking, "I'm going to do it one time." I've seen it myself. (Redd, Black, female, U.S.-born, 26–45)

The rich are getting richer, and the poor is getting poorer. This economy is suffering today, and in the near future what they plan on doing is taxing a certain bracket. The bracket that they're taxing is going to suffer. Why can't they tax rich people instead of the middle class, who are struggling? Why can't they tax just the rich, the rich people? If they do, the economy will go up. Somewhere down the line, it's going to be a tax write-off to these rich people. The rich doesn't lose. When they do fundraising, when they give, when they donate, that's tax write-offs. This money comes back to them. We can't do this, because we don't have that money. (Chino, Latino, male, U.S.-born, 46–65)

I worked the floor of the Stock Exchange for thirty-five years. My firm got taken over, and I got laid off as a result of this takeover. We had too many guys over 60, so they got rid of us. We threatened to sue based on age discrimination, but they said you can sue us, but then you're not going to get your severance package. We needed the severance package, so we didn't sue. (Michael, white, male, U.S.-born, over 65)

When General Motors went bankrupt, people came in these big suits [and] gave them $50 billion to save the cars, but people buy cars from GMC every single day. It's like they couldn't do something where they could raise their own money, as in building more cars. It's confusing.

There's just so much money being dished out. It's not necessary. You paying people on Wall Street, whatever million, $12 million to resign. Why you paying somebody $12 million to resign? He made that error, so you're going to pay him to resign? He should be paying $12 million back to Wall Street! It's a waste of money. When Bloomberg was running for mayor again, with his illegal tactics on how he went about it. When you have money, money means everything. Regular people gathered around, but they didn't even give them opportunity to express themselves. In the hearings, they let five or six people talk and then just ended everything, which was very unfair. Since [I was] a little girl, I know that when you have money, money is power, and that's what they have. The police don't have respect for the civilians, so of course the civilians don't have respect for them. There was a time where you know you could see an officer and you think you could trust him. Now, there's so many cover-ups. They're corrupted, just like the politicians. A lot of it doesn't even make the paper. They try to keep everything hush-hush, but as long as you have money, you have power to do what you want to do to the people. The same people that voted you in your position, once you get in your position, you don't care. You're going to do what you want to do. That's what I see them doing. (Spankey, Black, female, U.S.-born, 26–45)

Isabelle (Chinese American, female, U.S.-born, 18–25) points out that we lack a common frame of reference for understanding class:

There is a large spectrum of how people define middle class. We need to adjust that. There's a problem in politics when people say, "If you earn $250,000, you are middle class." We need to figure out what middle class really means!

Some participants speak to the ways that the economic situation is more difficult for some groups and less difficult for others:

I don't think the American Dream is accessible to all people, because immigrants aren't able to achieve certain things that people who are citizens here can. There's a lot of trouble for them to get real jobs. They don't have a lot of opportunities that someone who has legal documents [has]. (Kris Stewart, Black, male, U.S.-born, 18–25)

These days, you need eight Ph.D.s just to live! (Cinnfox Pebbles, Black, female, U.S.-born, 26–45)

That's not true, because half the time it's who you know. It can get you places. Having a positive attitude and knowing somebody who's in a good position can get you places. (Geneva Diva, Black, female, U.S.-born, 18–25)

I'm talking thirty years from now, girl. The way this economy is going, the way this recession is going, you're going to need, like maybe fifteen Ph.D.s just to have a job. How much competition is there going to be? Do you know how many there is now? It's going to be hard. It's going to be very competitive. (Cinnfox Pebbles, Black, female, U.S.-born, 26–45)

A lot of kids can't go to college, because they keep raising the tuition. (Nee-Nee, Black, female, U.S.-born, 18–25)

If it hadn't been a decline on Wall Street, tuition and things of that nature would not have been going up. (Spankey, Black, female, U.S.-born, 26–45)

The authorities are trying to push it off on immigrants, but they are not the problem. It's a lot of smoke and mirrors. But my father told me also to be careful about communism. (Layla, Asian, female, U.S.-born, 46–65)

Respondents universally agree that things have gotten more difficult for ordinary people, and most participants hold the wealthy, Wall Street, or the government responsible. They speak of an increased polarization of wealth, though not explicitly in those terms.

The Presidency of Barack Obama

The Obama presidency evoked hopes among many that we as a nation might be able to transcend politics as usual, but it was complicated by the desire to end the disastrous reign of the Republican Far Right. Some were fearful of throwing away their vote by taking a chance on the romantic appeal of an Obama win, because they believed that too many whites would refuse to vote for a Black person for president of the United States.

When Obama decisively defeated John McCain in the 2008 presidential election, there was much discussion about the meaning of this unprecedented political achievement. If Obama's election marked a new era in national *and* racial politics, to what extent has this been actualized? What did the outcome signify? What sense do people make of this historical moment? Some speak of the changes in the electorate, in particular recognizing that while the majority of whites overall did *not* vote for Obama in either presidential election (and the percentage dropped between 2008 and 2012),[3] the majority of whites under 30 did vote for him in 2008 but not in 2012:[4]

The [2008] election was so important, because so many young people were awakened to the need for change, and we were discussing this the other day—that they see things in a whole different light now. (Ina, white, female, U.S.-born, 46–65)

Obama being elected was a very big thing in this country. It shouldn't have been such a big thing, just the fact that he was Black, but it was. Somehow, change had to come, and a lot of people are ready to support different policies (Tony, white, male, U.S.-born, 46–65)

They're doing that out of fear, not because they want to. We had the choice of an even older, white guy. The United States is controlled by old white guys, and this was an older guy with the same views. Everyone was saying he's just an extension of the Bush and Cheney policies. That's the only reason why Obama actually got elected, and I'm glad. I love the hope he brings to everyone. He has a hell of a lot to live up to, but it was like "the lesser of two evils" type of deal. That's not a good way to start a social revolution or a social change. It's about time for social revolution, because we have gone so long with these ideas that once used to be very grand and glorious things. A nation run by the people for the people. The people that we used to be fighting with we're now fighting against, because now they're the suppressive power. The American government has gotten just too full of themselves to let anything go. The American people are smart enough to know when something has to happen. We could have elected McCain. (Andy, white, male, U.S.-born, 18–25)

It doesn't mean the fact that Obama was elected that everybody has become so radical in the country, but there's definitely a movement toward changes—but this is not a revolutionary-type country. (Tony, white, male, U.S.-born, 46–65)

It used to be. It wasn't just 1796 [sic]. It was also the Civil War. (Andy, white, male, U.S.-born, 18–25)

People in America don't want socialism. In my opinion, there isn't going to be socialism, but maybe there will be hopefully health care for more people. Eventually, we'll get to the idea, it really should be everybody. That doesn't seem impossible. Even addressing climate change that Bush ignored, to respond to that. (Tony, white, male, U.S.-born, 46–65)

I was thinking of a mental revolution as far as people's behavior toward each other and their surroundings. In that sense of a social revolution. I happen to be reading Lenin's *The State and Revolution* right now, so it was funny that you said that. If McCain got elected, I was done. I was going to move. I was going to be like self-hating Americans. I would hate to be an American under a McCain presidency, because that is one step too far. Bush was elected through the funny business the first time and then through fear the second time. (Andy, white, male, U.S.-born, 18–25)

We've changed since we went into Iraq. They don't think we're so great anymore. They might still want to come here, but we don't look as good. If it wasn't for Obama—he really saved us, because it really shows how far we've come and what we can do, voting in a Black president. It's sad it took us this long. (Cora, white, female, U.S.-born, 18–25)

Respondents spend considerable time discussing the implications of Obama's election for African Americans and for racist practices in the United States. This is a difficult discussion, navigating the parameters of the opening to the professional-managerial strata among racialized groups in the post–civil rights era and the hardening of racial oppression among the lower strata of the racialized groups as a means of social control. Indeed, a historically informed analysis of these trends might recognize the significance of social control throughout this whole process—not only during the current period but also throughout the nation's history. When FBI Director J. Edgar Hoover argued in 1964 that the nation was in the midst of a social revolution, with the racial movement at its core, he spoke of a long-standing trend in U.S. society.

Barack Obama is significant for the future. He opened more doors and opportunities for the African. If you do what you have to do, there could be a chance for you to get in this place. You thought that you could never make it. He opened doors for a lot of Black people. (Ziana Zania, Black, female, U.S.-born, 18–25)

Black people is going to have a more positive outlook on life and on their families. Over the years—and I don't want to make this a racial issue, but over the years—black people have been so torn apart between how white America sees them and how it really should be. That now that they have a person of color, they would have a better outlook. (Scorpio, Black, male, born outside the U.S., 46–65)

Many emphasize that change takes time and that we as a nation should be patient and not expect Obama to fix everything right away:

A lot was put on Obama to be the superhero and save us. That's unrealistic. It's not going to happen. If our economy can stabilize so there's the creation of jobs and more emphasis on, like, health care and things that have been sort of lacking, extricating us from Iraq little by little. It took us time to get into this whole mess, and it's going to take time to get out of it. I feel encouraged that enough people were willing to take a change and try something different. (Ellen, white, female, U.S.-born, 46–65)

Everybody thought that he could not do it, but he did. It's a big accomplishment. It's a new beginning. When you start something new, it's exciting, it's adventurous, it's great, it's awesome. You have this whole new way of looking at the future and saying, "Maybe we have a chance to survive after all." But whatever he's going to do, it's going to take time. We have to be patient. It's going to take a lot of work to fix a lot of stuff, and he can't do it alone. He's going to need a lot of people to back him up, supporting him in the election and with his views. Bush sabotaged as much as he could so the next president could go through a lot of trouble to fix it. Eventually, it's going to get to him. (Genesis Ruth, Latina, female, U.S.-born, 46–65)

We need a new face for our country. Obama is not going to do it. He's going to make some changes, but we are just too far gone. We are hated in the world. We [are] thought of as cheaters. We owe everybody. We owe our ports—Baltimore harbor and another port in Seattle, we've actually loaned or leased those out. The Saudis own them now. They are pawning some of our monuments and using those as collateral with the Chinese. The thing is that we have no respect. None whatsoever. We own nothing. We are living off credit cards. You've got the same haves that have stolen, and they're still stealing and they're sitting pretty. They don't even know there's a problem. Obama changes the way other countries view the United States, because right now they see us as a bunch of cheaters, liars, and crooks. You can't really fault them. My biggest fear is that he can't do what he said he's going to do, and we might not see another Black president for another hundred years. They'll say, "We gave you all a chance; you messed it up. Let's go back to what we know."

The real reason Obama's in office is to change the face of the United States, because we have no integrity overseas. We have somebody who may have the ability to go into the Middle East, and if they see another old white man, they're fixing to set the world on fire. They have got to the point where they can accept a Black man as president so they can keep their money, and that's a big deal right there. They were like, "Hey, you can be president as long as I keep my money and keep the trade still open." Like, who is it, Chavez? Have you ever seen him on CNN? He talks so bad about the U.S., and he talked about Bush. He said, "How can you vote for somebody who is so damn stupid?" He said it just like that. I mean, Chavez is off the chain. He said, "You all don't care nothing about the little people. All you care about is your money." He said, "You're greedy. You're a bunch of liars." Chavez had me dying. I mean, he told the truth. There are still haves and have-nots, but now you've got a Black man in office. (Harold, Black, male, U.S.-born, 26–45)

Sam Cooke said that a change is going to come. I was in Trinidad, maybe 15 or 16, and wanted to know what America is about. I would listen to King speak, and I would listen to President John F. Kennedy, and I wanted to know what is America about. We're seeing the dream and the Promised Land with Barack Obama. This is something we were looking for a long time. (Singing Dianne, Black, female, born outside the U.S., 46–65)

Let's be real—a Black president. You know what I mean? Like, something had to have happened. Those are changes. The difference in the way we view our leader. What was the change? What do you believe was the change that allowed this? Was it that Bush really f'ed up that bad? We really couldn't do another four years with a Republican? What was it? But it was something. It started with the people, and that's what it comes down to. Obama will probably tell you, "I feel like the American Dream right now." (Rome, Black, male, U.S.-born, 18–25)

The danger of the election of Barack Obama is that we thought that just by electing him [it] makes everything better. White America cannot just put [out] a hand and say to black America, "Are we cool now?" There's a danger in thinking that we automatically are equal now or that we're more equal. There were people who voted for Obama who still didn't like blacks, but they honestly thought he was the better choice. There were people who were racist against people of different races who voted for Obama just because they couldn't stand the opposition or because they just held their noses and did it. Does it really reflect how America is? What if the person on the Republican ticket was Black and the person on the Democratic ticket was white? Would it have happened? No. President Bush and John McCain's campaign was nauseating and awful. I would love to see a person of color on the Republican ticket. There are not that many in the party, especially not in office, and so a lot of it is circumstance. The Republican Party has had a lot of problems and was traditionally this intellectual, WASP-y party. Ultimately, economics determines votes more than anything else. (Jon, white, male, U.S.-born, 18–25)

This exchange suggests that perhaps Obama's wins are most powerful in their symbolic achievement:

My sister said, "We're going to get a Black president." I say, "You're crazy; what's wrong with you?" She said it to a principal, and they said, "Not in this nation will you ever see a Black president." When she heard the news, she went crazy. Obama earned it. He worked hard for it, and it's our duty as a Black American, right, to help build up that American Dream—and not to stop and say, "Oh because we have him there, he's just one person." It's all of us in it. (Bebe, Latina, female, born outside the U.S., 26–45)

There's always going to be something you don't expect someone to achieve. Everything is impossible until somebody does it. They've done it like anybody who has done it, then it doesn't seem like that really matter[s]. People aren't taking an initiative enough on their own lives, and that's part of the problem, too. They're expecting somebody to lead them, and nobody wants to get up and start leading. There's a lack of courage when it's needed. Speaking as a young person, I can't say I feel hopeful. I feel scared is more like it. (Pike, Black/white, male, U.S.-born, 18–25)

Table 5.1 shows survey respondents' thoughts on the impact of Obama as president. Most survey respondents do not think Obama's election indicates that there is no longer a "race problem" in the United States, but they are less certain about whether he will make achieving the American Dream more likely. Written survey comments affirm this cautious approach:

Barack Obama has been given the opportunity for traditional greatness. He is dynamic, smart, focused, upstanding, a man, a human being, an excellent politician, but not a savior or a stopgap. He is not an answer, he is a chance for us all to do the right thing. To get rid of the view where being a patriot means to follow blindly, allowing the TV to shape our future. It is a chance, at last, for us collectively as a nation [to] shine!!!

The "symbolic" victory of Obama's election must be distinguished from the imagined "material" gains that people of color will achieve as a result of this. Obama's election does signal that a biracial, Ivy League–educated,

TABLE 5.1. THE ELECTION OF BARACK OBAMA AS PRESIDENT OF THE UNITED STATES

	Strongly disagree	*Disagree*	*Agree*	*Strongly agree*	*Don't know*
Proves that we no longer have a race problem in the United States	56.4%	37.7%	2.8%	0.4%	2.8%
Will make my achieving the American Dream more likely	10.3%	30.6%	23.9%	6.1%	29.0%

highly successful Black man who spent over $350 million (I believe) on his campaign can be elected president. For many, it does mark the achievement of the American Dream, but we can't overlook the extraordinary circumstances that made this possible—his father was highly educated, he was raised primarily by his white grandparents in white communities, etc. We should not generalize from the symbolic victory that Obama's election holds specifically for African Americans to all other people of color. Just because Americans voted for a Black man does not mean that this will improve the social status of Latinas/os, Arabs/Muslims, American Indians, Asians, etc.

Regarding Obama, I am in the unpopular position of viewing his victory as a collaboration of sexist men. A lot of "liberal" white males now have legitimacy for whatever they do, because they voted for a Black man. It's really fucked up (pardon my vehemence) that he paid all his female staffers thousands less than his male staff.

What exactly does the election of Barack Obama imply, *if* indeed it does make the achievement of the American Dream possible? That you have to forsake you[r] cultural roots, be light-skinned, and surround yourself [with] powerful whites to achieve the American Dream. I don't think the election of Barack Obama in and of itself will actuate change in the current structural system of inequality embedded in America; however, I do believe it will incite hope in the many young males and young females who are themselves racially disadvantaged or who *want* to believe in the American Dream. Sometimes belief will take you much further than you expect. Until the people of America change the ground rules to playing the game of the American Dream, the AD is as closed today as it was November 3, 2008.

I don't think Obama has anything to do with me having the American Dream. That's all up to me.

Race and country are imaginary things, social constraints. While I realize they "exist" to the extent they have very real repercussions on people's lives, I reject them personally and define myself as a human and that is it.

Obama's administration is faced with some serious issues. I'm not sure whether even in eight years they can begin to make the Dream more possible for the disadvantaged, but I do believe they will make a dent. However, the public will forget the current economic hardships and go back to "values" voting after two terms. We'll see another cycle of conservatism. So, I'm hopeful but lacking a little in faith.

The election of Barack Obama shows that we have made progress, but racial inequality is still apparent. Racism has been a part of our culture for hundreds of years and institutionalized for decades. Although we are changing, there is still a lot of work to be done. White/European ways of knowing, language patterns, and so much more are still the norm. Until we embrace other cultures' language patterns, ways of knowing, history, etc., we will not have a multicultural society, and racism will still thrive and affect education, access to work, religious institutions, etc.

These comments acknowledge that Obama's election as president of the United States represents a change and the potential for a shift in the racial dynamics and political orientation of the United States. However, most participants are quite reluctant to convey wholehearted belief that this potential will ever be more than a minor shift. Participants express a significant degree of ambivalence about whether the course of history has been critically altered. More so, their sentiments articulate a wary view of the future.

What seems most clear, however, is that despite their wariness of any occupant of state power within an inherently polarizing social system, the mentality of the electorate has undergone a significant change, and that is the story that most matters in the long run. We dare say that this shift has been a long time coming, but now its reality indicates a true systemic crisis, when the system itself is in question. It is not for naught, either, that the system is widely associated with the power of "old white men."

During the 1990s, the patriarchal nationalism of the United States seemed at its shakiest, as illustrated by the incapacities of LAPD Chief Darryl Gates during the explosion of outrage in South Central Los Angeles when the police who were caught on video beating Black motorist Rodney King were found not guilty of assault with a deadly weapon and use of excessive force by a jury from an all-white suburb. Jon Katz attempts to summarize his sense of the zeitgeist, the fall of the all-mighty white man:

> In the end, when the movie is made of the long and bitter struggle against the white men who ruled America for three and a half centuries, it will not look anything like *Doctor Zhivago*. Instead of troops clubbing demonstrators outside the White House, there will be frantic producers and killer bookers battling it out on behalf of Larry King, Bryant Gumbel and Oprah Winfrey. Instead of white men being hunted down and imprisoned, they'll be standing in their suits and ties at press conferences, looking decimated and unnerved, muttering about patriotism, lamenting the new realities and wondering what the hell happened to centuries of entitlement.
>
> Just two weeks after forty-five people were slaughtered in Los Angeles, the long reign of the Last White Man in Urban America came to end on a Wednesday afternoon, when Daryl Gates traded in his gun for a talk-

show sofa and kicked off the tour for his book, *Chief*, on *Donahue*. Gates could not have picked a more apt way to say farewell. He would fill his last public days the American way, taking calls from Marlene in Sioux City.

For more than a generation, pictures of countless skirmishes have been streaming across the TV screen: civil-rights marches, feminist confrontations, gay-pride demonstrations, Native American occupations, academic boycotts, civil disturbances, an uncountable number of attendant lawsuits, appeals and settlements.

The media have faithfully recorded all the battles but haven't yet recognized the war or figured out what to call it. Yet these conflicts are not unrelated; they are all part of a historic whole, a conflict whose outcome will determine the kind of country and culture we are, who has power, who shares it and who doesn't.

The rhetoric of the Sixties has become the reality of the Nineties. The revolution is here—it's just less ideological and more fragmented than predicted. It isn't really against the system but against the white men who mostly run it. Now everyone is sick of white men: the white men who destroyed Native American culture, the white men who practiced slavery and fought to preserve it, the white men with clubs in Birmingham, the white men who beat up gays and raided their bars, the white men with briefcases who launch and carry out every war, the white men on campuses who cling to self-serving curriculum and control tenure, the white men in corporations who ravage the environment, the white men who dismissed Anita Hill's complaints, the white men who talk about family values while overseeing policies that ravage the lives of millions of family members, the white men who beat Rodney King.

Almost every other sexual and racial group in the country is fighting them with every means at hand—deploying lobbyists, lawsuits, voter-registration and fund-raising campaigns, mailing lists and PR people. Sometimes, as in Los Angeles, the weapons are lethal. And the battlefield is the most American element of all: TV, where opposing forces converge in an angry, raucous, electronic din.[5]

Wallerstein argues that the decline in the efficiency of the state structures in the core zones, combined with the increasing mass of the "third world within" in the core zones, meant that the populations of the core states would become increasingly dismayed by a sense of social disorder quite different from the protests of the 1960s and 1970s. The overall social context in which this crisis was occurring was also quite different than the period of ascent and expansion in which the social democratic state expanded from 1945 to 1975. One hallmark of this neoliberal period was a general consensus, promoted by global and national elites, that states were increasingly unable to protect their citizens from the ravages of the world economy and have not been able to guarantee their citizens an increasingly higher standard of living.

The situation that has evolved is not merely a conjunctural transition of an economic cycle; it reflects a powerful structural strain as U.S. hegemony, white world supremacy, historical capitalism, and the historical world-system itself approach their limits. Social disorder was most marked in the United States, with its very large and increasing complement of the "third world within." This social disorder has been widely misunderstood as simply an increase in crime. In reality, what we are seeing is civil warfare.

As we proceed deeper and deeper into our "time of troubles," people will become more, not less, dismayed, because the forms of opposition that we will see will not be the forms to which we have become accustomed. Thus there will be an increasing scramble for protection that cannot be provided by the state, which lacks the financial resources and the legitimation that are needed. In New York City, supporters of Mayor Rudolph Giuliani, a law-and-order centrist with strong connections to the police, were disappointed when they began to see that the tough policing that they desired was not the solution to the city's problems.

Giovanni Arrighi, Terence K. Hopkins, and Wallerstein (1992) detect a declining significance of states as sovereign entities that are key organizing centers of historical capitalism's patterns of development. State networks, they argue, are abridged by trans-state networks, state authority is defined by sectional and secessionist (and drug lord) interests, and business and consumerist interests serve as intermediaries in the election of lawmakers and the construction of the law. The state as a site for the betterment of all is increasingly losing legitimacy within this context. These phenomena are intertwined with the ongoing centralization of capital and the polarization of wealth within historical capitalism.

6

Perspectives on the American Dream

Whether celebrated or condemned, the American Dream
endures, though always ambiguously. We are forever
describing and defining, analyzing and assessing the concept,
and with each attempt to clarify, the idea of an American
Dream grows more incoherent yet more entrenched.

—JENSEN, "THE PAINFUL COLLAPSE OF EMPIRE:
HOW THE 'AMERICAN DREAM' AND AMERICAN EXCEPTIONALISM
WRECK HAVOC ON THE WORLD"

Every nation requires a story—or many stories, which taken
together form a national narrative—about its origins, a self-
defining mythos that says something about the character
of the people and how they operate in the larger world and
among each other. The strength of these stories lies in their
shaping power, the ways they illumine aspects of character
or embody ideals that, in turn, affect individual or collective
behavior.

—PARINI, "THE AMERICAN MYTHOS"

When in the Declaration of Independence the assertion was made that
"all men are created equal" and "endowed with certain inalienable
rights," the articulation of an American Dream also began to emerge.
This idea, of course, referred to only some men (and no women), yet it became a
symbol of the possibility represented by this new nation, tied to a construction
of "freedom." Franklin Roosevelt said, "Liberty requires opportunity to make
a living—a living decent according to the standard of the time, a living which
gives man not only enough to live by, but something to live for."[1]

Throughout the twentieth century, diverse groups in the United States navigated their particular positions in society as the nation rose to the position of
global leader with hegemonic power to define all that is worthy. The logic of
location was meant to justify the positioning of different people in different
places in society. The American Dream was held up as the distinguishing character of this nation. And, indeed, for many whites, especially those of eastern
and southern European roots, the mid-century did mark a period of intense
upward mobility. However, for most communities of color, a brief opening of

opportunities following the "second Reconstruction" during the 1960s began to disappear almost as quickly as it appeared. Among Blacks in the United States, a small percentage was provided access to the expanded wealth of the nation, but most remained firmly at the bottom of the "well" (Bell 1993). At the same time, some in the professional-managerial strata benefited, as one might understand in terms of the logic of class formation within the core states of the capitalist world economy and the particularities of geopolitical and geocultural factors in both the internal structure of the U.S. social system and in its relations to the larger social world in which it operates.

It is best to look at the trends starting in the 1940s, as the United States embarked on the American Century, but we should also take a brief look at the impact of the War on Poverty. As the most high-profile program of the civil rights era, the War on Poverty is believed to have had a striking impact, though of course it did not end poverty. Overall, the total number of poor fell from 18 percent in 1960 to only 9 percent in 1972 (Quadagno 1994, 175). This was a consequence of a substantial expansion of social-welfare programs, including social security, unemployment compensation, Medicare, food stamps, and public assistance. Child-poverty rates declined from 27 percent in 1960 to 15 percent in 1974. The percentage of Blacks enrolled in college increased from 13 percent in 1965 to 22.6 percent by 1975. Jill Quadagno argues that if this trend had continued, Blacks would have established parity by 1983. Similarly, by 1989, the number of Blacks holding white-collar jobs had increased by 522 percent (1994, 176).

But poor Blacks did not fare nearly so well. Between the early 1970s and the late 1980s, the percentage of two-parent Black families fell from 63.4 to 40.6 percent. The labor-force participation rate of Black high school dropouts fell by 25 percent. Jobless rates for Black men rose from 4.7 to 13.6 percent, and the percentage of Black children born out of wedlock increased from 35.1 to 62.6 percent. From 1970 to 1990, the rates of racial segregation, measured by the average geographic level of racial concentration, remained basically the same; in 1970, the average was 84.5 percent, and by 1990 it was slightly less, at 77.8 percent. Quadagno argues that segregation systematically builds deprivation into the residential structure of Black communities and increases the susceptibility of the neighborhoods to spirals of decline. A harsh environment is also said to create an oppositional culture that further separates ghetto residents from the majority of society.

In *American Apartheid*, Douglas Massey and Nancy Denton argue that segregation undermines support for jobs and services in the ghetto, because it deprives inner-city residents of the allies needed in a pluralist society where groups form alliances on the basis of mutual self-interest. Only ghetto residents gain when services and jobs are provided for the inner city, and only ghetto residents lose when they are removed.

When Ronald Reagan took office in 1981, he rolled back the welfare state. Funds for job training declined from more than $6 million in 1980 to less than $2.5 million in 1984. In 1981, federal aid to cities was reduced to 1968 levels.

Support for low-income housing was reduced markedly, from 183,000 starts in 1980 to 28,000 starts in 1985 (Quadagno 1994, 178). But, as we indicate above, we should look at more long-term trends, which complicate the kinds of empirical analysis that we often get. In a 2011 article in *Politics and Society,* William Sites and Virginia Parks argue that racial inequalities diminished significantly from 1945 to 1975 but have not changed very much since then. They point out that sociologists have often argued that economic restructuring led to a dramatic decline of employment in heavy mass-production industry, as indeed we have also argued. They do not believe, however (nor do we), that this is solely due to changing skill demands, as is classically argued in William Julius Wilson's *The Truly Disadvantaged.* Sites and Parks argue that the data that they have reviewed from the 1940s onward suggest that racial earnings inequalities have been significantly influenced by political and institutional factors—social movements, government policies, unionization efforts, and public-employment patterns—and that racial employment disparities have increased over the course of the postwar and post-1970s periods for reasons that are not reducible to skills.

The Fair Employment Practices Act of 1943 was a consequence of the overall strategy of the organized Black community. World War II juxtaposed the realities of U.S. racism and government acquiescence to it against the U.S. claim that it was fighting a war for democracy against an enemy who preached the doctrine of a master race. But the Black movement knew the situation on the ground in its struggle for U.S. government action on the claims of Black people. In opposition to the "Closing Ranks" position[2] that W.E.B. Du Bois and the National Association for the Advancement of Colored People (NAACP) had taken in World War I, the Black movement adopted the "Double V," calling for victory against international fascism and victory against domestic racism. The sense of militancy that pervaded Black America in the face of the recalcitrance of the federal government under Roosevelt led to agitation for mass pressure, leading eventually to the March on Washington movement. In calling for this protest, A. Philip Randolph argues, "Only power can affect the enforcement and adoption of a given policy. . . . Power is the active principle only of the organized masses, the masses united for a definite purpose."[3]

It is also important to note that the war created a demand for Black labor, which was increasingly filled by southern Black immigrants. The industrial boom stimulated by the war created a situation of relatively full employment, which reduced the intensity of job competition and thus of the opposition to Black entry into some segments of the labor force. This situation bolstered the self-confidence of the Black working class vis-à-vis white society, despite the continued existence of a racial division of labor that relegated Blacks to the lowest rungs of the labor force.

This period of increasing militancy on the part of the Black working class formed the context in which Malcolm X grew up. During this period, interracial violence increased, leading finally to the bloody summer of 1943.[4]

One Harlem leader argued, "If we don't fight for our rights during the War, while the government needs us, it will be too late after the war."[5] The Black press highlighted evidence of Black exclusion from defense jobs, blood plasma segregated by the Red Cross, abused Black soldiers, and white hostility and violence. With its circulation increased by 40 percent during the war, the Black press served to prod the increasing militancy and racial solidarity and embarrass America's "war for democracy" by publicizing its Jim Crow practices and policies. The NAACP's membership increased tenfold. The Congress of Racial Equality (CORE) was formed in 1942, inspiring sit-ins and other forms of direct action.

On the intellectual front, a steady stream of articles, books, letters, and speeches by such people as Pearl S. Buck, Eleanor Roosevelt, Wendell Wilkie, and Henry Wallace disputed scientific racism and condemned America's hypocrisy. This movement reached its peak with the publication of Gunnar Myrdal's *The American Dilemma* ([1944] 1964). Myrdal sidesteps the socioeconomic issues around which racism revolved and highlights instead the moral issue of the conflict within the American creed generated by the practice of racial discrimination. It had become clear that American hegemony would require racial liberalism as a central feature, especially given the emergence of a large cadre of Black intellectuals and antiracist intellectuals and activists who had close connections to the World Left (Ahmad 2007; K. Baldwin 2002; Biondi 2003; R. Bush 1999; Bush and Bush 2008; Césaire 2010a, 2010b; Cruse 1968; Du Bois [1903] 1986, 1928; Duziak 2000; Horne 1986; R. Kelley 1990; Makalani 2011; Marable 1986a, 1986b; Markowitz 1973; W. Maxwell 1999; Mullen 2004; Plummer 1996; Robinson 1983; Singh 2004; Solomon 1998; Von Eschen 1997; West, Martin, and Wilkins 2009; Q. Wright, 1955; R. Wright 1956). Importantly, this social force, which viewed itself as national in form but internationalist in scope, crosscut the nationalism of empire that was so central to U.S. national identity and inserted tension at the heart of U.S. hegemonic designs that was incompatible with U.S. national identity.

The patterns of changes in racial inequality since the civil rights revolution of the post-1945 period represent not only responses to internal social relations but also rejoinders to geopolitical and geocultural relations embedded in the larger global economy and social system. The evolution of the social system since the end of U.S. hegemony in the 1970s and the desperate attempt to establish a new American Century since the 1990s present us with a situation in which the multiple social times in which we all live become compressed, and what we normally take to be the time of the conjuncture blends into historical time as we move deeper into the structural crisis of historical capitalism. As this occurs, the stakes take on an urgency and immediacy that require us to focus all our energies and visions to determine the direction in which we will construct a new world. We are aligned against powerful forces who would take the world backward into a new barbarism that would reflect our worst dystopian nightmares, with armed vigilantes empowered to execute anyone who seems threatening.

This struggle will be protracted rather than quick, but the stakes are high, and so we cannot underestimate the urgency.

The experience of both Asians and Latinos in this struggle has been very mixed. Some Asian communities have mirrored the expanded wealth and incomes of whites; others have found themselves located among the poorest communities in the United States. The National Council of La Raza, partnering with the National Urban League, reported that 25.8 percent of Hispanic America lived below the poverty line in 2011, compared to 11 percent of whites. At the same time, the median household income for Hispanic America was 72 percent that of whites, while the unemployment rate was 70 percent that of whites (National Urban League 2013, 45). The Pew Research Center reported that the wealth gap between whites, Hispanics, and Blacks had reached record highs; in 2009, the median wealth of white households was twenty times that of Black households and eighteen times that of Hispanic households. It also reported that 35 percent of Black households and 31 percent of Hispanic households had zero or negative wealth.

For the last half of the twentieth century and the beginning of the twenty-first century, most populations except the very wealthy have increasingly struggled with joblessness, foreclosures, and debt. This situation positions people to wonder whether the American Dream is rhetoric, reverie, or reality. Ideas about what this dream entails vary enormously, with associations being made to economic mobility (home ownership, education, wealth, endless opportunity), family and community ties, political notions of freedom, and/or spiritual well-being. It is in this context that we explore how individuals perceive and think about their location, the position of the nation globally, the stories that frame and explain structural realities, and reflections on the American Dream.

The story of the American Dream is historically grounded in the European conquest of the Americas and the manner in which this led to the emergence of the world's major social power, the United States. The existence of the United States as a "presumed" white nation for most of its history is of great significance to the maintenance of the story of the American Dream. The demographic transitions of the past fifty years reveal much about this story that had previously been locked into internal debates among separate groups of Americans. The participants in this study offer a variety of perspectives on this story.

This tale of American (European, white) success had enormous implications worldwide. European colonialism racialized and gendered the economic structure throughout the globe. This was justified in similar terms, as those in positions of wealth and power were presumed to be in their social positions due to their inherent superiority and worthiness. The idea that upward mobility is not just possible but limitless provided just the rationale to garner loyalty to ideological rules and principles of capitalism and white supremacy. This justification implied that those who succeed are worthy, while those who do not succeed are not worthy or deserving.

A 2009 national study of political ideology conducted by the Center for American Progress found that people's beliefs about the American Dream reflect the following ideas:

A full two-thirds of Americans (67 percent) report that their family's income is falling behind the cost of living, with 23 percent saying their income is staying even and only 6 percent saying it is going up faster than the cost of living. The belief that family income is failing to keep pace with rising costs is uniformly held across ideological, partisan, race, and income lines.

Despite the harsh climate, many Americans continue to believe that they have achieved or will achieve their own understanding of the American Dream in their lifetime. More than one-third of Americans (34 percent) say they have already achieved the American Dream and another 41 percent believe that they will achieve it in their lifetime. Roughly one-fifth of Americans (18 percent) say they will not achieve the American Dream in their lifetime.

Significant education gaps exist on perceptions of the American Dream. Fifty percent of post-graduate educated Americans say they have achieved the American Dream and only 5 percent say they will not achieve it. In contrast, only 30 percent of those with a high school degree or less say they have achieved the American Dream and nearly one-quarter believes that they will not attain it in their lifetimes.[6]

In 1938, a Roper Organization Poll found that only 30 percent agreed on the idea of imposing a top limit on income, while 61 percent said there should not be one (Roper 1938). Despite the conditions of the Depression, there was a strong belief in economic prosperity through hard work (Hanson and White 2011). Sandra L. Hanson and John Kenneth White cite historian James Truslow Adams as referring to the American Dream in 1941 as the "glue that kept the country together" (Adams 1941, qtd. in Hanson and White 2011, 5). In our discussions, we explore whether that perception is still the case. How do people view this significant symbol of economic, political, and social success? Do people look to the "system" for explanations for lack of success, or do they blame themselves? How do people define the American Dream? We now share some of the participants' comments.

With regard to the many formulations of the American Dream, some argue that it is not just a dream but a reality for most people in the United States. Many, however, qualify their beliefs in a variety of ways. Even among those who "believe," most have difficulty describing the terms of the "dream."

The Dream Is Relative

Bruce (Chinese descent, male, U.S.-born, 26–45) points out that the notion of success being measurable in material ways is relative both in perception and in actuality. He argues that the "dream" is not necessarily attached to a specific lifestyle and that there are advantages to having to struggle:

> If you have been here for a hundred years, you're well off, and your name is Vanderbilt the fourth, then your American Dream—well, you are born into it. You are living your dream, unless you define your dream as having twice of what you already have. The American Dream is for everyone, and it doesn't matter what cultural race you are. It might be harder, but there can be some advantage in that. For Chinese people it's harder, but this is why we bond as a community and help each other out. It's like the deck of cards that everyone is given, but I think everyone is given a fair chance.

Tara (Chinese/Latina, female, U.S.-born, 18–25) echoes Bruce's sentiment:

> My grandmother came here, got a high school education, and then worked at a Chinese food restaurant. She thinks she actually did well in her life. People now would think that that wasn't enough. This is a big thing nowadays—people just want more. They can be making $100,000 a year, have a nice house, a nice car, but then they see a person making $200,000 a year, with two houses and three cars, and they feel that they have not achieved the American Dream. People always feel they can get more.

A discussion among women over age 46 focuses on how the idea of the American Dream has changed over time:

> Patrice (Black, female, born outside the U.S., 46–65): The American Dream is changeable and reflects the time. In the fifties and sixties, when my parents aspired to that, it was a very well-defined goal. It was if you work hard, you achieve economic success.
>
> Ina (white, female, U.S.-born, 46–65): The American Dream would be to go to college; to have some sort of social status; to get married, have children and a big, beautiful house, and be away from my family. I loved my grandparents dearly, but they were immigrants, and they didn't speak English. I guess I felt—I don't want to use the word "embarrassed." I didn't support some of the things they wanted, because my grandmother was very into social causes. She was very much a part of the civil rights [movement]. She loved me, but I held back from that, because I used to say, "I don't want any part of this." I'm still looking for what the American Dream is. The American Dream is always changing.
>
> Janice (white, female, U.S.-born, 46–65): The American Dream is being optimistic. The American Dream embodies the potential, but

there's so many factors in achieving that potential. The only part of the American Dream that I've truly achieved is the education. I've never owned a house. I'm 55 years old. I did not want my life to be consumed by material things. I have a good job that I love. I enjoy getting involved in human-rights issues, so my life is full.

Patrice: It is quite elusive, and look at our words, you know, "bling." That's what success is now. It's bling. It's buying things. It's baubles and cars.

Janice: That's promoted as the American Dream. But who profits? When you hear something or you see something on television, you ask yourself, "Who is profiting from me knowing this? Why should I buy into this concept?"

Subsequently, the following exchange occurs:

Patrice: Everything leads to America, and the whole world is seen through our prism, our perspective. One of the things about Americans as good, bad, or indifferent is a sense of ownership of the world, a control of the world, and more than anything it is what drives the American personality. We don't even consider for a minute collectively that we might not be loved or that life can be better elsewhere. In our arrogance, we don't consider that other people live much better other places and that basically we're a nation of workers—that we work our asses off. All the time. I mean, we work nonstop. People in Denmark have families who take care of them. I can't take a minute to walk my baby. Basically we're a nation of—

Ina: Arrogant people.

Janice: In France and Italy, you get five weeks per year mandatory vacation. If you have an elderly person, a mother or someone, in Italy, you're given a stipend to take care of that person, as opposed to putting them in a home.

Ina: I mean, in other countries, you get naps and child care. We really are backwards.

In another discussion, participants also express that an element of the American Dream is struggle and that what people strive for has changed:

I remember when it was land; owning something was a sign of making it. Now it's rental apartments, loans, you know. I came from a time where my grandmother kind of owned that apartment. She couldn't get kicked out. Back when we had the block associations, you felt entitled to your property. Now it doesn't seem the same. We have more government projects, and it's not the same as actually having a piece of our so-called American Dream. If I come out of the hood thinking that everything about the American Dream is my reality and I pursue life that way, working hard, then it shouldn't be too hard for me to grasp that concept.

But if I'm that person that ha[s] all the strikes against me, I'm at the bottom of the barrel to start off, and I don't have the belief in this American Dream system, then it's not fair to say that I'll achieve. You have to overcome something. The renaissance and civil rights movements and things of that nature cannot be taken for granted, because it's actually had its benchmark in our lifetime as far as rights, equality, the whole equal-rights movement. I have relatives who would never dream of that; that's long gone right now. If I had the opportunity to wake them right now just to let them see that, for me, that's like wow, that's the American Dream. (Rome, Black, male, U.S.-born, 18–25)

Another group recognizes that the idea of the American Dream looks different in different contexts. For example, Lisa (white, female, U.S.-born, 26–45) says:

The Chinese, for example, have always been oppressed. There was a time when the Irish and the Italians would get killed for being Catholic. It has always been selective, and they have more of [a] chance to achieve their dreams.

Breana (white, female, U.S.-born, 18–25) expands on this idea:

You can't tell the people that were slaves about the American Dream. The idea of the American Dream covers up the actual poverty issue because of the global competition. By doing this, we are trying to make ourselves look better. It gives us a better rank among other countries that look to us.

Some participants question the origin of the American Dream, asserting that the idea was created to entice immigrants to come to the country at a time when labor was needed:

At the turn of the century, when my grandfather came here, America needed labor. People can sometimes make a mistake and sort of have misty eyes about dreams. There is the underlying economic structure underneath. (Carmella, white, female, U.S.-born, 26–45)

Some note that the American Dream motivates migration to the United States. Alice (white/Asian, female, born outside the U.S., 18–25) says:

I always felt that the American Dream was [for] someone who's from a "troubled" country or escaping something—they come to this country to, you know, to have opportunities and whatnot.

Aria (South Asian/Desi, female, born outside the U.S., 26–45) argues:

The American Dream is a cliché—that anyone can do anything, a reason why all the people are here. The flipside is that anyone who does not make it because of the multiple circumstances—it is not because they are not trying hard or that they are lazy. There is a devaluation of people's life if they do not achieve it, do not succeed, or do not follow a certain ladder.

Other participants strongly believe that opportunities exist and that being rich or poor is a straightforward matter of choice:

It is a matter of choice on a subconscious level—people choose to be poor. If people are poor and they are looking for people to feed them or hand them a welfare check, then that is a choice. On some level, they are saying, "I want to be this way."

I lived in the projects, and I came out of it. I see people on my days off and wonder, "Why are there still so many people here?" It is because no one is working. These people may want to be rich, but how much are they willing to sacrifice? You have to be open to the opportunities in front of you and willing to make the sacrifices. A lot of Chinese people grow business communities and trade amongst themselves. They become rich together. You just have to be smart about it and network your way into it. (Bruce, Chinese descent, male, U.S.-born, 26–45)

This position inevitably invites debate:

Rich people make themselves richer—it's easier to make $5 million when you already have $1 million than to make $5 when you start off with $1. To make the initial million dollars, you have to sweat for it—after that it is not too bad. (Joe J., white, male, U.S.-born, 26–45)

I agree! My friend buys a two-week Metro card, and I tell him to just buy the monthly one, as he'll save a few dollars. But he says, "Who has the money to put down right away to buy the monthly one?" The Native Americans, they never had a chance. (Tara, Chinese/Latina, female, U.S.-born, 18–25)

My mom, who is successful, would attribute people being poor because they had poor financial planning and that we have a commodity fetish. But they are too busy surviving; they don't have time to think about the American Dream. They are not represented when we think about America overall. They are not accorded the American Dream. We don't pay attention to the fringes. It is the media; the rich keep getting richer, obviously. It is such a weird systematic Darwinism where we just don't pay attention to the poor. There are eight hundred million people that are not taking part in any success. These are people who are being abandoned. We just want to hear about success, the pleasure principle—we don't want to face the fact that there are so many people living on a dollar a day or [that] even in America there are thirty-five million people below the poverty line. (Kendra, Asian, female, U.S.-born, 18–25)

In a conversation with other college students, Betsy (white, female, U.S.-born, 18–25) speaks to another aspect of the American Dream that suggests this idea targets immigrants and is grounded in imagery:

In America, it's all about product placement. People from other countries see America as this land of opportunities. It's more like an advertisement. It's like, "Come to America—we have our own dreams, and we can make your dreams come true for you."

Carl (white, male, U.S.-born, 18–25) takes this thought a step further, saying that it not only is now but has always been about imagery:

The American Dream is not alive today. It is not vital. If you ask someone today what the American Dream is, they can't give you a straightforward answer. People are confused; 150 years ago, it was all about propaganda, too. It was a "Come over here and get all the land for your farming and such." . . . It is all about social mobility for many people.

If you review the last fifty to sixty years, you can notice that we've been in and out of constant war. I want to live in a community that doesn't do that, and that ties to the basic idea of [being] isolationist. But the fact that we don't live in such a nation and that I so strongly disagree with the choices that this country makes really destroys my perception of who I am as an American—it really destroys my idea of being an American.

Meryl (self-identified as "other," female, born outside the U.S., 18–25) questions the relevancy of the American Dream to different populations:

When you guys say that the American Dream has diminished, it is not true. In other countries, people still see America as the land where you can find opportunity and find freedom and equality and jobs. People still dream about coming to this country. People that grow up here don't see it, or they forget it, but people that are in other countries definitely still have it alive in their minds.

Kendra (Chinese descent, female, U.S.-born, 18–25) explains:

My father's conception of the American Dream, we discussed it one time
at dinner. I asked why he wanted to come here, because he was a part
of the Cultural Revolution; he was one of the students. He said in one
sentence that back in China at that time, you couldn't eat until you were
full. So you were always hungry there.

My mom came here on a student visa. They had this idea that the
American Dream was financial stability and the ability to move upward.
They did not have that in China. My mom earlier said that the American
Dream had expired for the Chinese, because now a lot of my relatives
are still in China and we'll tell them, "Why aren't you applying for the
visa?" because sometimes it takes up to ten years to get it. They say, "We
don't want to come to America!" Ever since Deng Xiao Peng opened up
China, America is just not as appealing to them. They have no desperation to come here anymore.

Two winters ago, my family and I were sitting around the living
room, and my aunt said, "I don't know why I came here! I don't know
why I am here. I am just not happy here." It's not only with the Chinese,
because I taught the pre-GED class [and] a lot of my students were from
Africa. Their goals were to go back, after they saved up some money. Like
my mother said, "The American Dream expired about ten years ago."

There has been a shift. Even though people that came here in the
eighties and nineties didn't fare well here, though they weren't very
prosperous here, they would buy a lot of gifts, clothes, when they visited China to kind of fake like, "Oh I am doing so well in America!"
Saving face is very important to the Chinese. Now with the decline of
the American empire and the rise in China, there is less of a veil of the
American Dream, and they are not applying for their visas.

Many people express that the American Dream is not just about consumption but also about the opportunity to contribute to society and to work for a
better world. Some speak about how the dream inspires a feeling of community
and well-being and has to be disassociated from the quest for material accumulation. Adams articulates a concept of the "American Dream" in his 1931 book,
The Epic of America: "It is not a dream of motor cars and high wages merely,
but a dream of social order in which each man and each woman shall be able
to attain to the fullest stature of which they are innately capable, and be recognized by others for what they are, regardless of the fortuitous circumstances
of birth or position" (415). He understands that the "dream" was never solely
about economics.

Rashida, an African American woman in her 20s who grew up in Harlem,
argues that the American Dream of having a family, career, and house with a
picket fence and of being well-off is unrealistic and unattainable:

I call it artificial, because not everyone has equal opportunity. For me, it is not attainable. I do not really believe in the American Dream. We say "the land of opportunity," but not everyone has the same opportunity. It depends on class, gender, race, economic status, and history.

Her comments are met with mixed reactions from others in the focus group who are of Haitian descent:

I never, ever thought of the American Dream until today. The American Dream does not exist for people who were born in the lap of luxury. You should have been born in misery [to come from the bottom] to *need* a nice house, etc. If you were born in a rich family, you do not want a house, because you already have it.

The American Dream is a dream, purely in the mind of the person, and stays there unless they choose to follow it and make it a reality. For me, the American Dream is more of a mental liberation than actual liberation; I feel pretty free—yet racism is an issue that will not be resolved or settled in my lifetime.

People come here in the land of opportunity to be happy. My teacher said that we are taught what makes us happy; we were told what the American Dream is. I refuse to be told what will make me happy or what my dream is. I want mental liberation to escape the media that is trying to move me. I talked to a coworker and said that both my parents have bachelor's degrees, and they were surprised. (Jodel, Haitian, male, U.S.-born, 18–25)

Jodel articulates his belief that we must take individual responsibility for what we pursue and ward off forces that attempt to shape our worldview or sense of worthiness.

For Jerry (Jodel's brother, 18–25), the American Dream is fully economic:

I had a happy childhood but felt shame and sadness to see other people's misery. My parents did everything, came here, bought a house, sent us to private school; I took everything for granted. So much was given to me that other people do not have—I feel guilty and a sense of shame when I see other people. I can take a loan for a college, for a car. My father cosigned for me and said that this way, he will teach me to pay money. Some people do not have fathers to do that [or] do not have a person with this economic status.

Their mother, Bobola (46–64), was born in Haiti and moved to the United States at age 24. She went back to school to get a GED and eventually a college degree. For her, America is the land of opportunity. She believes that there are some barriers, but as long as you are determined, you can succeed:

The reason I like the American Dream is whoever wants to do it, he can do it. You have to search for it. You cannot sit down and wait for your parents to provide it. Rich kids have nothing—they do not understand American Dream, they have the opportunity. They believe that because you were born here, you will have everything. But being an American— if you set your goal, you will see the dream, you will see what America offers.

Jodel raises another issue:

People from other countries tell us they do not like us, but they come here. Everybody says they do not like the U.S. It is possible not to like U.S. but to be here—the whole idea of freedom and its attainability.

What is represented in his statement? Is the American Dream economic? Political? Is it relevant to only those who strive for upward mobility? Is it the projection or embodiment of the "ideal" life? Bobola responds with mixed emotions:

The vision that we have is to come to America. When we are kids in another country—America is the best place until you come. People say, "Money is everywhere; houses are so beautiful." . . . When people come back from America, they look very nice—nice hair, nice clothes—their dream came true. But when I came here, I lived on the twenty-first floor; nothing impressed me until I came to Manhattan. The American Dream is Manhattan. But the school system should have more diverse interactions with kids from other countries.

In another exchange, other participants similarly discuss tensions in the American Dream. Audrey (Black, female, U.S.-born, 26–45) speaks to changes that have occurred in the last few decades:

The American Dream idea is becoming smaller and smaller for people. People are getting selfish. They are just worrying about themselves and their families and/or their race. It is becoming very competitive.

Carol (Black, female, born outside the U.S., 26–45) moved to the United States from Barbados and explains that she moved back and forth between her mother, who was poor, and her father, who had land. Her education included public schools attended predominantly by African American students as well as private schools attended mostly by Jewish students:

I am my mother's American Dream. When she came to this country, she wasn't seeking the American Dream for herself; she was seeking to achieve it for me. Do I believe in the American Dream? Do I think that it is something special? I am going to say, "yes and no." I say, "no," as there are a lot of other countries in the world where you can go and achieve economic happiness. "Yes," in the sense that there is definitely something in this country that attracts people. They see some chance of improvement here. It's the poor people that leave and the rich people that stay. So do I believe in the American Dream? I don't, because ever since I was little, I saw that you don't have to work hard to become wealthy.

Audrey (Black, female, U.S.-born, 26–45) echoes sentiments about the shallowness of this "dream" and how it is particularly associated with materialism:

The American Dream really is about things, whether it's about wealth or actual material things. It evolves from just having things to what type of things you have, like name-brand things. It becomes the image you're trying to uphold. People put themselves into debt trying to attain a certain image and upholding like they are making it. But they [are] not, and they are not necessary fulfilled. I went to Puerto Rico for one of my friends weddings, and when I went to the store, it hit me how privileged we are. They had one peanut butter and one jelly. This was a big store, and I was thinking we have too much choice, and that what's it about, and I think that it's about having choice. Like Gabriel in *Lost Boys*—I was crying about how touching it was to see these guys going to refugee camps where they can barely eat, and here they go down an aisle where they have different types of pet food, and they stood there in awe.

Andrew (Polish, male, born outside the U.S., 26–45) comments:

When I was a kid, one of the ways to make money was to travel from country to country and buy things, sell things, and we would go to Turkey, to Russia. In one trip, you can make like $400 in American dollars. I remember going into a store and seeing what kind of soda I wanted to drink. I remember seeing three different kinds of bread; I was like, "My God, this is like heaven."

Equating material wealth and endless choice in material goods with the American Dream is a common response among participants; however, as demonstrated above, many readily offer the opinion that their idea of a good life is different:

My brother and sister wanted material success, so they chose careers that would provide that kind of comfort. I pulled away from that at a fairly young age. I had a sense that wasn't going to give me the peace and deep fulfillment that I was looking for, so I wound up going into special education. I'm very happy I did. I'm very glad for the path I took. I chose a mate that had similar kinds of values. I made the choice early on not to pursue material wealth in the way that people around me were doing. If you don't make that choice, then you lose out. There's not enough support for people that are looking to live just, you know, simply but gracefully. We're kind of always struggling. We didn't even have health insurance or a car. (Ellen, white, female, U.S.-born, 46–65)

It's kind of all or nothing. (Tony, white/other, male, U.S.-born, 46–65)

A participant in a discussion with people over 60 explores how material success is valued and measured. John (white, male, U.S.-born, 46–65) says that if you have material wealth, people look at you and say, "This man is somebody. He's important." At the same time, he realizes that he could continue to work and accumulate more wealth but chooses not to:

If you don't stop someplace and enjoy what you have, what have you achieved, what have you worked for? It's got to stop. I'm where I need to be; I'm happy where I am. You have to think about the American Dream in your own terms.

Mandy (Black, female, U.S.-born, over 65) agrees and elaborates on this point:

The American Dream to me is the way I'm being treated by other people and the way that I relate to other people. With Barack Obama being elected as president, to me that was the beginning of the dream. I can now say our grandson won't know anything about how we felt and how we never dreamed that anything like this would ever happen. He will think this is the way it's always been. Our daughter never knew anything about the civil rights movement, only what she read and what people told her, but to me this is the beginning of the dream. As far as the house, the car, whatever, it's not me.

Often interwoven in discussions about the true character of the American Dream are questions about the meaning of success and the relative value of viewing wealth accumulation as a priority. For some, the American Dream of economic advancement and material success has never been accessible. Joseph (Black, male, U.S.-born, 46–65) describes his experience:

The mainstream American Dream is the white picket fence around a nice little house. The *Father Knows Best* type of house, which I grew up watching. Which is fine, but not everybody has access to the dream because of racism. I didn't become aware of racism until my teen years from reading but also personal experiences. Other kids would call me names, like darkened jokes. The darker you were, the more you got joked on. But for me, the American Dream has been fulfilled in that I blazed my own trail, so to speak, and carved out my little niche. To me, the American Dream is more, is not necessarily a house or a wife and a car, but it's just living a satisfied life and being able to contribute to society and be happy, go to a job that you don't hate, have a job or a livelihood where you can't wait to get to the next day. But most people work at jobs that they don't like.

Many wonder whether one must surrender quality of life to achieve the American Dream:

Money and success, it's all good, but it's empty. You have all this wealth, you can get anything you want, but it doesn't really mean anything. I have some friends that definitely lived in lower-class neighborhoods and worked harder than I did in school. They knew that getting a good education and job is key. I quit my job about two years ago and got married. I want a family and stuff like that. The American Dream for each person changes as they develop as a person. I want financial security, but I don't want to spend the first ten years after graduating pursuing that, because you miss out on a lot. A person should spend more time finding out who they are than just pursuing the all-mighty dollar. (Joe, Chinese, male, U.S.-born, 26–45)

Yuan (Asian, female, born outside the U.S., 26–45) came to the United States from China to attend college. She questions whether other elements to a successful life are equally or more important. Her comments reflect ambivalence about traditional notions of the American Dream:

In China, you don't have a lot of money, but I still dream for that lifestyle. In the morning you eat breakfast, do some exercise, and go to work. You finish at 11:45 A.M. and go home to cook and have a snack. Then you go back to the factory and work again from 2:00 until you go home at 5:00. Then you cook and eat, and then you can go to school after that. You have a little nice lifestyle, but here never. Here, the education system is different. Children only stay in school until 2:00; after that, they don't know what to do. They [are] bored every day. So, they develop a lot of afterschool programs, but you have to pay.

People live here, and many don't live with their parents. Parents are working so hard, and even though they are tired, they are still working. In China, school starts at 8:00 A.M., but the kids come home at 5:00 P.M., but in between, they go home to eat.

The life is really different, still here there is more chance, but I don't know how. Sometimes it [is] very hard. When we came here, we really had nothing. Our ticket was borrowed from somebody, so we worked hard and then earned the money. It is a little different in China. You don't have the ability to work hard; you only live just for a living. But here, education really makes the class change too, so you have more money because you have a little higher education. I don't know what kind of class I can define myself [as], but really, when we came here, it was really nothing, but now I have a little.

Yuan's experience in the United States has been mixed. She acknowledges her upward mobility, particularly as a result of her access to higher education. However, the quality of her life is focused on work rather than on family or community. She describes the challenges that this poses. Her access to material goods provides some comforts, but she reminisces about a time when she was able to go home for lunch, when her family was together during the day and in the evening, and when schooling was a full-day experience.

Perhaps encouraged to speak more freely by her husband Edward's open criticism of the American Dream, Yuan talks more about the aspects of her life that she finds difficult:

When we come here, you work very hard in the morning. You didn't see the sun; you never see the sun, because you came out the door about 6:00, and you come home, it's night, so the whole day, life is very hard.

So the lifestyle in China, I'm still dreaming if you can have that. Here, it is true you have more opportunity if you work hard. I don't think if I stayed in China that I would get a college degree. I never can get a master's. I have more dream[s]; I can buy a house soon.

But people [here] don't live with their parents, and their parents [are] working so hard, and even though they [are] tired, they still [are] working.

She offers the perspective that in the United States, people are working harder and have higher wages but don't have time to spend with families or to enjoy their relative wealth. Families are more separated; children have more formal education but spend less time in school. She seems distressed by this paradox.

Ideas about what constitutes the American Dream generally focus on material acquisition. However, some participants are able to outline other components, such as self-actualization, contributing to one's community, spending time with one's family, and living a more satisfying life—a truly *good* life:

Most people think of the American Dream [as] mostly a material thing and housing, opportunities for education, and employment. Those are three major elements of the American Dream, attaining those things and being [a] self-sufficient nuclear family. A lot of that came out of the post–World War II era. You have the bread winner and the homemaker, which was traditionally the mother, the wife in the family. That was generated post–World War through the G.I. bill, home ownership, and now you definitely have less of that. Why that is unique to America, I don't know. There's lots of great things about this country that make it unique, especially democracy and our Constitution, but as far as quality of life, I don't, I don't see it being exponentially better than a lot of these other countries, Western European countries. (Joe J., white, male, U.S.-born, 26–45)

Martin Luther King and Barack Obama have expressed better than I can the varied aspects of the American Dream. I have achieved many of the material aspects, but there's a long way to go in human relationships founded on reciprocal empathy. Narrow identification creates almost insurmountable obstacles. Ethnicity and race make elevating status more difficult. It is still possible, as shown by many remarkable people, but stereotyping and ignorance cause many problems. Certainly, harassment, violence, and antisocial behavior only retard progress. There is a shortage of empathy in the highest seats of power. (Stanley, white, male, U.S.-born, over 65)

It's kind of interesting that we've talked about escape from poverty. None of us [have] really talked about escape from oppression. Not everybody came here so they could have a huge house or drive a Mercedes. Some came here so they wouldn't starve to death and [some] people came here so they wouldn't be shoved in ovens or whatever. We kind of forget often, like, how bad it was for a lot of people wherever they came from. They weren't hoping for a Mercedes. They were hoping for a place to live and enough to eat and not getting killed and the Constitution. (Carmella, white, female, U.S.-born, 26–45)

While racialization brings privilege for people of European descent, those who have migrated to the United States after 1960 are often shocked by the more complete commodification of everything in the United States, resulting in a fast, frantic pace that has removed much of the joy from life. Many of the themes described above are echoed in the words of Louise (Italian, female, born outside the U.S., 46–65):

I was born in a small town in Italy, a town of six thousand people right by the water, and it was a lovely place. In this town where life was so simple, every, every little thing would bring you joy—even if it was to take a walk to the beach and you find a rock that looked different, you were happy. We were happy, for little or nothing. You were happy. Now you see kids, they have everything, and they want to cry and complain like if they got nothing.

My sister got married and came to this country. My other sister came to this country, so only myself and my brother were left there with my parents. I got engaged to this fellow who was in the navy—that's how I met him. I was supposed to come to this country, too, so my mother said, "Oh no, that's it. I got no life anymore." She said, "I'm dead," so my father decided, "Let's go there."

It was a big shock to me when I came the first time. We couldn't wait to go back home. I stayed for three months. I had my ideas of coming to the United States, like whatever [I had] seen on television. Whatever we saw, like beautiful place, like different, you didn't think much of the mentality that the different people [have], because you think about going there. When I came the first time, it was a shock to me, because I saw how different was life. It was overwhelming.

I found out life was so rushed, pushing. Oh my god, you got out of work, and it was already night. Oh my god. Everybody's running. Everybody here is rushing and running. Why? When you got out of work, it was dark. Why don't you slow down? Because in Italy, you eat in the afternoon, you go to rest about an hour, and then you get up, you're nice and refreshed, you do other things. So my sister says, "No, no, no, take it out of your mind. Here, you don't sleep during the day. You sleep at night—if you're lucky!"

When I came back, I was going crazy, because I felt like I was empty. I felt like, "Oh my god, my life is work," going to work, come home, going to work, and come home, and the weekend [would] come, and I didn't have that many friends. I missed my home. I felt like I was going to choke to death at night. I missed my balcony. I missed my beautiful, you know, my rooms. You know, you are born in another country. You bring [that] with [you] all the time. You carry [it] inside, and no matter how good the life can be here for me, I always carry my Sicily and my, my background is always in me.

This sentiment—that the dream allows for material accumulation but not quality of life—is echoed in the comments of other participants. They express different opinions about what is achieved through hard work.

Louise (Italian, female, born outside the U.S., 46–65) and Deidra (white, female, U.S.-born, over 65) discuss the differences in the quality of life between the United States and Italy:

> Louise: In August, most everything shuts down in Europe as people take a break. Stores are closed on Sunday, providing time for families to get together.
> Deidra: In Italy, it's a better life in that people take vacations more than they do here.

Louise: The American Dream was years ago, when Europe was much poorer.

Deidra: The feeling was to come here, you'd get a better life. It still is for a lot of cultures.

Louise: You don't find so much immigration of Europeans now.

Deidra: They have a pretty good life in England.

Louise: The immigration from Europe was a lot in the fifties and the early sixties, when that was really the American Dream. When my sister came, everybody thinks that you get off from the airplane and you find the big car waiting for you. It's not like this. You've got to go to work, and you've got to work hard to reach the famous American Dream.

Deidra: Our kids have grown into a comfortable life, and we just want to expand on the comfort level. They're not pursuing anything, because they have it.

Stefan was born in a small town in Poland and moved to the United States at age 17, where he attended high school and college. He "always thought of the American Dream as materialism and obsessing over things and wanting to succeed." Questions about the meaning of quality of life, family, and what is important emerge continuously in these discussions. If you start rich and gain more, you are successful; if you start poor and gain a little, you are successful. Are other elements of a successful life equally or more important?

With regard to the American Dream, Thomas D. (Italian American, male, U.S.-born, 18–25) argues that the idea that one could be whatever one desires if one works hard enough is a mythology that overlooks the stratification system and discrimination. Personally, he has done well but has incurred a lot of debt attending college. While emphasis is often on freedom, there is a great deal of pressure for conformity and for those outside our borders to subordinate their own aspirations to the desires of the United States. He suggests that the American Dream is always viewed from an individualistic perspective:

It is always about what can each individual person achieve, and growing up you kind of get indoctrinated with the mythology of America, that America is supposed to be the beacon for humanity.

Thomas D. goes on to say that this original idea is no longer relevant:

[Now] it's not about spreading or allowing people to emerge as independent and unique individuals, not just this country but throughout the world. Internationally it's about imposing positions on people and countries to kind of meet whatever it is the United States is at today.

Eddie C. (Latino, male, U.S.-born, 18–25) takes this position a step further:

Anyone can achieve it, but at a cost. There's something called the big sacri-fice. The big screen portrays that the underdog can overcome and rise to the top, but most of the time there's always a price to pay. That's the fall. There's a rise to the empire, and there's a fall to the empire. The price is normally your freedom, so that American Dream, you give up a slice of it. You give up a piece of that pie. What you sacrifice, you're actually giving up the whole pie for just a piece of it. What do you really gain? Even some hard workers, you know, get the short end of the stick. So it's not guaranteed. I don't want to sell anybody a façade. I don't want to sell you a dream and say, "You know what, if you believe and put all you into this, what I'm saying, regardless of whether it's hard work or you're just making that sacrifice, [is] that dream will be there for you." You within yourself have to know whether you can believe that much into it and get what you put into it out of it. I don't want it to be about a social thing, because we don't even carry ourselves socially anymore. We don't worry about the next person and how, you know, if they're getting by. We've got to worry about ourselves, so honestly, if I tell somebody what I believe in the American Dream, am I really giving them something or am I taking something from them? It affects me in a negative way to see somebody feed into an American Dream, but I know where they're coming from—they don't have much; the movies just make it [seem] more attractive [and] being possible. Even people in America have their discomforts. We're here supposedly amongst the American Dream, but we're not satisfied. We want more.

I wasn't raised to believe that what you work for was the American Dream. People lose sight of exactly what the American Dream is, and I'm an example for that, because I'm sitting here before this actual sit-down, I'm thinking of it in terms of a negative way, like, you know, it's just something to believe in, the great white hype. Not just a white man has a family, not just, you know, the Chinese man has a family, but all races and all differences of people have families, and that's the symbol or goal is to be able to provide beyond means for that family, whether that means working overtime, double shifts, grave shift. If that's the embodiment of the American Dream, I think anybody can achieve that with hard work. It just has to be a fair economy. If you're struggling and all that hard work is just to get by paycheck to paycheck like you said, that's not going to get it. Just being able to pay the bills and keep food, just to keep the household going but not being able to live. If you have what you need and more so, in my eyes, if you are living the American Dream, I pay more attention to what the more that you have, what do you do with it? Do you become socially responsible, so you'll be able to share that dream with the next person that's helping you pay taxes in this world? People glorify it, but do they really understand the responsibility that comes with it? If I were successful, I would be, like, trying to give back to the community, like, really bring [about] that social change. I watched the middle class dissolve into either lower class or upper class. At least if I could see myself kind of bridge the gap between the lower class and the upper class or even bring back for some type of assistance that middle class where people can live above, you know, poor. We get caught up on how people view us and how people judge us as far as our level of success. People that don't even have that still try to do it. People living in projects who got the Cadillac Escalade sitting on it in the projects' parking lot, and you're still living with your momma.

Others offer these thoughts:

Everyone has a dream—but the American Dream is about materialism and that corrupted U.S. society. People here are extremely corrupted, impure, and materialistically driven. What is disclosed in *Gatsby*: The materialistic drives of a personality go along with his or her own decay; materialism will not lead you to anything good. The American Dream is all about possession, the tangible goods. Therefore, the economic situation is so disastrous. Everyone during the last decade was striving for more; we see, due to technology, that we can always have more and want more and more. Suddenly the economy collapses, because one nation cannot only be driven by the material things. The American Dream is maybe not a good thing; everyone has a dream. It is a great thing to believe in something and want to achieve it. The American Dream is all about a house, a car, the picket fence, and a good job, but what about the moral values and spiritual things of life? Too materialistic for me. In American society—there is such a huge gap between the lower and upper class. Only the upper class can achieve the American Dream. People who are not economically well cannot achieve it. Public schools cannot compare to private schools. (Victoria, white, female, born outside the U.S., 18–25)

There's a lot of propaganda, stuff coming out of the U.S. media-wise that attracts people who have come from a simpler way of life, where you fish for your own food, and you work thirty hours a week, and it's seventy degrees year round. They come here from what I would consider a better quality of life because of opportunities for material things. It's a kind of ugly sort of thing going on. A lot of people that come here regret it sometimes. I mean in certain ways, you know, or they are kind of nostalgic about their life prior to coming here. (Joe J., white, male, U.S.-born, 26–45)

There Is No Truth to the American Dream

The thing about the American Dream is that everyone thinks that they can achieve it. There is a misguided belief about that. We saw with Hurricane Katrina that people in southern Louisiana were living in huts. We claim that the U.S. has equal opportunities, but we don't see those equal results. We all say everyone can be wealthy, but in all honesty, if people don't have the means to get a good education, then how far can they really get in life? It's not as easy [as] for people who come from wealthy backgrounds, where their parents are doctors, and so they can go to a good school. I think that education makes a big difference. (Linda, white, female, U.S.-born, 18 25)

The idea of the American Dream is a bit hyperbolic. There is a chance for everyone, and other countries have more of that oppression feel to them. (Breana, white, female, U.S.-born, 18–25)

America has a powerful freedom and an advanced system of democracy compared to China, yet the Chinese can do great things like [host] the Olympics. A lot of people outside the country migrate here. They want to enjoy their freedom, but they forget that this freedom is only under the control of the United States' government. I understand what Americans do, the politics behind everything, and why Americans always have a war. They create war every single year. A lot of wars. Is this the American Dream? Is this the freedom we wish for? What does freedom mean when many people die? My mind is international and not only for the American group. I don't think it's fair to everybody—freedom only for Americans? (Edward, Chinese, male, born outside the U.S., 26–45)

In the article "Goodbye to My American Dream,"[7] Tiffanie Drayton explains that after graduating from college at the New School University, she decides to return to her place of birth, Trinidad. She says, "My relationship with the United States of America is the most tumultuous relationship I have ever had, and it ended with the heart-rending realization that a country I loved and believed in did not love me back. . . . I have found freedom by leaving the land of the free."

Changing times also lead to changed minds about the possibility of social mobility in the United States. Dan (Italian American, male, U.S.-born, 18–25) speaks to this transition:

I used to think it was achievable too, [now] maybe not so much. A lot of the American Dream is really bound up with wanting to be the quint-essential consumer of everything, consuming houses, consuming cars, just wanting to have . . . why one house, [have] two; why one car, have three. It's becoming apparent that the American Dream was purchase[d] on credit, now our credit is drying up, the country, people's individual credit, poverty, and wealth. There [is] something to be said about the American Dream and the American vanity as everyone wants to self-identify as closer to the wealthy than they are to the poor.

Dennis (white/Latino/Puerto Rican/Italian, male, U.S.-born, 18–25) agrees:

Our consumption patterns are becoming more vulnerable because of the breakdown in credit. We bought so much stuff we identify with that we thought was part of achieving this dream. That credit, which was false—people don't make a lot of money to buy what they want to, so they need credit. Now that the credit gone, credit is becoming more difficult to attain for most people. Yeah, the dream is becoming further out of grasp.

Paul (Black/Latino, male, U.S.-born, 18–25) agrees as well:

Back then, that was the American Dream, a family-owned business. You didn't need to rely on the economy. You *were* the economy. You stabilized the production in your community. Now we rely on big business to carry us through, and we're not involved in that big business, so we're kind of, like, just falling for the crumbs that come off that big corporate cookie. You know? Right now, we [are] giving them our crumbs between us bailing them out and stuff like that! Back in the day, we were more in control of our economy, our American Dream, as opposed to now, we're just going with what we have to. We have to pay our taxes. You have to pay your bills.

Stan (white, male, U.S.-born, over 65) explains his point of view:

Over the last fifty years, radical changes have been made in the United States, from segregation in the South to the lack of women's rights to the beginning of emergence of some of those civil rights. But for immigrants coming into this country, there's a great deal of discrimination. My parents were able to come here and weren't concerned about a green card. It was America [that] opened its arms and embraced the immigrants. Now we no longer need cheap labor, so they no longer embrace them, and they're building walls to prevent people from coming here. And over a million minorities—for the most part, young men—are in jail. We say the American Dream, but very few other countries have so many people in prison.

Another point made is how we can talk about an American Dream when the people on whose land we live are struggling to survive. Denise (Black, female, U.S.-born, over 65) speaks passionately, saying that Americans do not really want to talk about the American Indian. Michael (white, male, U.S.-born, over 65) attributes this attitude to a lack of leadership among Native Americans:

So were the blacks, but yet Martin Luther King stepped up, and, you know, they had leadership. Now you've got the president of the United

States. The Indians have no leadership. There's nobody fighting for Indians, I don't think.

Tim (white, male, U.S.-born, over 65) agrees:

You're absolutely right. As a matter of fact, the Bureau of Indian Affairs is run by white people.

As for where responsibility lies, Michael is unequivocal about his opinion: "I blame George Bush for the death of the American Dream!"

While speaking of the young people he works with in an organization providing support for homeless youth, Andrew (white, male, born outside the U.S., 26–45) notes that "the American Dream to them is the reality TV and becoming famous. About 70 percent of the people who come here, they would say, 'I want to be big; I wanna be famous'; that['s] what I hear over and over again."

The American Dream means there [are] certain things we are supposed to obtain, like having that house, that car, that marriage, that child. For me, none of that has ever been important. I have built my own American Dream that has nothing to do with the mainstream idea of the American Dream. I write, publish; I have [a] hard time calling myself an American, so it is just my dream in America. A lot of the American Dream is based on whiteness. I am not white. It is the history of this country—how far it has gotten because of imperialism. People are not looking at the fact that they have destroyed other countries to get ahead. All they see is that the U.S. has gotten ahead. It was able to get so far because it destroyed other countries to get ahead. (Pat, Black, female, U.S. born, 26–45)

The American Dream? Damn, yeah, yeah, I'm definitely going to get it, because I feel like it's a secret society. I've seen the middle class get phased out; you're either going to be rich or poor (Paul, Black/Latino, male, U.S.-born, 18–25)

This comment opens a discussion of the contradictions embodied in the concept of the American Dream. Though the American Dream represents opportunity, it does not necessarily offer the achievement of middle-class status or an easy lifestyle. Ziana Zania (Black, female, U.S.-born, 18–25) responds to Paul by explaining her experience:

I have two kids, and I'm young. The American Dream means you wouldn't have to be on welfare and have public assistance helping pay your rent. It shouldn't be so hard to find a place to live where people accept two young children and the parent. It's such a struggle. It's not having enough money during the week to get what you need. It's hard in this world right now. I'm on my way to it. I've just got to keep striving. That's why I came back to school, to get me a good job and live the American Dream. I have two kids to live it for. They're going to have the American Dream. I didn't have it for my life. They're going to have it for theirs. I have to.

Scorpio (Black, male, born outside the U.S., 46–65) shares this ambivalence—the feeling that if the American Dream is a reality, life should not be so hard. He compares his experience in his native Grenada with that of living in the United States:

In America, you're always hustling. You go to work, you come back, you do your chores, you've gotta take care of your kids. Back home it's pretty, it's not like that. If you go to work, you come home, you're at a slow pace. You grow your little garden. It could have a few things that you eat. Here is a constant, everyday struggle, but financially it's not as burdensome. There is more income coming to you that you could do a lot with in a much quicker time. It's been a struggle, but like she said, it's an everyday commitment. I would like to go back to my country and just retire.

Participants debate whether the responsibility lies with individuals or whether there is something inherently inaccurate in the idea that the American Dream is achievable by all:

A lot of people don't know how to get things done. They don't have the information or even confidence to think that they can ever make it that far. A lot of people just put their selves down. They can't do something instead of trying and going out and doing it. Friends and family could even give confidence, encouragement, and resources and [let] them know that things good can come. You have to want it. (Ziana Zania, Black, female, U.S.-born, 18–25)

Genesis Ruth (Latina, female, U.S.-born, 46–65) responds:

Sometimes people that feel so sorry for themselves, they hide in the back of liquor, they take drugs, they drink, they [are] so self-pitying, and they just drown themselves. Sometimes it's hard. We live here and it's hard, so it's just not people with immigration.

Geneva Diva (Black, female, U.S.-born, 18–25) comments:

The American Dream is not to be the richest person, just to live a little bit above comfortable and to have stability. In case I decide one day to have children, I want them to have it better than I do.

Cee East (Black, female, U.S.-born, 26–45) echoes this perspective:

Everybody thinks it's living in a mansion and driving a fancy car. To me, that's not it. To me, it's setting goals in your life. I never really said, "I want to live in a mansion." Money doesn't make you happy. That's my description of the American Dream. Setting a goal, sticking with it, becoming the profession you set out to become, and having a nice family, having a nice husband, somebody supportive, no one negative, having your environment negative-free. A nice home, a nice husband, a couple of kids, one nice car, maybe one for the snow. Just being happy. Not having money and every time you're depressed, you go shopping. That's not happiness to me.

Spankey (Black, female, U.S.-born, 26–45) takes this idea one step further:

I'm living the American Dream now. I have my health. I have my strength. I have all four of my children, who is everything in my life. As far as achieving my dream, from where I came from to what I have now without a GED, I'm living my American Dream. I have a beautiful apartment [where] I can come and go as I please. I have insurance. I'm able to pay my bills. I'm just blessed for the little things. I thought the American Dream was a house up on the hill looking over the coast, but that's a fairy tale, and I don't want that. What I want is a peace of mind. What I want is to be happy. If I want to go in my refrigerator and have whatever I desire, [then] I can do that. I took so many things for granted. I want to achieve my GED so I can go further. Then I can put some more treats into my American Dream, just a few more, you know, treats. I don't want all the money in the world. You can have all the money in the world and be miserable. You've done shopped till you drop and still [are] not happy within.

Chino (Latino, male, U.S.-born, 46–65) agrees:

My American Dream is I'd like to get my GED. I'd like to land a good job, be self-sufficient, and just continue to live a happy life.

Some people, like Joe (Chinese, male, U.S.-born, 26–45), assert that "even illegal immigrants feel that the dream is alive and well, even though they have had to go through barbed-wire fences or swim under rivers." However, their story is not so simple. Marisol (Latina, female, born outside the U.S., 26–45) explains:

We were very poor. I came here and really had no dreams of getting rich. My only interest was in getting money so my family would have food. I was the single one in my family, so it was up to me. I grew up very poor and lived in a small house that was clay with soil on the floor. There were three rooms—I lived with my grandparents and parents and six brothers and sisters. We had some blankets but no mattress. We were very poor. There was no electricity or water—we got the water from the river or a well. We cooked outside.

We didn't eat good food, as there was no money to buy. My grandparents planted corn, vegetables, and beans, and that's how we ate. We didn't buy food, just oil and salt. We had chickens but ate that only when we had a party. We had a cow and sold her milk and some of our mangoes to buy the oil and salt. My grandparents couldn't read—my parents could, because they went to the second or third grade. My grandma spoke only her language.

I finished the third grade and then went to the city to go up to sixth grade. I took a bus. Most people in my town went only to second or third grade, and maybe one or two children went on to the sixth. It has changed, though, as now people work as carpenters, plumbers.

When I went to school in the city, I saw that the other girls had everything—pretty clothes and good food in their lunch. They were rich but didn't want anything to do with us who were poor. It made me very sad. They inherited their wealth—that's how it happens. If your family is rich, you will be rich; if your family is poor, you will be poor, too.

Marisol continues her story, saying that since she was the single daughter, it was up to her to come to the United States to try to get money. She speaks of her travels and what was on her mind during this time:

When we got close to the border, the *paleros*[8] went to the top of the mountain to see if there were police, and then they told us to run and hide and seek. Quickly, quickly. My heart was pounding in my throat. I have never been so afraid.

But we finally made it, and the people who were to meet us were not there. They told us we will sleep on the rocks while it was pouring rain, and if the people weren't there in the morning, we would have to walk another ten hours, but I couldn't. I was soaked everywhere, my head, my clothes, my shoes, and I had no strength to go on. I kept thinking about whether I would be caught and sent to jail or sent home to gather money again to come.

When we woke, the cars were there with dark windows. We were only eighty then, since the police had picked up twenty of us on the way. It was so heartbreaking to think of those people. My heart hurt for a long time and still now when I think of them. We packed into cars so tight we couldn't move—like an onion. While we drove, the police passed, and

I was frightened. We were brought to a house to deliver the remaining part of the $13,000. My brother-in-law's family lent me the money.

We waited at the house until the money arrived and then were brought to the airport to get on the plane to wherever we were going.

My brother-in-law was waiting for me before my plane arrived, because they said if someone is not met, they will be questioned by the police, so we took no chances. I was nervous because it was so dangerous.

I wasn't coming because of a dream. I was coming because my family had no food. I had no choice. When I arrived, it was very different than my home. I felt nothing but exhausted. I didn't feel happy, just tired. I needed to get work to pay back money. It took three years. I am a single woman, so I am the one who sends money every month for my family and gives my sister with four children money for food. I just work, and sometimes I go to church if I am not too tired.

I am in school. I have money, but I have no family or no life. I miss them so very much. Whenever I think of them, I cry. But there is no other way, as they have no money to eat. There is discrimination here, but nothing we can do about it. One lady took my name and said she will give me papers. She took about $800 or $900 from me, and then her sister found out and got angry at her and made her give it back. But she can do anything at any time, so I am never safe. The way it is now is not fair.

We often presume that the driving force for migrants is the pursuit of upward mobility but rarely consider the level of desperation that so many people feel that precipitates their migration. Marisol speaks of her grandmother, whom she longs to see. She cannot get the image of her, hungry, out of her mind. She speaks of being propelled to do anything to prevent her death from hunger. Marisol describes her living quarters and lifestyle, which is focused on survival rather than any fantasy of a picket fence. She acknowledges her vulnerability but adds that it would be a luxury to entertain concern over that for long.

A different experience, yet also one worth reflecting on, is expressed by Bessie (Black/white, female, born outside the U.S., 46–65):

I'm someone who lived all her life, well into her early 20s, in the Caribbean, who always stood by the roadside hoping that some American tourist driving down the dirt road in that little pink jeep would see this pitiful-looking little girl on the side of the road and say, "Wow, she looks so pitiful, I really want to take her and adopt her and take her away." But that never happened.

She came to the United States seeking the American Dream, the road to Broadway, and the big home with a Jacuzzi. Once here, she realized that education was not the only prerequisite for achieving the American Dream. Stefan (white, male, born outside the U.S., 26–45) concurs:

It takes more than hard work; one has to make connections with the right people. America is the only place built by immigrants, but illegal immigrants do not find it easy to make good money. They leave places that's so poor and come up north and with the thought of being here for just a year and making enough money to send back for their family, and then either bringing their family here or going back there to them. Neither one happen[s], because being an illegal immigrant, it's not easy to make the money that you would need to do what you dreamed of doing.

Following are related written comments submitted in the survey:

The American Dream is a discourse used to maintain ideologies of meritocracy and individualism so as to hide the impacts of racism, classism, sexism, and homophobia.

The notion of the American Dream seems to implicitly buy into a leveling myth that is inextricably tied to teleological notions of capitalist modernity. It's also tied geographically to American nationalism, which occludes many forms of social hierarchy.

The American Dream is a crock of shit. We live in a white supremacist, capitalist patriarchy, and as a man of color, that's what I have in mind. My parents immigrated to the U.S. during a moment of easier immigration from India and capitalized on shifts in U.S. racial policy to become middle-class U.S. citizens and business owners.

The American Dream is more of a myth than a reality. Indeed, there are occasional cases of "rags-to-riches" stories, but persistent race, class, and gender barriers have prevented anything like what some call the American Dream to be achieved on a widespread basis.

The American Dream is to have power to dominate and a set of ethics to enjoy real or imagined superiority.

I do not believe the American Dream exists. It is a national narrative used to justify inequity, maintain the status quo, and blame the lack of success of people of color on their genetics, race, communities, etc. Basically, it perpetuates deficit thinking.

I don't think the American Dream is so great. It's more about money and houses and upward mobility. I'm more interested in quality human relationships.

The traditional American Dream is like hoisting your hopes solely on winning the lottery or betting your bills on being struck by lightning.

What the hell is "the American Dream"? I have achieved some material affluence, but I am bitter and disillusioned about the possibility of equality and democracy.

"American Dream" is constructed mythology. It essentializes a field of ambitions and aims for which there are no normative values.

The things I dream about are not contained within the United States; they are mostly about changing the country. My American Dream is about justice and peace.

Survey results are also notable in that, despite the economic crisis, respondents significantly agree (62.4 percent) more than disagree (30.2 percent) that they have an easier chance at achieving the American Dream than their parents did and that this is one of the many factors that make the United States a special nation (59.8 percent versus 31.1 percent). However, they disagree more than agree that the American Dream can be achieved by anyone who works hard (58 percent versus 38.7 percent). (See Table 6.1.)

Some interesting yet somewhat predictable differences emerge between groups in their responses about being treated equally and the possibility of achieving the American Dream. Whites are significantly more likely than Blacks to believe that people of color are treated equally when applying for jobs or housing and when being approached by police (5.4 percent versus 2.5 percent). Latinos are significantly more likely than Blacks to believe that all people have an equal chance of succeeding (33.3 percent versus 10.9 percent). Whites are more

TABLE 6.1. QUESTIONS ABOUT THE AMERICAN DREAM

	Strongly disagree	Disagree	Agree	Strongly agree	Don't know
Compared to my parents, I have an easier chance of achieving the American Dream	5.0%	25.2%	36.6%	25.8%	7.4%
The American Dream is just one of many reasons why the United States is a special nation, today and historically	15.0%	16.1%	40.9%	18.9%	9.1%
The American Dream can be achieved by anyone who works hard	22.6%	35.4%	22.6%	16.1%	3.1%

likely than Blacks to agree that all people can be assimilated into mainstream U.S. society (43.5 percent versus 25 percent).

Protestants are significantly more likely than agnostics and atheists to expect to achieve the American Dream (48 percent versus 19.4 percent versus 21.2 percent). Respondents whose family income is less than $50,000 are less likely to believe they have already achieved the American Dream compared to all three higher-income categories (6.5 percent versus 16.5 percent versus 25.9 percent versus 36 percent). Respondents whose family income is more than $200,000 are significantly more likely to believe they will ever achieve the American Dream compared to those whose family income is under $50,000 or between $50,000 and $100,000. (See Tables 6.2 and 6.3.)

Respondents with family income of more than $200,000 are more likely to believe that people of color are treated equally to whites when applying for jobs or housing and when being approached by police compared to those with family income under $50,000 (16 percent versus 2.6 percent). Respondents with family income more than $200,000 are more likely to believe that the United States is a land of equal opportunity compared to those with family income under $50,000 (32 percent versus 16.1 percent) and to strongly believe this about the United States (20 percent versus 2.6 percent).

For Anna (Latina of Puerto Rican, Dominican, and Danish descent, female, U.S.-born,18–25), achieving the American Dream has been complicated. She is clear regarding what it is but has had difficulty achieving it:

> The American Dream is having a really good job, a job I am happy with, that pays well. Coming from a homeless background, the American Dream is being financially stable, having my own apartment, being able

TABLE 6.2. TO WHAT EXTENT HAVE YOU ALREADY ACHIEVED THE AMERICAN DREAM?

	Less than $50,000	$50,000– $100,000	$101,000– $200,000	More than $200,000
Not at all	28.1%	14.9%	14.8%	12.0%
Somewhat	65.4%	68.6%	59.3%	52.0%
A lot	6.5%	16.5%	25.9%	36.0%

TABLE 6.3. TO WHAT EXTENT DO YOU EXPECT TO EVER ACHIEVE THE AMERICAN DREAM?

	Less than $50,000	$50,000– $100,000	$101,000– $200,000	More than $200,000
Not at all	13.7%	13.3%	12.3%	4.5%
Somewhat	52.3%	56.1%	52.8%	31.8%
A lot	34.0%	30.6%	34.9%	63.6%

to take care [of] myself, being successful and happy. I have been home-less since three years ago. I moved into a new apartment; the next day I lost my job. I had no money, stayed with my grandma, then I looked around shelters to find a place to live. I finished high school a year early, went to a community college, then wanted to go to a state university.

I have not yet achieved American Dream; I am still working on it. Right now, I am unemployed—it is a little unsettling. I do not like not having a job, not doing anything. When it comes to money, I have to hold on to every single cent I have. I am looking for a job, sending résumés to everyone, posting it on Craigslist, reaching [out to] my friends to help me. The economy is awful—so hard, difficult to find a job. It is not just me—so many people looking for a job: It is so competitive. The typical American lives from paycheck to paycheck.

Some people believe that the American Dream promotes an external image of success that keeps people striving:

They don't know who they are, so they're looking for all these other dif-ferent things to put together as a collective to make themselves. By them buying things, all they're caring about is that they look good. They're feeling because they have low self-esteem inside, so they feel like doing the outside out will make them feel like they are the American Dream, because they have all this fancy stuff, nice cars, a nice house, but inside they're dying. They're miserable. (S. Westmoreland, Black, female, born outside the U.S., 18–25)

And others believe that the challenges will be overcome in time:

The U.S. demographics will change and power will shift ethnically, hopefully on the highest moral plane. International collective action for the general welfare of diverse peoples is likely to increase, and hopefully change brought about by the gun will decline. (Stanley, white, male, U.S.-born, over 65)

Rhetoric, Reverie, or Reality?

In a focus group of whites born outside the United States, participants struggle to define the American Dream and are hesitant to endorse it as something unique to the United States. Frost (white, male, born outside the U.S., 18–25) says:

The U.S. has contributed the American Dream to the world; the Ameri-can Dream involves universal values—self-reliance, materialistic ones also, uniquely from the U.S., but it can be applied globally.

To which Annelise (white, female, born outside the U.S., 18–25) responds:

The American Dream is a little pretentious; it is like a mission statement that you write before the whole thing is built, but you do not write a business's mission statement before you build the company. The American Dream is not something that is preordained; it is what we come up with; it is vapid without the individual and without the ambition and the social means by which to achieve it. It reverts back to the success of the individual, to whatever their objective is.

It is the pursuit of happiness. It is sort of burnt into you—that you have all these options and opportunities—but I think certain people have certain opportunit[ies] due to the nature of their abilities. Whether or not you achieve [the] American Dream is not given. You have to obtain it, and if you are not capable [of] obtain[ing] it in the fashion you want, there is always another avenue. There has to be some level of ambition if you want to participate. There is sort of a laziness—you cannot think [the] U.S. will give you something; you have to obtain it yourself.

Study participants in other groups share similar concerns:

A lot of people emerge from different countries over here to live the American Dream. There's so much to offer in America that you can't get overseas, because in the other countries, a lot of 6- and 7-year-olds work. Instead of being in school, they're working. Their moms and dads is dying every day, and the oldest child has to take care [of] the rest of the siblings, and it's really, really sad. That's just how it turned out to be. The poor countries just have to immigrate over to America and achieve their dreams, because over there, they can't even dream there, because everything is a nightmare. Every day is a nightmare. The kids can't even lie down and have a dream. Not to lay down, you have to pray that you have fresh drinking water the next day. You pray that maybe it's two biscuits or two slices of bread that you could share with your mom and your siblings. I've been watching these shows for, like, over thirty years, but my heart still weighs so heavy. How could they really know how to go out to that dirty, dirty water and try to fetch water and bring it back to the hut? America has so much money, so why nobody is [sic] trying to help these poor countries? If people would send in all these millions of dollars overseas into the country for these kids, where's it going? My heart just really goes out to them. The children as well as the adults, because the adults don't be nowhere near my age. They be looking 80 years old because a disease just deteriorated their bodies. (Spankey, Black, female, U.S.-born, 26–45)

Everyone believes America has the American Dream. We have over nine million immigrants in this country alone, so there has to be something here that they're coming here for. There's something they're here for, and believe me, when they come here they do achieve what they set out to do, because, believe it or not, they are very smart people, very smart people. I've been around some that's very smart, but they just didn't have the instruments that they need to get ahead. (Cee East, Black, female, U.S.-born, 26–45)

Rome (Black, male, U.S-born, 18–25) responds:

Not everyone has it in them to believe in the American Dream. Some people need that role model to set the trend for them to believe in it. I can't honestly say that I've believed all my life in the American Dream. People utilize a role model to have something to look forward to in life. People connect the American Dream to, like, a lavish lifestyle, living beyond your means. The American Dream is that guideline that hard work and perseverance, everything that you put into as far as working, you get out, you know. Some people, because they start off lower on the ladder, they're still willing to believe in it. People around me believed in working, paying bills. I'd never seen nobody rise above what everybody else is doing. To achieve that American Dream, you have that house in the hills, you have those cars in abundance, and you know bills aren't even a question. Like, if you buying things, you don't ask how much it costs. That kind of lifestyle. The American Dream, that's what it is. Personally, I look at the odds. It's a façade. A state of mind. I don't want everything to seem monetary, but when you look at it, successful people are people who have some type of sufficient amount of funds.

Aria (Desi, female, born outside the U.S., 26–45) grew up in India and at the age of 14 moved to the United States with her family to California. She attended university in the Northeast and then moved to back to California. She argues:

The American Dream is a cliché: Anyone can do anything, a reason why all the people are here. The flipside is [that] anyone who does not make it because of the multiple circumstances—it is not because they are not trying hard or that they are lazy—there is a devaluation of people's life if they do not achieve it, do not succeed, or do not follow a certain ladder. My brother is 21 and all-American, dropped out of college, and started a job, tells me: "Look at all these people who got out of nothing and did it." But where are the people who did not do it?

Dennis (white/Latino/Puerto Rican/Italian, male, U.S.-born, 18–25) comments:

Many of the immigrants I've spoken to tend to be more conservative, in terms of being not nationalistic, especially not all, but some have more reverence to the U.S. But living here and seeing how hard it's been, I've had to fight tooth and nail. I've always had the rug swept out from under me. So in some sense, I do think that there are things that you can achieve in this country that are great and perhaps not in other countries, I don't know. On the other hand, it just seems absurd that anyone can achieve the American Dream when it's very difficult; it really depends on where you're coming from. It never entered into one of my cousins' mind of how his school gets paid for. He's two years into his degree, and it just never occurred to him how his school is paid for. On the other hand, all I can worry about is how my school is paid for, my rent, and stuff like that.

As journalist Robert Jensen (2011) has said:

The American Dream is born of and maintained by domination. . . . While put forward as a dream for all the world to adopt, it clearly isn't. Some of the people of the world had to be sacrificed for the dream, as has the living world. Dreams based on domination are, by definition, limited.

Several themes emerge among participants' beliefs about the American Dream. Most recognize the potential for the acquisition of material goods and upward mobility in the United States. However, they simultaneously acknowledge that these are accessible only to some. They recognize that the higher one is positioned in the social hierarchy, the more likely that mobility and those goods are available.

While White and Hanson find that the dream is not "in doubt," they recognize that people believe it is harder to achieve, with 75 percent claiming it is not as attainable as it was in 2000 and 59 percent believing it will be harder for the next generation to achieve (2011, 11).

In 2011, scholars at Xavier University found that "the American Dream remains remarkably resilient despite a continued wave of bad news." Roughly 63 percent of respondents indicated that they were extremely or fairly confident that they have already or will achieve the American Dream (Center for the Study of the American Dream 2011). However, they also found that 69 percent thought the dream was harder to achieve for the millennial generation, and 59 percent believed it would be much harder for future generations.[9] Problems in the educational system were the most frequently cited reason for difficulty, along with a lack of appreciation for the values of hard work and responsibility. It is notable that the definition of the American Dream has shifted. Focus on family, financial security, and happiness has increased, while emphasis on opportunity, a good job, and wealth have decreased (14). Interestingly, "48% of immigrants rate the dream in 'good condition' compared to only 31% of the population overall" (19).

However, 65 percent of respondents indicated their belief that the United States is on the decline (23).

These figures are consistent with other studies, such as one by the Economic Mobility Project that found in 2009 that 68 percent of those polled thought they either have achieved or would achieve the American Dream.[10] It is also notable that "going back to 1820, per capita gross domestic product in the United States has grown an average of 52 percent for each generation. But since 1973, overall median income has grown on average 0.6 percent per year, with a 17 percent increase in the average family's income for each generation."[11]

Furthermore, despite rhetoric regarding limitless opportunities for upward mobility, the greatest guarantee of being middle or upper class is having a parent in that group. Also, counter to common belief, people in the United States actually have less upward mobility than people in other industrialized nations: Germans are 1.5 times more mobile, Canadians nearly 2.5 times more mobile, and the Danish 3 times more mobile.[12] Additionally, roughly one-third of Americans raised in the middle class fall out of the middle as adults, with 38 percent of Black men versus 21 percent of white men doing so. Race and gender play a critical role in social class.

Despite these figures, studies show that people in the United States dramatically underestimate levels of wealth inequality in the United States. They tend to believe that there is a much higher degree of equality and appear to prefer the existence of such equality. A recent national study indicates that people in the United States prefer to live in a country more like Sweden than the United States, with ideal wealth distributions that are far more equal than they estimate those in the United States to be. Additionally, there is more agreement than disagreement about this across the political spectrum, although there are real differences in the parties' beliefs about the underlying causes for inequality (Ariely 2011).

In January 2012, a Pew Center survey found that 66 percent of respondents believed that strong or very strong conflicts existed between the rich and the poor in the United States. This figure is 50 percent higher than it was in July 2009 and higher than the number of people who believed that tension existed between races or between immigrants and the native-born. This perception was particularly true among women, African Americans, Democrats, and immigrants. In particular, the increase was evident among whites, whose belief in the existence of tension jumped from 43 to 65 percent in two years (Morin 2012).

Jensen (2011) asserts that "our task is to tell the truth about the domination that is at the heart of the American Dream so that we may face the brokenness of our world." These research participants surely offer cause to challenge the typical narratives and seek an alternative truth.

Here are some final quotations from the written portion of the survey:

The American Dream ended with the Great Depression—sometime during the Hoover presidency.

This American Dream mythology is a little much. . . .

The American Dream is pretty bogus. You have to debt yourself to death so it just *APPEARS* that you've made it. Pulling yourself up by your bootstraps never happens. No one does anything without the help of someone.

I don't think the election of any president will make my dream come more true. That is up to me and my willingness to go out there and do it.

It is not just the American Dream, it is the human dream—very human thing (in whatever culture you are) to try and be the best version of yourself. People like the idea that people are coming to U.S. to live the American Dream—they think U.S. is the place where they can get it. It is hard for people to imagine that U.S. is not the best thing and that you cannot get everything.

7

Expressions of Revolt
against the Systems

In this chapter, we explore participants' critiques of the system as it stands
now, as well as their visions for the future. Anticapitalist sentiments, critiques
of the idea of the American Dream as a means of social control, and a deep-
rooted desire for a dramatic reorganization of society routinely emerge in discussions. Some participants speak to a belief that education fosters social change;
many express a desire for a "dream for all humanity" rather than just people in
the United States. Themes for a reimagined future are expressed by participants
as they challenge rhetoric, confront realities, and embrace their reveries.

In other words, the dream of a good life is real and valid—where needs are
met, community connections are strong, caring for the common good is assumed (the actualization of all human rights?)—yet it is also reverie, because it
is "a fantastic, visionary idea."[1] The rhetoric that the quest for a good life is solely
"American" is increasingly transparent, as working people (poor and middle
class) struggle more to make ends meet and the demographics of the United
States change. Responses to the question "What does the American Dream mean
to you?" generally cluster into three views. First, the American Dream is, in fact,
about the ability to stand up for one's beliefs, whether they include the desire for
material goods or more philosophical strivings. In this way, participants express
the importance of this ability as an inspiration. Second, this striving is, in fact, a
Global Dream (not solely an American quest). Last, many participants question
the idea itself and whether it is a ruse to elicit compliance with an unequal and
unjust system. Their responses evoke the notion that the endless accumulation of
capital is an anarchic runaway tidal wave engulfing and devouring everything in
its path. Regardless, most participants believe that we are in the midst of a crisis
and that change is coming, whether for the better or the worse.

The American Dream Is about Ideals and
Fighting for One's Beliefs

For some, the narrative of the American Dream is a symbol of being willing to struggle for what one believes rather than achieving material comfort. In this way, striving for the dream defines national character symbolically, leaving individuals with a sense of dignity and pride that is not necessarily problematic:

> Part of the American Dream is that desire, that longing, that fighting that we go through to achieve something because it's just within our reach. We don't look at the impediments that come up, and if we do, we persevere. (Janice, white, female, U.S.-born, 46–65)

> That's part of not the American Dream but of the whole thing with the American Revolution. It's the spirit of this country. Of fighting, of going forward and not giving up, that there's a goal. (Ina, white, female, U.S.-born, 46–65)

Indeed, the ambiguous nature of how the dream is defined leaves it open for more radical interpretations. Lana (Asian/Jewish, female, U.S.-born, 26–45) explains her view:

> The American Dream is overthrowing capitalism. For me, that's what it is. I appreciate the natural environment, because I grew up surrounded by it and appreciate its natural beauty. I am really homesick in New York, really miss my home, think about the destruction of the environment, the structure of people/community, and how intimately this destruction is tied to capitalism. A friend of mine told me that New York City and the U.S. is constructed around apartheid in terms of access to resources—communities of color have so much less resources than upper- and middle-class white people, [and] segregation by race and class has torn apart communities. The U.S. is built upon racism—that is all tied to capitalism—the destruction of the Earth, natural resources. While we could be growing food nearby, it is getting imported from third-world countries. This is the American nightmare!

In line with this less common interpretation, several participants raise critiques of the American Dream that speak to their belief in the need for resistance. For example, Dennis (white/Latino/Puerto Rican/Italian, male, U.S.-born, 18–25) questions the role of this concept in eliciting compliance with a structure that is inherently unequal and unjust:

> Part of me feels like the American Dream is just bullshit. It feels like an idea that is sold to you to in order keep the capitalist wheels rolling.

It's sort of like the carrot on the stick—when you're riding a horse, you put the carrot right in front of the horse, and it'll keep moving, in spite of the fact you'll never be able to achieve that. Even if you are wealthy, it's never going to be enough; you still have to become wealthier just to keep everything moving and growing. So part of me feels like that, and another part of me. . . . When I speak to my friend from Haiti, he said he has to fear for his safety every night. There are people in this country who have to do that, but I guess to some degree maybe there are things here that would be much more difficult to achieve in another country. I don't know.

Pike (African American, West Indian, and European descent; male; U.S.-born; 18–25) is very clear on his thoughts:

The American Dream is a form of social control. It is held up as an ideal that people should live up to. Instead of getting up each morning so that you can live your life, you are trying to follow the example of this or that celebrity or style. You are taught to try to be something that you are not, even if it is uncomfortable. It is a form of social control. The government tried to control people. People try to rebel. Some don't care, and there are politicians who try to use that as a way of getting into people['s] heads. They do studies to figure out how to manipulate people. It is vicious, and people who are doing it don't care as long as they are getting a paycheck. You should want that paycheck, too.

The imagery of potential unlimited riches and unbound opportunities is a compelling draw for many. Frizzy (self-identified as "other," male, U.S.-born, 46–65) agrees with Pike's point about the American Dream being a form of social control:

Companies try to hold control over massive numbers economically. If they can pull your chain strings in your pockets, then they can pull the way you act. If you can talk sweet enough, you can make shit smell sweet in this country. People have a hard time recognizing what is the truth.

Some participants question the relationship between Martin Luther King Jr.'s famous "dream" and the American Dream. Was it the same or something very different? They wonder whether everything comes down to economics or whether the American Dream is also an articulation of political principles:

When I think of the American Dream, I don't think [of] freedom. I think of wealth. Martin Luther [King] was wanting opportunities, but I don't feel he was focused on wealth. (Diego, Black/white, male, U.S.-born, 18–25)

King's was the true American Dream. It was freedom for all people, regardless of skin color or ethnicity, to be able to achieve the same level of wealth, the same house with two cars, the same right to sit in a restaurant and eat together, and the same right to use the same toilet. That was the American Dream. (Bessie, Black/white, female, born outside the U.S., 46–65)

One World, One Dream

Many participants express opinions that the dream is real and valid but not solely "American." They believe it has no national boundaries and articulates a vision of the kind of world that all should have access to. The Olympics held in China made a significant impression on many, more firmly positioning it in the minds of people as a rising power, with ideological power.

For example, Joe (Chinese, male, U.S.-born, 26–45) explains:

The American Dream is very alive and real. It used to be that America was one of the few places that you could get it, but a lot of other world countries are becoming first-world countries. It is a lot easier for China, for example, to have a Chinese Dream. You know, "one world, one dream," the Olympics phrase!

Speaking about the Olympics, they were an important factor in showing that China is also a world power, and they deserve respect. In the past, I rooted for the U.S. and my parents would root for China, and I would think, "Why are they rooting for China?" But 2008 came around, and I found myself rooting for China first and America second. You feel kind of conflicted when they are playing against each other. I ended up cheering for China, because I know that if I were to go to China, people would say, "Hey this guy is Chinese; let's show him some respect." But if I were down on my luck here in America, people would say, "Hey this guy is Chinese; screw him."

Other participants of Chinese descent echo this critique of U.S. nationalism:

I have a very negative view, because people use democracy only to benefit and profit for themselves; they are selfish. "One world, one dream" is what I dream of! The American Dream is false, because the American Dream doesn't help people; it fools people. The politician fools people. People believe that only Americans have this dream. They fool people.

The American Dream is false; it is not a dream for me. The American Dream [is] only a dream for others. I don't agree with that. You enjoy one world, one dream equally, because we are *all* created equally, not just all *Americans* are created equally. (Edward, Chinese, male, born outside the U.S., 26–45)

Other participants also express their belief that the notion of an American Dream is nationalistic and arrogant:

The American Dream doesn't just exist in the United States.[2] There are other places that are considered places where you can get ahead. People follow the idea of economic opportunity—there may be additional reasons, but that is the main one. People from India go to London and Dubai. (Aria, South Asian/Desi, female, born outside the U.S., 26–45)

If it's an American Dream, it's only available to the United States because it's American. In other countries, like the U.K., they can have their own dream. They may call it the English Dream. (Kris Stewart, Black, male, U.S.-born, 18–25)

We need to drop the "American" part from the dream, because I don't think that we're the only ones that live the way we do here. I live much more differently than my cousins in the DR [Dominican Republic]. My mom is not rich, but at least here they try to give you financial aid, supposedly to go to college, so that would be the American Dream. It's the options that you supposedly have. When I was working at a community organization, we used to have a legal clinic where many homeless people would come. If they had a ticket or a summons, they'd get legal advice on what to do. It was surprising to me. Why would you ticket a homeless person? You know they can't pay it. Why wouldn't you find another way for them to fix the problem? I learned that the system is set up to keep people where they are. (Damaris, Latina, female, U.S.-born, 18–25)

Lisa is an Italian American woman who was born in Queens but moved to Long Island at the age of 4. She, too, is critical of the mythology:

The American Dream is not just American; it goes back to the folklore this country turns to. If you go all the way back—it was not the same, a lot of disparity [in] how the country was set up and how it is actually run. It is not just the American Dream, it is the human dream—a very human thing in whatever culture you are to try and be the best version of yourself.

Lawrence and Paul echo this theme:

The American Dream is a human dream, to be happy. I do not care if you are in France, Italy, Kenya—most countries are family-oriented. It is really the *human dream* about being fulfilled as a human being and as a family person. (Lawrence, white, male, U.S.-born, 46–65)

The American Dream is advertised all over the world, but it originated in the United States. They went to different countries—even with the countries that the pilgrims came from. They was like, "Yo man, check it out. We got this here." I don't know if it was called the American Dream back then, but they was advertising pictures, and then they came over. But these people come, and they be like, "Dang, it don't feel like it," but it's embedded in their mind. My family, my grandmother and my mother, came up to the city to better themselves. They brought their families up here. My grandma from Puerto Rico, she brought her family up here knowing something was better. When you look at it, though, you really don't have to come to America to do all that. There's probably better opportunities elsewhere in different countries. The American Dream is cool, though, but they really don't have to just look at America. (Paul, Puerto Rican, male, U.S.-born, 18–25)

Breana (white, female, U.S.-born, 18–25) asks:

Anyway, why is it the American Dream and not the British Dream?

Change Is Coming

Some respondents are clear that the recent polarization of wealth has reached a point of no return. The system is in crisis:

Even though the majority may not be aware, I look at it kind of like *The Matrix* at another level. It's going to be an awakening. You're always going to have that group of sheep that are just going to go with the flow, but then you always have that one or two that says, "Hey, why am I even walking *this* way? Why can't I walk *that* way?" Oh man, these young cats are going to be off the chain. When the group that does wake up and realize it's not what they thought it was, it's going to be a whole other thing. It's going to be something big.

I don't even know if it's going to be people of color. It's going to be more so the haves and have-nots. That's what it's going to come down to. The race thing is going to play itself out, because now you have a new common enemy. You know? The money man. That's who do what they want when they want—the rich. The oppressive. Now instead of only having a culture being oppressed, you have a caste that's being oppressed. You have millions of people who have lost their jobs, but the CEOs are still getting their bonuses and golden umbrellas. Come on, man. What is that about? They are vulnerable, because this country was founded on robbing, stealing, and killing, and they're *still* robbing, stealing, and killing. Neo is going to jump out there somewhere and there's going to be a—Neo is the main character in *The Matrix*. He doesn't know that he is going to be the—and I won't say that he is the savior. He's the catalyst to the jump-off spot. Anytime you've got too many people out of work, you're going to have people that have and the people that have not. There is no middle class. The middle class is slowly getting eradicated, and that's due to deregulation. Anytime you take away regulations, you're going to have chaos and mayhem. There are no rules. That's going to be the issue, and it's going to jump off, and it's going to be one of these young cats. I'm telling you now. They're going to get tired of not having. Somebody's going to wake up and be like, "Say what?" (Harold, Black, male, U.S.-born, 26–45)

These sentiments are echoed in what Carmella (white, female, U.S.-born, 26–45) has to say, reflecting a growing understanding of the tensions between the haves and the have-nots and the changes that occurred in the last decades of the twentieth century. Both of their comments reflect a recognition that positive social change occurs as a result of pressure from the masses of people:

My parents are hardcore New Deal Democrats. . . . I grew up with this implicit understanding that the reason things were good was because of Roosevelt and the unions.

Harold describes a situation that occurred when he was a university student: He and other Black students were trying to get funds to organize an activity, and the student government attempted to block them:

I was learning if we want to do this, we've got to submit a request, and student government tells us yeah or nay. I said, "Well then, if that's the case, how can they deny our petition, no matter what it is?" How can you deny it? Really, they can't, so, I mean, the same thing with taxes. If my money is going to taxes, how can you deny me health care?

I was really hot. Instead of just being angry for nothing, I was angry with a mission, so now, you know, I had just cause to be upset. You know how you know something is wrong but you don't know why it's wrong. You just know that's wrong, and so now he explained it to us, and I said, "Oh." So it was on then. We submitted again and said, "Hey, this is how many students that go to the school; this is how many students [are] Black; this is Black History month. This is our budget. This is what we want." They said, "Well, we need you to itemize." I said, "No, we're not itemizing it." Then we had one little bourgie: "Well, what is it going to hurt?" I said, "I am so sick and tired of you." I said, "You why we stay down. . . . I bet it was your great-great-great-granddaddy, he was the main one telling us the master good to us. You know? He feed us on Monday. You know? He only beat us on Tuesday. Come on, man.

Don't you see it? You're slowing down the process." He really didn't see it, though. He thought I was just over the top. So okay. All right. We finally got it.

Harold speaks about another experience in school that increased his understanding of how power works in society:

I went to school ROTC, which opened me to really showing out, because we were still active duty but we were going to college. They made sure. They said, "Anything you do wrong, we're going to send you back to the fleet," and dah, dah, dah, dah, dah, and the guy was talking to me, and I was like, "Hold on, partner." I said, "What you need to do first is take some bass out of your voice." I was all about that "I'm a man" thing. I'm a grown man, and I'll tell you that in a minute. You are not going to talk to me any kind of way you want.

They kept going on about you're in the navy. You've got to conform. I said, "Well, conform to what?" I said, "Why? Whatever I do outside of my personal life, you know, you can't hit me for it." "Well, it's the military. We own you." I said, "Hold on, partner, you don't own nobody," but really I did know once you sign the papers, you actually are government property. They can write you up. You are truly government property, so being that's the case, well, if you read the fine print, it'll tell you you're government, and they can do what they want to do to you. I'm just trying to help these people understand, you know, hey this is not just white folk no more. I said, "What is that about?" They just cut my scholarship right then. They put me out of the navy. They gave me my discharge papers from inactive reserve from the ROTC unit so I didn't have to go back to the navy.

Many participants speak eloquently of the critical role of resistance. Debates ensue about whom to struggle against and why:

There's a lot of people that are fighting to save the Earth and stop global warming, stop companies, and all this. Then there's a lot of people at the same time who want what I feel has become the American Dream: the glitz and the glam and these technological advances. They're a form of overindulgence. People are wearing out the Earth, and soon they're not going to have much to live on. But there are people that recognize that and are trying to fight back. I think we need some freedom fighter to stop companies assuming control over people's lives. (Pike, Black/white, male, U.S.-born, 18–25)

Pike says "companies" and I think more to myself "government." I mean, that's the same thing, I guess. (Diego, mixed, male, U.S.-born, 18–25)

I say "companies" because companies have leverage on the economy, which interferes with government, and companies also have leverage over society through advertising, so whether it be government or just society, they have control over whole degrees, and that's why I feel that they have more of a, pose more of a threat to people than just government alone. (Pike)

In another exchange, Carmella (white, female, U.S.-born, 26–45) suggests that most people are fed up with the system as it stands:

I wonder how much further materialism can go with people who have enough. Does it reach a point where people are like, "This is not it." I'm sure you've heard of research by the Center for the New American Dream. They found out that, like, overwhelming amounts of people, people who are comfortable, middle-class Americans, say, "I don't need more stuff. I need more time." But then on the other hand, you have people who don't have enough to eat in the world. You know? Even in America, people don't have enough to eat, so less materialism is not very appealing for people who, like, don't have shoes.

You know how there's all these shows now, like *The Real Housewives*. It's kind of ridiculous to me, because they live in this world, like, it's all about where you buy and what you're buying, and they have a house in the Hamptons. I feel like, "How can you live in this bubble and not concern yourself with someone else? Like, someone else is not eating, and you're here spending I don't know how much money." It's okay to be comfortable, but it gets to a point where you're a little too comfortable, and it gets ridiculous at that point. More people have to be made aware and be involved. Of my friends, I'm the most political, and that kind of bothers me. I would like them to be interested in the world and to want to go and vote or to listen to someone at a lecture. I would like to encourage them a little more to go out and ask questions and be curious about how our country is run and how the world goes on every day.

Damaris (Latina, female, U.S.-born, 18–25) responds and mostly agrees:

After I started seeing all these people suffering in the world and you're not told that, and that was an eye-opener for me. That's when I started caring. Many of them were suffering because of us, because of this country, and because of the way we run our politics. That's when I decided. When you start caring, you can't stop caring. If it's signing a petition or learning more about the issue, you want to get involved in any way you can, so I guess that is the second step afterwards. Then there's obviously much more things you can do after that on a bigger scale.

Some participants take this idea a step further and begin to talk of the vision of what they want to see enacted. Carmella (white, female, U.S.-born, 26–45) describes her ideas:

The American Dream originally started much more modestly, like with my grandparents and with people before them. People wanted safety, enough to eat—basically just a decent life from a material perspective and safety from persecution. Even the beginning of this country, like the Constitution and what it was supposed to guarantee. People back then had much simpler lives. Because of advertising, consumer culture, and all that, it's like the American Dream has sort of been built up into having a lot more than you need. That maybe it needs to sort of go. The American Dream is not having a huge house and a Bentley and this, that, and the other thing and having a new wardrobe every season. We need to get back to think[ing] globally. There should be some kind of Global Dream that everybody has adequate shelter, and enough to eat, and seasonally appropriate clothing, and public transportation, a decent standard of living, as opposed to, like, more, more, more, more. It originally started out much more modest, and it's become kind of ridiculous. I don't know. Somehow, that future needs to be more realistic, I guess.

Joe J. (white, male, U.S.-born, 26–45) agrees:

Hey, that's what I was going to say! We're such a consumer culture. The way we use up most of the resources in the world with a very small population! We need to encourage people not to use so much stuff.

Some people are more hopeful:

Things will change through grassroots organizing, talking one on one, or having intimate discussions with people, like, about elections. The paradigm is starting to change. It's starting to shift a little. Maybe. Hopefully. If Malcolm, Martin, John, and all those folks had not been assassinated, what type of world would this be? People of that persuasion are starting to come—it just seems like some more of those folks are starting to come forward. Maybe it's just wishful thinking on my part, but it just seems like maybe things are starting to shift. There's not going to be this same kind of corporate greed that they used to be. They're really scrutinizing spending now in corporations, in the private corporations, unlike any other time I've seen. They're coming down on people. Why are you flying jets, and why are you doing this? Before, all the spending was behind closed doors, and nobody knew about it. It was a gravy train. (Joseph, Black, male, U.S.-born, 46–65)

Deidra (white, female, U.S.-born, over 65) reflects on the source of the problem and what is needed for things to change:

This man fell off a crane where seven people got killed. There were no inspectors there. Why don't you hire inspectors? Why are fines are so little in this country that people die for no reason? If there was more of a sense of responsibility . . . that's what this country is lacking. People are not responsible and accountable for what they have to do. If you have more accountability, you wouldn't have half the problems we have today—whether you're going with the market, whether you're going with Congress, you're going structurally on this country. Things got worse because Bush didn't live in a real world. He came out of a very comfortable background, and I don't think he understood how the average person felt. He just was a person who was interested in his own world and that's it. It's heartbreaking to see the soldiers and families and so many lives ruined for his being arrogant, for his feeling that he's above the law. The pity of it is that nothing will ever happen to him. Some of it will change. I don't think everything but pride will be put back into doing things.

Another strand of this conversation that runs through many of the discussions is what determines whether the United States is generous and lives up to its ideals. This issue is particularly important, as it signifies what would be needed to create a Global Dream. In this exchange, the participants are simultaneously cynical and hopeful about the possibilities for change.

Cee East (Black, female, U.S.-born, 26–45) is more critical:

With America, if that country don't have nothing they can gain or use or take, like Iraq with the oil, they're not going to help. They're not helping Haiti, because Haiti has nothing that they want. The U.S. is so rich and other countries so poor because of robbing countries. Robbing like Robin Hood, but they don't steal from the rich and give to the poor.

Singing Dianne (Black, female, born outside the U.S., 46–65) responds:

They cannot help the whole world. Let's remember that. You can't help the whole world. Right? I think that America tried to do their best. When Grenada had this war, when they overthrew the government and stuff, America came to their aid. They helped them in whatever way that they could. America came to Grenada's aid. They need to get something back. You understand?

Redd (Black, female, U.S.-born, 26–45) comments:

I'm agreeing with Cee. They help countries that they know they're going to get something back. Look at the story with the kids crying for money. You never hear on the news, "The United States sent a million dollars to this country for clean water," or whatever. Most of the time, you hear the United States saved the oil, did something, went to war, or whatever to take, but you know, it's just like here, we have hungry people, and you know how hard it is.

To this, Chino (Latino, male, U.S.-born, 46–65) responds:

I'm quite aware of how wealthy the United States is. We've sent millions and millions of dollars to other countries throughout the world. But I can't understand how the United States neglect[s] their own people. I can walk in my neighborhood within the five boroughs and see the poverty that we have today in our own backyard. It is there. I would like to know when the United States is going to pour this money into our own country. I think it's political. They want to hold the people down. That's what I do believe. Why is it that they are so willing to spend millions and millions of dollars [on] other countries?

Look at the news and the soup kitchens in the United States. Pretty soon, homeless people, they're not going to have nowhere to go. These soup kitchens are going to close. The pantries are low. Pretty soon, public assistance in this country is going to be cut off. Social Security, it's going to be just a matter of time that that's going to be cut off, whether they're going to go onto disability and other funds that is open to the public, that's going to be cut off, but still, after this happened, we're still going to continue to support other countries.

The dialogue continues with Cee East's (Black, female, U.S.-born, 26–45) response:

If people want to come over here for a better life, I'm all for it. I'm all for people living good. I'm all for people coming over and helping themselves and creating a better life for themselves and their families.

Singing Dianne (Black, female, born outside the U.S., 46–65) then comments:

People who are making an honest living shouldn't have to wait eighteen or twenty years or if the president has a heart to give them amnesty. As long as they're not committing no crime. The people who commit so many high crime[s] get away with it. These people here just here for a reason. And they are a part of building this country.

Redd (Black, female, U.S.-born, 26–45) agrees:

Leave them alone. They come here and they want, and all the ones I see, they work. I done seen ten of them in one apartment, and out of the ten, eight of them is working, 'cause the other two be kids. They work, and they struggle. They work for hardly nothing. Look how many lives be taken when they swimming out there in that ocean trying to make it through the Florida Keys. They go through so much!

Chino, Singing Dianne, Cee East, Redd, Nee-Nee, and Spankey expand on their thoughts about the relationship between the American Dream and the challenges faced by immigrants. In different ways, they articulate concern about the contradictions of this construct such that the rhetoric implies that upward mobility and the "good life" are accessible to all, although the reality tells another story:

Chino (Latino, male, U.S.-born, 46–65): I'd like to believe that this country is open to anyone that wants to come here. However, they should follow the proper procedures. We speak about the United States not providing for their own country. The economy is poor. They're trying to make it better. How is it going to get better if the borders in our country are very weak? How is it that other countries are coming in here and taking the jobs that we need for ourselves? There's going to have to be a solution to this. You can't continue to let these people just come sneak in here.

Singing Dianne (Black, female, born outside the U.S., 46–65): Are you going to go in the Korean store and work for thirteen, fourteen hours for maybe $5 an hour? Are you going to do that? Are you going to go in New Jersey and work in the white people's house and take care of their kids for them for maybe $200, $250? You will say you don't want that job.

Cee East (Black, female, U.S.-born, 26–45): And how [are] they taking from the economy? The economy is poor. If they're illegal and don't have documents and get paid off the books, how are they taking from the economy?

Singing Dianne: The legal are not going to do the jobs. They don't want it. They want to work in an office and the computer and things like that.

Chino: It's going to be a brighter future. In my heart, I feel that this economic, this struggle that we're going through, the poverty that we're having today, I don't think it's going to last forever. People are going to get together. They're going to open up a lot of doors. The economy is going to blossom. There's going to be a lot of jobs in the near future. They're going to support the education, the hospital. Our medical is going to come down, our salaries are going to go up. I see this future blossoming. That's how I feel in my heart. And we ready for change. We want change.

Singing Dianne: I cannot predict the future, but for what I'm seeing right now, I am seeing a change, and I see even a great change coming. The change has to come from within us.

Redd (Black, female, U.S.-born, 26–45): I live one day at a time, so I'll see when it gets here. I can't say I see the future, because so much is happening, and it's like to me nothing is getting better, so I don't know how it is going to get better or worse, so I just take one day at a time. That's it.

Nee-Nee (Black, female, U.S.-born, 18–25): I'm just hoping for a change, because I need a job. I need a better education, so hopefully it will be a change for the good, better than what it was.

Spankey (Black, female, U.S.-born, 26–45): I'm just going to be praying and hoping for the best in the future. It's like too much tension on poor Barack—that, you know, he's only one person. He's only human. I have faith that he can endure the challenges. He's only a man. Some people have this superficial thing, like he would change the world in a blink of an eye. That's not going to happen. We as a people have to come together and do the things that we need to do. Because if you don't stand for nothing, you fall for anything. I'm going to maintain and keep my head above water like I've always done. The sky is the limit for me, and I'm going to keep reaching my goals, because I see the light at the end of my tunnel.

Singing Dianne: We never thought we would have a Black president. My father, if he was alive today, and my grandmother just died last year in February; she was eighty-five. So I can't even get into how they was, but it's like they would never believe it. She would never believe it. My father would never believe it.

Spankey: I idolize my mom to a certain extent. She showed me her hands that she picked cotton with. She didn't know what it was to have a new outfit, because she got the hand-me-downs. There was seven of them. You know what I'm saying? She was the second youngest, so she didn't know what it was to go get a new pair of shoes. She got what was passed down to her, and, you know, if they could make it, that's what lets me know that I, too, can make it.

In the voices of the participants of this discussion group, it is clear that hope and despair reside side by side. While their problems are immense and their difficulties many, they reflect on the changes that they have seen in their own lifetimes, and this reflection leads them to consider that things could change again, even possibly for the better.

In the final set of comments in this section of the chapter, the values of participants resound loudly regarding what they want to see for the future:

We were like a "one love."[3] We might not all have money. But we had a lot of love in our community. So that's why I like to give. I like to give back, especially to elderly people and children. I don't care who you are. But you know, some people don't look at it that way. Holiday time, we know all the sisters, the brothers, and all the grandchildren get together, so we know what is one love. We know how to give back to the community. (G. G., Black, female, born outside the U.S., 46–65)

I believe actually there's a group of people who actually run the whole world. I think it's a set of thirteen people. They're called the elite. Am I correct? They actually give you a rundown of how they want everything to run, how they want the society to actually look. This is where the brainwashing comes in at. Why do you think they have all the rappers out now who are cursing, who are rapping about shoes and sneakers and killing people and drugs? They don't have rappers who are talking about getting your education, finding out who you were, finding out who your history trees are. They're pushing those to the side. They want to push the rappers out who are trying to brainwash our kids. Everything brainwashable—it's all about controlling. You control the mind, you control everything. I was reading a Willie Lynch speech, and part of his speech said, "You control the mind, so you can control the body."

You know, they took the Black male, beat him in front of the wife and kids, and put fear in the woman, so that—because they knew the woman actually controlled the family, so if she's raising a child, she's going to let her child know, "You listen to this person, because you don't want what happened to your father to happen to you," so she's going to protect her child, of course. You know? So with that, it's all about brainwashing. If you can get into somebody's mind, that's Psychology 101, if you can get into someone's mind, you can control their whole life. We can do what we need to do, but we all have to be on one page. (S. Westmoreland, Black, female, born outside the U.S., 18–25)

Data related to public opinion about social supports reveal some interesting patterns. Although many people approve of the idea that all people should be cared for, there is less explicit support for "socialism," however it is defined. (See Table 7.1.)

A 2011 Pew Research Center survey[4] also evidenced important distinctions in the support shown by different demographic groups, with younger people, Blacks and Hispanics, and people from lower-income sectors indicating more positive views toward the idea of caring for the common good than older, white, and higher-income groups. (See Table 7.2.)

Furthermore, a November 2012 Gallup poll found that among Democrats and Democratic leaners, 53 percent said they had a positive image of socialism. Ironically, of this group, 55 percent expressed positive views of capitalism, 75 percent expressed positive views of the federal government, and 88 percent expressed positive views of free enterprise. Clearly, these views may appear contradictory

TABLE 7.1. BELIEFS ABOUT SOCIAL SUPPORTS

	Strongly disagree	Disagree	Agree	Strongly agree	Don't know
The government should make sure everyone has access to a living wage.	2.8%	4.1%	28.0%	63.3%	1.8%
The government should make sure that everyone who needs healthcare receives it.	2.0%	2.6%	19.1%	75.7%	0.6%

TABLE 7.2. VIEWS OF "CAPITALISM" AND "SOCIALISM"

Reaction to . . .	Capitalism		Socialism		
	Positive %	Negative %	Positive %	Negative %	Difference in % positive
Total	50	40	31	60	+19
White	55	35	24	68	+31
Black	41	51	55	36	−14
Hispanic	32	55	44	49	−12
18–29	46	47	49	43	−3
30–49	50	40	34	58	+16
50–64	53	39	25	68	+28
65+	52	32	13	72	+39
Family income					
$75,000+	68	28	22	71	+46
$30,000–$74,999	52	43	27	68	+25
Less than $30,000	39	47	43	46	−4
Party and Ideology					
Conservative Republican	66	29	6	90	+60
Moderate/Liberal Republican	54	40	25	66	+29
Independent	52	39	32	60	+20
Conservative/Moderate Democrat	42	49	37	51	+5
Liberal Democrat	46	47	59	33	−13
Occupy Wall Street					
Support (44%)	45	47	39	52	+6
Oppose (35%)	67	28	18	76	+49
Tea Party movement					
Agree (19%)	71	26	12	85	+59
Disagree (27%)	53	39	37	53	+16
No opinion (50%)	42	46	35	55	+7

Source: Pew Research Center for the People and the Press, "Little Change in Public's Response to 'Capitalism,' 'Socialism,'" December 11, 2011. Available at www.people-press.org/2011/12/28/little-change-in-publics-response-to-capitalism-socialism/. Reprinted with permission of the Pew Research Center.

and are certainly complex; however, they stand in contrast to those of Republicans or Republican leaners, who expressed positive views of the following: socialism (23 percent), capitalism (72 percent), the federal government (27 percent), and free enterprise (94 percent).[5] In April 2013, a Gallup poll found roughly 60 percent of those surveyed believed that money and wealth should be redistributed more equally in the United States, and 52 percent of Americans thought the government should redistribute wealth "by heavy taxes on the rich."[6] This viewpoint was divided along party lines, with 83 percent of Democrats and 28 percent of Republicans supporting the idea of wealth redistribution by taxation of the rich.

What Do We Make of the "Stories of My America"?

In Part II of this book, we have provided readers with the means for direct connection to the thoughts and reflections of those we spoke with. We have sought a deep understanding of how allegiance to capitalism and the idea that upward mobility, material accumulation, and individualism are created and then reproduced as well as when and how individuals come to question dominant narratives about race, nation, class, and capitalism as the only reasonable system.

Immediately apparent as we began this research was that those we spoke with had already thought about many of the issues we raised. While some felt certain about their own beliefs, many expressed uncertainty or confusion about how to make sense of commonly referred to explanations that did not really explain either their life challenges or good fortunes. Many appeared to be rethinking some of the assumptions on which they had built their lives thus far.

It became clear that numerous mechanisms enact loyalty to the standard ways that modern history is explained, even when some of them contradict the lived experiences of ordinary people. The emergence of the United States as a nation with narratives based on notions of benevolence, superiority, freedom, equality, justice, diversity, and being a superpower provides a strident image of strength with which most would like to associate. The expectation of unquestioning support for the military shores up this image of power and might. Who would not want to be on the "A" team?

Furthermore, the depiction of the United States as a land of no crime or poverty, a place where money grows on trees so anyone can live the high life, provides an incentive to "believe." Consumerism/materialism offers a goal that appears reachable to all (despite the debt that may be incurred). Such symbols as the flag with its stars and stripes, "patriotic" T-shirts, fireworks (bombs bursting in air), the Pledge of Allegiance, and the outward portrait of unity provide a sense of stability and strength. The orchestration of reasons to fear (crime, terrorism, youth gone wild) and a lack of safety often leaves people unwilling to take chances, to question, or to act in nontraditional ways. The stigmatization and suppression of dissent (in schools as well as in the public domain—for example, the treatment of the Occupy movement, the Dream 9, the Dream Defenders, and the protesters in Ferguson, Missouri) further encourage strict adherence to the party line.

Most reporting on the social world is done through an individualist lens with little historical contextualization; this situation limits our understanding, particularly of economic and political structure, but also of group differences. Segregation leaves us ignorant of the real experiences of those whose lives differ from our own. Cultural explanations are used as fill-ins. Among the privileged, this lack of understanding is compounded by self-interest—isn't it better to believe all are treated just like you are? Otherwise, you must recognize distinctions. Explanations of cultural differences are utilized to explain positionality, as if there is some essential nature among different groups that explains their specific places in the social hierarchy rather than history and context. Also, the social world is portrayed through decontextualized and constructed ideas about "rich" versus "poor" countries. Little is revealed about what led to this state of affairs, such as colonialism, imperialism, capitalism, and what is occurring in the contemporary social context to reproduce this hierarchy of nations.

We are misled about history based on who comes out the victors and how that happens. The role of Christianity in establishing and maintaining hierarchies is entirely invisible. We are told that the government makes independent decisions and are rarely privy to the thoughts and understandings of corporate lobbyists and wealthy male legislators who are rarely in touch with the lives of ordinary people.

Finally, unemployment for youth, particularly of color and from agricultural areas, leaves them looking for solid ground at a time of uncertainty. The military offers that option, if one believes in the idea that serving one's country is a great honor and deserves respect. The mainstream narrative affirms that notion and more, offering military members a sense of entitlement and specialness. Barack Obama's election offered hope that the narratives about democracy, justice, and equality (and post-racialism), however challenged in the past, indeed accurately depict the nation's character.

Simultaneous to these reflections, many of the people we spoke with made clear that they were questioning what they had been told and what they had believed to be true about the U.S. nation. There was a significant degree (both quantitatively and qualitatively) of challenging most of these notions. Many people expressed frustration and even anger at what they perceived to be hype about the United States. Heightened global awareness was evident as a result of access to information and because of U.S. involvement in global affairs, such as the wars of the last decade. Many people openly engaged questions of morality and believed that something was wrong with the current level of violence and poverty. They expressed a great distrust of those in charge, particularly of the government and corporate leaders, and an acute sense that these individuals were disconnected with the concerns and challenges of ordinary people in the United States.

Greater interaction between groups (however limited and segregated) seems to have led to more openness about the humanity of all people, especially among younger people. Detachment from religion seems to be symbolic of the willingness to question rather than accept what one is told to be true. Among immigrants, arriving in the United States, discovering that the streets are not paved with gold, and navigating the challenges of employment and discrimination seem to support a more critical understanding of the U.S. nation's character. Furthermore, increased numbers of immigrants mean more people with multiple national allegiances.

In the political process, while young people were more involved in the last elections, it has been apparent that the makeup of the government does not mirror the U.S. population, nor do government officials appear to be especially concerned with public opinion. The sense that politicians are generally corrupt or that they just do not care about "the little person" leads people to question the depiction of the United States as a democratic nation where the officials are representatives of the people. Scandals, whether financial or sexual in nature, deteriorate allegiance and loyalty to politicians and to the corporate sector as a whole. The responses to Hurricane Katrina, abuse and torture in Abu Ghraib, and the wars in Iraq and Afghanistan, with massive loss of life to the citizens of those countries and to people in the United States, have left their mark. The treatment of veterans; rising costs of health care, housing, and tuition; and minimum-wage stagnation have caused many to detach from their previous belief in "America, the Beautiful," the greatest place on Earth.

There is greater awareness of inequality and violence as part of the reality of everyday life in the United States and an increased feeling of vulnerability. The "spread the wealth" discussions of Obama's campaigns and first presidency raised the level of understanding of the economic structure of the United States. Younger people are more exposed interracially and express a lack of understanding of their parents' biases. However small the increase, there are more interracial marriages and individuals openly identifying themselves as being of mixed backgrounds. The challenges for young people, even those with college degrees, are leading some to question the narratives about work and lack of satisfaction from a lifestyle that means always being tired and rushing, with difficulty finding time for friends and family.

Finally, during this period of upheaval, there is a scarcity of widespread ideological explanation for the vast levels of inequality that leave many people questioning whether what they have been led to believe about capitalism, race, and the United States' place in history is accurate. Repeatedly evident in the different ways that people framed their reflections was a deep desire for a loving world where all were cared for, had a way to contribute to society, and were considered valuable. What that would mean in practice was rarely articulated, but the vision, the dream, and the soul were almost without exception voiced, loud and clear.

In Part III, we connect these "Stories of My America" to the question of whether the institution of nation reflects empire or liberation. Here we reflect on both the multiple crises of the U.S. nation and the revolts of the past decade to draw our final conclusions and provide our analysis about *Tensions in the American Dream*.

III

Tensions in the American Dream

Rhetoric, Reverie, or Reality?

8

Nation

Empire or Liberation

Though the U.S. trajectory from settler colony to global hegemony fits well into the narrative of U.S. exceptionalism, we have attempted to engage readers in a fulsome intellectual and political examination of how these presumptions and the realities are embedded in the concept of the American Dream. This dream of human possibility is not intended for all humanity and therefore does not consider how our practices in the global arena restrict the possibilities of others. In line with Melanie Bush's *Un-pledging Allegiance: Waking Up from the "American" Dream*, we argue that the nationalism of U.S. empire has been articulated through its historical constitution as a nation that colonized numerous populations and incorporated them as second-class citizens or as noncitizens within its polity. These internally colonized populations (of which African Americans constitute a significant segment) articulated a sense of their own peoplehood that cut across the nationalism of empire and gave social and political stability to the nation. As a social practice parallel to the construction of historical capitalism, it has also been the foundation of the gravediggers of this empire.

But the very creation of the notion of race during the conquest of the Americas and the capture of Africans as a labor force in this new world naturalized the difference between the socially defined superior populations of European descent and racialized populations within this new world. The settler colony British North America expanded from the Eastern Seaboard to the Pacific, fulfilling its manifest destiny and establishing an ideological formation that justified its expansionary policies. This is what we designate as the nationalism of empire, a system of pan-ethnic unity and pan-European racism that drew a firm line between socially defined whites and racialized others.

Such a contention is greeted with some skepticism in the political climate that has prevailed since 1980. However, the postwar era in which U.S. hegemony was constructed included the expansion of an internal social democracy that incorporated Blacks and members of other racialized groups.

President Lyndon Baines Johnson's June 4, 1965, speech "To Fulfill These Rights" made an attempt to address the tide of social revolution of the 1960s during a visit at historically Black Howard University. As he began to lay out his views about how the nation should respond, his commentary quite clearly reflected the problem of belonging that we have detailed in this book as continuing to exist today. This selection from his speech demonstrates the thinking at the highest levels of government during this period in U.S. history:

> Our earth is the home of revolution. In every corner of every continent men charged with hope contend with ancient ways in the pursuit of justice. They reach for the newest of weapons to realize the oldest of dreams, that each may walk in freedom and pride, stretching his talents, enjoying the fruits of the earth.
>
> In far too many ways American Negroes have been another nation: deprived of freedom, crippled by hatred, the doors of opportunity closed to hope.
>
> In our time change has come to this Nation, too. The American Negro, acting with impressive restraint, has peacefully protested and marched, entered the courtrooms and the seats of government, demanding a justice that has long been denied. The voice of the Negro was the call to action. But it is a tribute to America that, once aroused, the courts and the Congress, the President and most of the people, have been the allies of progress. . . .
>
> But for the great majority of Negro Americans—the poor, the unemployed, the uprooted, and the dispossessed—there is a much grimmer story. They still, as we meet here tonight, are another nation. Despite the court orders and the laws, despite the legislative victories and the speeches, for them the walls are rising and the gulf is widening. (Johnson 1965)

Where have we gotten to as a nation if a former president who is known for extending the New Deal social contract to racialized groups who had not been fully included during the heyday of the New Deal is viewed in hindsight as a wild-eyed radical whose thinking is not acceptable in the mainstream of U.S. social thought?

Some will argue that it is simply the political cycle. However, we argue that such cycles are symptomatic of longer-run structural changes. Most scholars acknowledge that the period from 1945 to 1970 was the height of U.S. hegemony within the modern world-system (commonly known as the "American Century"). In August 1963, at the historic March on Washington that had been approved by President John F. Kennedy, Martin Luther King Jr. called on the United States to live out the true meaning of its creed. In this moment, civil rights became a part of the American Century, possibly its crowning jewel. However, below the surface lay cracks in this sense of national unity. After 1970, the price of hegemony began to take its toll, as the economic leadership of the United States was increasingly challenged by Germany and Japan. The victory of the national liberation movement in Vietnam had signaled the unruliness of the third world, which the Reagan doctrine attempted to stabilize. The collapse of the European arena of world communism did not result in the triumph of capitalism, as some have argued, but in the removal of the Soviet Union as a key stabilizing agent in the system based on the agreements at Yalta (Wallerstein 1989, 2000a, 2000b, 2003b, 2004). George H. W. Bush's idea of a new world order with a thousand points of light was revealed as a false promise in the very limitations of the first U.S. attack on Iraq, as was clear to a cadre of neoconservative intellectuals who formed an organization that they called "The Project for the New American Century" (PNAC).

In their 1996 *Foreign Affairs* essay, William Kristol and Robert Kagan call for the "remoralization of American foreign policy," arguing that only a morally based foreign policy could win the support of the American people. Moreover, a moral makeover of U.S. foreign policy would contribute to the "remoralization of America at home." According to public documents by PNAC and its associates, the moral fundamentals guiding their foreign-policy vision are those declared by America's founding fathers. They make the strong argument that the "principles of the Declaration of Independence are not merely the choices of a particular culture but are universal" or, as the founders themselves asserted, "self-evident" truths. PNAC's "statement of principles" is unequivocal: "The history of the 20th century should have taught us that it is important to shape circumstances before crises emerge, and to meet threats before they become dire. The history of this century should have taught us to embrace the cause of American leadership."[1] This is the doctrine of "Pre-emptive Strike" and "Benevolent Hegemony."

While neoliberalism had proved to be a temporary measure that could not really impose a permanent freeze on the share of the income going to the workforce, the neoconservative intellectuals have argued for the establishment of a democratic empire to stabilize the world situation in which U.S. hegemony would be ensured by using its military power to destroy and intimidate potential and real challenges to its authority.

During the postwar period of 1945 to 1970, the national liberation movements came to power throughout the formerly colonized world, generating an echo within the pan-European world itself (including among the third world within the pan-European world) that shattered the centrist liberalism that had constituted the geoculture of the world-system from 1848 to 1968. But political independence did not enable most of these new nations to break through the economic domination of the core states. The end of the postwar expansion was hard on these nations and on the socialist states as well. By 1989 to 1991, the communist regimes of Eastern Europe had imploded, and the descendants of the national liberation movements had succumbed to the neoliberal program of structural adjustment. But we should be clear that the counterrevolution of the late 1970s, which some called "an attack on labor," was an attack on the entire Left worldwide, whose growing power had challenged the prevailing power of capitalism, white world supremacy, and U.S. hegemony.

The failures of the erstwhile antisystemic movements created disillusion among the popular masses throughout the world-system. One of the major blocs of nonsubaltern discourse in the world-system was the Muslim world, where opposition to the hegemonic designs of the pan-European world emerged as a political force, although the national liberation movements in this area had been targeted by U.S. imperial operations seeking to make this zone hospitable to its corporate, geopolitical, and hegemonic designs. In the wake of the destruction of the secular national liberation movements arose movements that operated under the banner of varieties of political Islam. Although these political Islam movements were often anti-imperialist in their opposition to U.S. hegemony, they were often viewed by secular progressives in the West as being to the right of traditional antisystemic movements. They were thus viewed with some ambivalence by the cadres and intellectuals of these movements.

On January 1, 1994, the rebellion of the Zapatistas in Chiapas, Mexico, raised high the banner of the most oppressed segments of the world population—the indigenous peoples—and laid claim to their right to autonomy and well-being. This action was significant in its denunciation of the neoliberal program of the upper strata and its lack of interest in state power and was an example of the possible for all to see, especially in its claim of the moral high ground. Latin America has moved significantly to the Left since the Zapatistas' rise to public prominence in Mexico. This movement to the Left is partly a function of the mobilization of indigenous movements throughout Latin America, which—as Elizabeth Martinez (1998) notes in a chapter entitled "Be Down with the Brown!"—is an increasing influence among Raza youth in the United States.

The Latin American arena of global capitalism is significant in this regard because of the longer historical process that we have been at pains to demonstrate in this book about Americanity and because of the middle-run strategies of global capitalism dominated by the United States as the hegemonic power (Quijano 2000). Gerardo Renique locates the foundational moment of what he deems the "Neoliberal offensive" in that other September 11, in 1973, when General Augusto Pinochet, with the backing of the U.S. government, led a violent coup d'état against the Chilean government of Salvador Allende, the first elected Marxist president in Latin America. Renique (2005) holds that Pinochet's coming to power provided a space within which a segment of global capital could begin to implement reactionary free-market policies intended to reverse the global Keynesian orthodoxy enforced by political compromises with social democracy and organized labor that had been the common coin of post–World War II global capitalism. This offensive was guided by economist Milton Friedman and the "Chicago Boys,"[2] who were supported by a multinational cadre of followers educated in U.S. universities and who held key positions in multilateral institutions, such as the International Monetary Fund, the World Bank, and in Latin America central banks and ministries of economy and finance (Renique 2005). Pinochet is said to have not only enjoyed the admiration of Henry Kissinger and Margaret Thatcher but also served as the model for the subsequent adoption of conservative economic measures, such as privatization of social security as a component of an emerging neoliberal orthodoxy.

According to Renique, neoliberalism, also known as savage capitalism, reached its peak during what was called the lost decade of the 1980s in Latin America, during which demands for labor rights, basic social services, free education, land reform, and national control of strategic resources were devastated. This chaos led in short order to the dismantling of the "developmentalist states" in Latin America and a dramatic impoverishment of the population, wherein 225 million people (44 percent of the population) were reduced to poverty.

It was in response to this onslaught, Renique offers, that new social actors emerged who came together with existing activists to create new social movements and revitalized older class-based organizations to defend the popular classes and strata in the region. Strikes and mass mobilizations in Peru in 2000, a popular insurrection in Argentina in 2001, and rebellions of indigenous populations in Ecuador and Bolivia have undermined the authority of corrupt and repressive regimes and made possible the election of left-wing governments in Argentina, Brazil, Venezuela, and Uruguay. Their reestablishment of diplomatic and economic relations with Cuba represents a dramatic reversal of a long-standing subordination of Latin American states to the will of the U.S. government, which has long attempted to isolate, strangle, and dismantle the Cuban Revolution.

For those who argue that this is simply another upsurge that will eventually have to surrender to the dictates of global capitalism, we have to respectfully disagree. To understand the basis of our disagreement, we must look back at the issue of temporalities—that is, to the plurality of social times.

The Plurality of Social Times

French historian Fernand Braudel (1982) argues that time is a social creation. It is not just marking the dates of battles fought, treaties signed, and administrations' ascent to power. It is therefore of the utmost importance to understand the multiple forms of social time. First, we have the short term—that is, the time of the event, of our illusions and rapid judgments. It is the chronicler's and journalist's time. It is the most capricious and deceptive form of time. Braudel (1992) argues that the event is like "dust in our eyes."

Second, we have the middle run (cyclical or conjunctural time—ten, twenty-five, fifty years). It is the narrative of the conjuncture or cycle. We might think here of the long economic cycles of expansion and stagnation in the economy.

Third, there is the long term (or *longue durée*). It is here that structure becomes key. The word "structure" for observers of social life implies organization, coherence, and fairly stable relationships between social realities and people over historical or long periods of time. Braudel calls on us to pay attention to the enduring structures (economic, cultural, and structural) that over the long term frame the context for our collective behaviors, our civilizational patterns, and our modes of production.

Historical capitalism is a durable social structure whose workings have governed the world-system for five hundred years. Historical systems experience a birth, a rather long period of normal functioning, and a demise when secular trends, such as mechanization, polarization, and so forth, move toward an asymptote that begins to undermine the social system's ability to function. As long as the system is functioning normally, efforts to change it make only minimal differences. Even very strenuous efforts, such as revolutions, may alter the relations of force in a given area for a time, but capitalism is a world-system, a historical system, a structure of life. The balance of forces is always in its favor as long as it is in a period of normal functioning. But once the system enters a period of structural crisis, which is the case today, then the agency of people is most effective and most important.

One of the great demographic shifts in the rich nations of the capitalist world is increased immigration from the Dark World, creating what some call a "third world within" these countries. The increasing size of the "third world within" polarizes these societies internally but also fundamentally alters the foundational system of pan-European racism that is central to the justification for social inequality within historical capitalism. So as the "third world within" continues to increase as a proportion of the population of core states (a situation that is most pronounced within the United States), these societies will increasingly face the challenge of creating an effective rainbow coalition and a political strategy for undermining not only pan-European racism but also the fundamentally inegalitarian nature of historical capitalism, which has entered a period of structural crisis during which human agency will determine the direction of transformation of the system.

Nationalism and the American Dream in the Twentieth Century

To understand nationalism and the role of the American Dream during the middle and late part of the twentieth century, we have examined the increasing power of social movements of oppressed social strata from the European immigrants of the late nineteenth and early twentieth centuries and from the migration of people of African descent from the U.S. South and the Caribbean from 1910 to 1930 that created a new social force, the New Negro. Following W.E.B. Du Bois, Rod Bush (1999) argues that the era of the New Negro was also the era of war and revolution on a world scale and that in the United States it brought about the "Blackening" of U.S. radicalism. In Du Bois's writings during the 1920s, whiteness comes to signify class as much as race. This is an important and significant change in radical thought, as Du Bois begins to articulate his own understanding of what was at stake in the debates over what was called "the national question" by members of the Third International and of the Communist movement of the early part of the twentieth century, such as V. I. Lenin, M. N. Roy, M. Sultan Galiev, and others.

In his fictional work *Dark Princess,* Du Bois enters this debate through dialogue among characters who are in the process of forming an organization called the Darker Peoples of the World. While Bill Mullen argues that this organization derives its name from the International League of the Darker People, formed by A. Philip Randolph, Marcus Garvey, C. J. Walker, and Japanese representatives, it seems to reflect Du Bois's attempt to explore the idea of a pan-African and pan-Asian joint solidarity, thus connecting the world's darker people into a single world-shaping force. In contrast to much of the work around the "national question" at that time and since, Du Bois takes an approach that resists the temptation to reify groups.

With regard to the debates about the "national question" animating the world Left during the 1920s, Du Bois agrees that African Americans constitute a "nation within a nation" but transcends that position by arguing that it merges with all the oppressed nations that together comprise the Land of the Blacks, which he also refers to as the Dark World (1999, 25). Muhammad Ahmad, a protégé of Malcolm X and founder of the Revolutionary Action Movement (RAM) during the early 1960s, articulates a similar concept that he refers to as the worldwide Black Underclass (1986).

It is important that we summarize our sense of what happened during the massive upheaval and transition in the United States during the 1930s and 1940s. The encounter with European fascism marked a critical transition in U.S. society and culture based on the confrontation of this nation in the process of becoming, of taking its place on the world stage with international(ist) roots in the cacophony of memories that merged into a new social and political entity—not so much exceptional but a historical entity that is defined by its timing and configuration. Jennifer E. Langdon points out that the "growing threat of fascism—at home as well as abroad—powerfully reinforced the 1930s elaboration of an American Way of Life and of an imagined community grounded in ethnic tolerance, national unity, and democratic traditions" (2009, ch. 2, 1). Hollywood films played a key role in articulating this antifascist popular nationalism, beginning in the late 1930s with a cycle of films that raise the cry of alarm to the American people about the dangers of fascism and usher in a new era of "political" filmmaking.

The 1930s and 1940s witnessed a dramatic growth in the social power of the lower U.S. strata, though unevenly across racial and ethnic lines. But despite

such unevenness, movement leaders (including some important representatives of the New Negro Movement) were able to build a multiracial Left that,
for the United States, was remarkable in its breadth and inclusiveness. The internationalist credentials of this U.S. Left were also remarkable, with connections in Eastern Europe, central Asia, eastern Asia, southern Asia, Africa, the
Middle East, the Caribbean, and Latin America. Unlike the sixties movement,
which was viewed as centered on an age cohort, the popular Left was so broadly
representative that it might be viewed as a hegemonic force within the nation,
what Henry Wallace would conceptualize as representing the emergence of the
People's Century, or the Century of the Common Man.

The more youthful and countercultural movements of the 1960s and 1970s,
which included a substantial segment of what came to be considered "a third
world within," formed a much more counterhegemonic force and were thus considered to be revolutionary rather than merely the acts of a dominant progressive
segment of the larger body politic. Though the Popular Front was strongly antiracist, it articulated a progressive nationalism in which racialized groups were
viewed as a welcome part of "The House We Live In" in the film *Race: The Power
of an Illusion*, produced by California Newsreel and broadcast by the Public
Broadcasting Service. At the end of World War II, as the struggle for the future
of the United States attained its full unfolding, the advocates for the American
Century unleashed their power on the left-of-center coalition created by the
Popular Front. With the end of the war and the transformation of the alliance
with the Soviet Union to a (measured) conflict with the Soviet Union, there was
no longer a need for a Popular Front.

The hegemonic strategy of the American Century required instead the destruction of the Left, with its strong connections to international communism
and the radical nationalist movements that became the prototypes of the national liberation movements that would arise in the postwar period. The forties was a
period of a struggle for the soul of the United States. From the perspective of the
Popular Front Left movement itself, it was broader, because the tensions between
the European immigrant Left and the racialized strata were not as polarized as
they would become during the 1960s and 1970s; the social distance between
the racialized social strata and the European immigrants was less extreme, because the pan-European social strata had not yet been fully incorporated into
the mainstream, and thus some of them were not fully considered to be white
people. So, though the racialized social strata were less numerous, they were not
yet considered a "third world within," though there had been substantial discussion about a Negro Nation within the Black Belt South due to what was viewed
as the fascistic character of the Jim Crow South.

The "nation of nations" vision reflected in the Left of the 1930s and 1940s,
and even in the later vision of President Johnson, was distinct from the nationalism of empire ideology that surged to the forefront during the 1940s' transformation of U.S. nationalism as the United States entered its postwar period of
global hegemony. While the emergence of cold-war liberalism departed sharply

from the Popular Front Liberalism that had partnered with New Deal liberalism, the rise of the Bandung Movement in the 1950s[3] and the subsequent unruliness of the third world destabilized the mature global liberalism that the United States sought to project in the midst of the rebellion against the old colonial powers of Europe. The global 1960s intensified the challenge to pan-European dominance and internationalized the struggle for social change, and the center of gravity of this developing movement became firmly located within a rising anticolonial construct that came to be known as the Bandung world, with strong support from the second world and from the "third world within" the pan-European world. In the United States, explicit manifestations of the rising arc of the Bandung world included the Student Nonviolent Coordinating Committee (SNCC); the Revolutionary Action Movement (RAM); the Organization for Afro-American Unity (OAAU); the Black Panther Party; the Crusade for Justice; CASA: Centro de Accion Social Autonomo, Comite Nacional Hermandad de Trabajadores; La Raza Unida; Katipunan ng mga Demokratikong Pilipino (KDP; Union of Democratic Filipinos); the Young Lord's Party; the American Indian Movement; SNCC's Greenwood Movement; the Patrice Lumumba Coalition; and the Nation of Islam. But it also included the older civil rights organizations, such as the Southern Christian Leadership Conference (SCLC) under King's leadership, the National Association for the Advancement of Colored People (NAACP), and the Congress of Racial Equality (CORE).

This examination was framed in an understanding of this particular world historical moment and looks at both the desperate acts of an "imperial nation" and the righteous demands for the "liberation of nations." Key to our argument is that this is not simply a moment in time but part and parcel of a long-term process within the social world that is based in the rise and decline of the modern/colonial/capitalist/Euro-centered world-system. We have explained at great length how race was used as a means of naturalizing the relationship between the conquerors and the conquered within this world-system and as a means of allocating people to social positions within this world-system. It was not class or gender that was new in this world-system but race.

From the point of view of the struggles of oppressed strata within this world-system, one of the most important imperatives is the need to break down the divisions and establish a sense of solidarity between the dominated groups, which are numerous, not singular. An issue crucially important to the continuing evolution of the social existence of oppressed strata is the issue of immigrants' rights, which is central to breaking the barriers to solidarity among workers. Within a context that accepts the reality of competition between workers as a fact of the natural order of things, one may argue that restriction benefits the members of the domestic work force at the lowest levels. However, capitalists seek to reduce their costs by employing workers at the lowest wage and with the fewest protections to the extent that they are able to do that.

It is instructive to review debates in the pages of *New Politics* and *New Labor Forum* around Stephen Steinberg's article "Immigration, African Americans, and Race Discourse." Steinberg issues a challenge on immigration, insisting on a consistent standard of social justice as few on the Left have been willing to do. At the end of the Civil War, he argues, four million emancipated slaves were, in theory, free to meet the great demand for labor in the North and the West. Why did they not have a fair opportunity to obtain those jobs? He is not the first to point out the dubious practice of social scientists in the United States, who thought this contradiction a great mystery.

For Steinberg, the answer to the mystery is simple: the immigration of some twenty-five million Europeans to the United States between 1880 and 1924. When immigration was cut off by World War I, it triggered a massive migration of Blacks to cities in the North and the West, resulting in the most significant economic advance for Blacks since the abolition of slavery. He then quotes an editorial in a 1916 issue of *The New Republic*: "The average Pole or Italian arriving at Ellis Island does not realize that he is the deadly foe of the native Negro. . . . It is a silent conflict on a gigantic scale."

He asks whether history is being repeated with the influx of twenty-five million legal immigrants since 1965, which have made African Americans superfluous at the very moment of their victory over Jim Crow racism and segregation. Here, he argues, is another missed opportunity to integrate Blacks into the economic mainstream. Instead of dealing with this long-standing promissory note, immigrant virtues are extolled, and invidious comparisons are made to Blacks, who are portrayed as culturally deficient and lacking the pluck that has allowed immigrants to pursue opportunity. And, too, immigrants are friendly and deferential, unlike unruly, abrasive Blacks, whose attitudes antagonize whites.

Steinberg methodically takes on a number of immigration scholars whose work he argues systematically defines racism out of existence and posits the defective culture of Blacks as the reason for their continued exclusion. Blacks are said to have adopted an adversarial culture, lack social capital, are obsessed with race and racism, and have problems of self-presentation.

Steinberg paints a stark figure and argues in the final analysis that an optimistic projection is that new immigrants may provide renewed inspiration and leadership in the ongoing struggle to erase the vestiges of slavery. But the weight of history is more ominous. One way in which immigrants avoid pariah status is to dissociate themselves from African Americans and their plight. "Tragically and ironically," Steinberg points out, "it is one way that immigrants 'become American.'"

Integration, Immigration, and Democracy

Integration as a philosophy is unique to the United States because it is the only country which has been built on the systematic assimilation of successive waves of immigrants into the American—i.e., the capitalist—system. Each of these waves of immigrants were assimilated into the American system by climbing on the backs of others, first and always on the backs of

Negroes, and then on the backs of other immigrants until each reached a status more or less equal to that of the Founding Fathers. The word "integration" was not used to describe this systematic process until the Negroes (who had come here at the same time as the Founding Fathers) began to demand assimilation on the same basis as the immigrant. It was only then that the concept of assimilation began to appear revolutionary, rather than a natural part of the system. (Boggs 1970, 33–34)

Here Boggs elaborates on an analysis that distinguishes between integration/assimilation and revolution that is quite characteristic of his work in the 1970s and 1980s. We know that Steinberg acknowledges awareness of Boggs's *Racism and the Class Struggle* in his 1995 book, *Turning Back: The Retreat from Racial Justice in American Thought and Policy,* so we will also assume that he would welcome the following discussion as being in the spirit of his own courageous insistence on a standard of social justice.

Boggs's point is that full equality for the U.S. African American people cannot be achieved by integration/assimilation, for given the centrality of African American oppression to U.S. nationalism, the struggle for full equality is not a question of assimilation into the existing system, which by definition marginalizes its racialized social strata. The fight for racial equality is thus a question of social revolution within the United States, based on solidarity with the righteous struggle of the African American people and other racialized populations.

During the heyday of the Black Power movement, according to Boggs, any serious Marxist had to advance the classical Marxist revolutionary framework from the nineteenth century to address historical situations of the twentieth century, where the underdeveloped (or superexploited) nations of the world, "which are in fact a world underclass, confront the highly developed capitalist countries in which the working classes for the most part have been incorporated or integrated into pillars of support for the capitalist system. Their integration into the system was to a large degree at the expense of the world underclass" (1970, 52–53), including the internally colonized Black population.

Regarding the Black Power movement of the 1970s, Boggs is critical of the confusion within the ranks of the Old Left radicals, who viewed the Black Power movement as a deadly enemy of their own strategy of "Black and White, unite and fight." Boggs holds that the "unite and fight" strategy is in error, since it assumes that Blacks and whites "had common issues and grievances, systematically evading the fact that every immigrant who walked off the gangplank into this country did so on the backs of the indigenous blacks and had the opportunity to advance precisely because the indigenous blacks were being systematically deprived of the opportunity to advance by both capitalists and workers" (1970, 54).

Boggs, however, is a keen observer of the time on the clock of the world and in his city, Detroit. Though the indigenous Native American and Latino populations have always constituted an important historical presence in the country, the immigration of peoples from Asian, Latin American, and Arab countries has

dramatically increased the multicultural diversity of the country, and a significant segment of the Black intermediate strata has assimilated into the existing
U.S. social system. Boggs argues that Blacks should not only work with greater
urgency to be revolutionary leaders but also create a common cause with their
racialized sisters and brothers and with whites to foster a revolution to transform
American society and its impact on the rest of the world.

At the same time, James and Grace Lee Boggs begin to question the basic assumptions of a revolutionary movement. The Black Power movement had been
really militant and revolutionary, but was it failing simply because many whites
did not accept their responsibility for fighting to rid society of the scourge of racism, as James Boggs had argued during the heyday of the Black Power movement?
If the working-class majority could not organize themselves to overcome the
domination of a relative handful of capitalists, maybe there was a deeper problem.

Boggs and Boggs argue that revolution is more than simply a struggle to take
power, to claim rights, or to improve material conditions. How could all these
objectives be said to be "revolutionary" in the context of people in the United
States, who live in a region that monopolizes access to the entire world's resources and whose geopolitical objectives are aimed at the active defense of that
monopoly? It is more than a struggle to correct past injustices; "it [is] a struggle
toward the conscious creation of a new expanded human identity" (Ward 2011,
2)—thus their emphasis on revolution and evolution. As revolutionists, the
Boggses accept responsibility for grappling with the fundamental social and
political challenges of one's society, "projecting a philosophy of change, and
developing a method or form of struggle based on the new ideology, and organizing to change society along the lines of the new ideology" (Ward 2011, 1).

The 1980s had been a period of counterrevolution in the United States and in
Europe as the neoliberal juggernaut of Reagan and Thatcher gained such traction
that many of the Left began to tailor their own projects to Thatcher's strident
war cry that "There Is No Alternative" (nicknamed TINA by some). Boggs and
Boggs then created an organization called the New Organization for an American Revolution. The strength of the counterrevolution caused many of the Left
to see the possibility of transformative politics, and many leftist organizations
disbanded, as some began to talk of a "crisis of Marxism."

We have traced the eventual rebound of the world's lower strata, spurred
by the rebellion in Chiapas, the rise of the antiglobalization movement or the
movement for global democracy, and the formation of the Social Forum movement in 2001 in Porto Alegre, Brazil. During the 1990s, some began to talk about
demographic changes within the United States as people of color became an
increasingly larger proportion of the country's population. Surprisingly for us,
there was not a great deal of discussion about the political implications of such
demographic changes among journalists and politicians.

While increased attention has been given to the demographic changes taking place within U.S. borders and their impact on the political fortunes of conservatives in the Republican Party, much less attention has been given to how

this demographic shift is inextricably intertwined with the ways in which the U.S. economic elite has imposed a global neoliberal social order that has spread the inherently socially polarizing logic of the capitalist system to every corner of the earth, what Terence K. Hopkins calls the broadening and deepening of the capital accumulation process. One hears with increasing force Karl Marx and Friedrich Engels's admonition that what capitalism creates most of all is its own gravediggers, because it cannot ensure the survival of its slave within its slavery.

One can hardly take exception to the standard of social justice demanded by Steinberg on this issue. But how can we seek to understand the issue of labor migration apart from the larger global division of labor imposed by economic elites, leaving the working classes of the peripheralized areas of the world economy at a disadvantage because these areas are by definition locations of low-profit, low-technology, and low-wage production processes? This means that the economic transformation of these areas by foreign capital displaces local labor, forcing them to migrate to areas where jobs are available precisely because of the displacement of living-wage jobs by low-wage jobs that U.S. workers believe to be unacceptable.

Indeed, Raul Delgado Wise (2013) argues that neoliberal globalization has entailed a massive assault on the labor and living conditions of the majority of the global working class, a major dimension of which is the strategy of creating cheap labor so that business can take advantage of its massive global oversupply. According to Delgado Wise, the implementation of structural adjustment programs in the Global South has dramatically increased the size of the labor supply available to capital, from 1.5 billion to 3.3 billion over the last two decades. This increase has led to the disproportionate growth of a global reserve army of labor, which absorbs between 57 and 63 percent of the global labor force. According to the International Labor Organization, the number of workers in conditions of labor insecurity rose to 1.53 billion in 2009, encompassing more than half the world's workforces, with 630 million receiving a salary of less than $1.25 per day. At the same time, the number of global unemployed rose to 205 million (Delgado Wise 2013, 28).

Historically scholars, intellectuals, and activists in the core states have viewed this process as one of integration/incorporation, as James Boggs argues in his writings during the late 1960s and early 1970s. Thus, regarding the unprecedented demonstration in favor of a just immigration policy on May 1, 2006, Ramon Grosfoguel and Nelson Maldonado-Torres declare that the United States fully entered the twenty-first century. In this remarkable article, Grosfoguel and Maldonado-Torres locate themselves on the trajectory that Du Bois describes in his speech at the closing session at the July 1900 meeting of the Pan African Conference. In his speech, entitled "To the Nations of the World," Du Bois declares that "the problem of twentieth century is the problem of the color line" (Lewis 1993, 251):

In the metropolis of the modern world, in the closing year of the nineteenth century, there has been assembled a congress of men and women of African blood, to deliberate solemnly upon the present situation and outlook of the darker races of mankind. The problem of the twentieth century is the problem of the color line, the question of how far differences of race, which show themselves chiefly in the colour of the skin and the texture of the hair, are going to be made hereafter, the basis for denying to over half the world the right of sharing to their utmost ability the opportunities and privileges of modern civilization. (Lewis 1995, 639)

Regarding the more self-conscious entry of the United States into the twenty-first century on this May Day march, Grosfoguel and Maldonado-Torres take pains to show that the issue of the migration of millions of Latinos into the United States is not a problem different from racism but intimately connected with it. The fear of the impending demographic shift has given rise to what they see as a neo-apartheid movement among some segments of the white population, especially those in border states. Though apartheid has been the reality faced by most racial minorities in the United States, the formal acknowledgment of equal rights codified in the Civil Rights Act of 1964 legitimized the claim that the United States is a democratic nation. With regard to Latino immigrants, Grosfoguel and Maldonado-Torres argue that many would support the reforms of the white neo-apartheid camp in order to have legal residence in the United States. These groups see other "minority groups" as rivals and sometimes reproduce racist discourse toward *themselves* and toward other groups. Clearly this applies to other groups as well, not only to some Latinos (2006, 16).

Grosfoguel and Maldonado-Torres argue that there is another position, which they characterize as a reformist de-colonial position that would support the rights of the undocumented and argue for equal rights for all people of color but also support the globally dominant position of U.S. imperialism (2006, 16).

A third position held by the social strata who have migrated to the United States from Central America, South America, and the Caribbean is what Grosfoguel and Maldonado-Torres deem a radical decolonialist position. This last group links the struggles of the undocumented immigrants to a decolonial antiracist struggle against white supremacy and the imperial state (2006, 16).

If we are to move toward a standard of social justice that Steinberg calls for, it must be based on a long-term strategy for a "borderless world, for a solidarity among people of color within the U.S.A. and link their demands to anti-imperialist positions against the U.S. Imperial role in Iraq and Latin America" (Grosfoguel and Maldonado-Torres 2006, 16). Grosfoguel (2008) argues further that this position requires that Latinos decolonize their own cultures and epistemologies and affirm their African, Indigenous, Arab, and Asiatic traditions to be able to serve as a decolonial bridge inside the United States toward the radical decolonization of the U.S. empire.

Similarly, but with a closer focus on Afro-descendant populations, Agustin Lao-Montes calls for closer attention to a transnational racial politics of Black self-affirmation and liberation, which he traces to antisystemic slave revolts of the eighteenth century (most notably, the Haitian Revolution) and the Black abolitionists during the nineteenth century and to the rise of a new wave of antisystemic movements in the 1960s (2007, 311). Lao-Montes seeks to utilize an Afro-diasporic perspective to allow us to rethink self, memory, culture, and power beyond the confines of the nation as a unit of analysis (and as the domi-nant form of political community). He seeks as well to develop a politics of decolonization not confined to nationalism (313).

Lao-Montes also views the African diaspora as a Black Borderlands, fol-lowing Claudia M. Milian Arias's attempt to reconceptualize Gloria Anzaldua's "borderlands" (1987) and Du Bois's "double consciousness" (1903) as a way to construct links between Black studies and Latino studies based on a relational theory of race. Here, Lao-Montes consciously brings into focus intertwined dia-sporas, the plurality of histories, and the world's historical entanglement of mul-tiple genealogies of diasporic formation (African, southern Asian, and eastern Asian, composing a Caribbean diaspora).

Lao-Montes argues persuasively that Afro-Latinidades are an important source of the decolonization of power and knowledge and that Black cosmo-politanism has been an important source of decolonial knowledge and politics since its inception. It is here that critical traditions of Black and Latino studies converge. Both areas of knowledge are based in a radical decolonial politics of liberation that are anti-imperialist and often anticapitalist as well. The everyday resistances, social struggles, and antisystemic movements from this long-term process of decolonization at the center of the capitalist/colonial world-system will be one foundation of the construction of an alternative future.

The alternative to the radical decolonial perspective offered by Lao-Montes, Grosfoguel, Santiago-Valles, Maldonado-Torres, and others is a conservative or centrist liberal vision that UCLA political scientist Albert Ponce suggests is to brandish the judicial category of illegality as a weapon to discipline the social strata involved in migration (2013). Ponce argues that the judicial category of illegality and the threat of deportability are used as mechanisms to discipline migrant labor and, we would argue, to deter them from associating with the long-time occupants of the lower rungs of U.S. society, who have adopted a cul-ture of resistance that actively defies those who would demonize them in the public discourse. Though the racialized identity imposed by illegality allows for the "legal" codification of "inferiority" and the maintenance of coloniality, as Ponce argues, it also maintains "borderlands."

These borderlands are enmeshed within the coloniality of power. Kelvin Santiago-Valles is critical of the inclination of many scholars and activists to accept the conventional definition of colonialism as "the formal, direct, and political rule of overseas territories by European countries" (2003b, 217). Santi-ago-Valles's rethinking of colonialism, race, African diaspora, and nationality has led him to conclude at least preliminarily, as he emphasizes, that race, mo-dernity, and capitalism together with chattel slavery and its legacy are all bound as coloniality.

According to Santiago-Valles, races are organized around unevenly structured populations or nationalities rather than necessarily being organized on
the basis of juridico political territories. This form of social order means for
Santiago-Valles that "race, modernity, and capitalism, as well as chattel slavery
and its legacy are historically and conceptually bound together as coloniality.
This includes both formal colonialism and neo-colonialism as well as the Oc-
cidentalist culture of both" (2003b, 218). This ensemble of structures has undergirded the modern/colonial/capitalist world-system.

Santiago-Valles avoids the pitfalls of most who view colonialism solely in
territorial terms by insisting that modern colonialism and colonial modernity
are synonymous with the creation and perpetuation of races. Against the outcry
of defenders of the well-intentioned nature of the pan-European social project,
he argues that this is not a consequence of the ill intentions of the residents of
the pan-European world but that the very existence of races "corresponds to
concrete socio-historical processes which are objectively organized around the
regulation, exploitation, and domination of specific populations." In the event
one misses the implication here, Santiago-Valles continues, "In other words,
they exist to extract surplus labor, as well as to control their—or rather *our*—access to social resources and physical spaces" (2003b, 220, citing Quijano 1998).

For Santiago-Valles, races are structured around and embodied by unevenly
constructed *populations* or *nationalities* rather than being organized on the basis
of juridico political *territories* (2003b, 220). His point here is that "the social
spaces that encompass these populations do not have to be structured" along the
lines of *their own* nation-state, its legal boundaries, and its citizenship categories
(2003b, 221, citing Shapiro 1997, 1–40).

Santiago-Valles takes pains to emphasize that he is not talking about stereotypes or labels that are attached to previously existing people *who are born* (not
made). His focus is precisely on the production of social subjects, who become
individuals only insofar as they are *racially fabricated* as dominant or subordinate within the context of what he refers to as colonial modernity. However,
as Ron Hayduk indicates in response to Steinberg, immigrants will grow in
number and disperse throughout the United States, so "it is not a question about
whether the millions of immigrants in the United States will be incorporated,
but how they will be incorporated" (Hayduk 2006). Wallerstein argues that despite the controversy over immigrants everywhere, they are indeed integral parts
of the workings of the *capitalist* (our emphasis) world economy. They are willing
to take jobs that are necessary to the economy; they contribute to pension funds
for the over-65 demographic group that is growing in the rich countries, which
must increase immigration in order to sustain a working-age population that
contributes adequate funds to the pension funds. They maintain the worldwide
system of differential labor costs on which the stability of capital rests.

We must be careful to remember where we are on the world's clock. We cannot freeze ourselves on the clock of the twentieth century and view the issue of
social justice as centered on the racialization of U.S. social strata. Though this

is an important historical legacy deeply embedded in the social relations of the force of historical capitalism, it is a manifestation of the inherent logic of the social system, which is a socially polarizing logic. We agree with Wallerstein's contention that we live today in an age of transition and that capitalism has entered its moment of structural crisis. Steinberg insists on a standard of social justice that is consistent with the logic of a transition toward a more democratic and egalitarian society rather than contributes to the emergence of a historical system that rests on the continued exclusion of those who speak truth to power and stand up for justice.

This debate reveals that we need to think more seriously about the issue of timing, for we are entering a crucial time in the trajectory of historical capitalism. Although Wallerstein has been critical of the inability of socialist states to change the world, as they had envisioned in their two-stage strategies (first seize state power, then change the world), he has in recent years cautioned us to pay closer attention to what Grace Lee Boggs refers to as "the clock of the world." In discussing the movement to the Left in Latin America, Wallerstein points out that although leftist intellectuals and some leftist movements are unhappy with what is not being done in Latin American countries where Left or Left-leaning governments have come to power, the United States is more unhappy with what they *have* done. What this demonstrates for Wallerstein is that the United States no longer has control (economic, political, or diplomatic) of its own backyard. This is an ominous sign. Wallerstein compares this process to an old Chinese torture called *Ling chi*, or death by a thousand cuts.

Regarding the labor movement, Steinberg's optimistic scenario may indeed develop. Although capitalists simply want less expensive and more pliable labor, historically, newly incorporated labor inevitably assumes the standards and stances of more established labor forces. But at this time in history, as the scale of immigration to the core zones is anticipated to increase dramatically, an immigrants' rights movement can dramatically accelerate the pace of change and thus strike at the Achilles heel of capital: working-class solidarity on a world or even regional scale.

We can scarcely believe the tone deafness of members of the U.S. Republican Right who thought that their social conservatism would appeal to the Latino electorate over and above what some refer to as human needs. When the 2008 presidential election returns from the Southwest in favor of Obama rendered the decision on this issue, we were surprised that the U.S. punditry did not make more of what seemed to be the obvious verdict on this question.

The "Open Letter to Our African American Sisters and Brothers" in the *Black Scholar* from Martinez and a long list of important Latino intellectuals and activists (Martinez 2006) is encouraging. If oppressed strata can think through a program for ironing out the dilemmas of immigration among themselves, it will constitute a giant step forward in undermining the false universalism of the dominant strata and the framework for a true recognition of multiple universalisms and multiple we's.

As argued above, scientific culture within the modern world-system has functioned as a form of socialization of the cadres of the world division of labor. It served to unite the world intermediate strata as a cohesive subaltern class in the service of global capitalism. It created a framework within which it was possible for individual mobility to thrive without threatening the very real hierarchal workforce allocation. Despite appearances, Wallerstein argues that meritocracy reinforced hierarchy instead of tempering it, as is the common perception. The emphasis on the rationality of scientific activity shaded from public view and, most of all, public understanding of the irrationality of the endless accumulation of capital hidden allow this structure to be reproduced. This is based on the particularity of scientific culture in the Euro-centered world-system, which is distinguished by the separation of the true from the good and the beautiful (which was viewed as the province of the humanities). Those cadre from the peripheral zones and internally colonized populations tended to be ambivalent toward this ideology of universalism, alternatively viewing it as a tool of true liberation and empowerment of their populations, as a means of personal mobility for themselves within the world-system, and as a trap set by the elites of the world-system to trap them as a subordinate group within the world-system with no means of seeing the truth, since they have been lured into the den of the world intermediate strata whose access to a so-called universal science was empowering to themselves and for those whom they served. Marx employs a similar tactic (with the same dangers) in distinguishing his views from those of other nineteenth-century socialists by using the designation "scientific socialism." In this way, Wallerstein argues that "anti-systemic movements have often served as intermediaries of the powerful to the weak, vitiating rather than crystallizing their deep-rooted sources of resistance" (1995, 88).

However, beginning in the twentieth century, and with increasing power since the 1960s, the theme of civilizational assertion and cultural resistance has been increasingly important in the theorizing of the antisystemic movements and its intellectuals. Wallerstein argues that the basis of this shift in ideology among the antisystemic movements is the increase in recruitment of strata more economically and politically marginal to the functioning of the system: "Compared with the profile of the membership of the world's anti-systemic movements from 1850 to 1950, their profile from 1950 onwards contained more from peripheral zones, more women, more from 'minority' groups (however defined), and more of the work-force toward the unskilled, lowest-paid end of the scale" (1995, 90).

There is thus a cultural crisis wherein the antisystemic movements are questioning the premises of universalist ideology, such that the movements are taking seriously the search for civilizational alternatives. Furthermore, the whole intellectual apparatus that came into being during the fourteenth century is being slowly placed into question (Wallerstein 1995, 92), and the pace of this questioning is accelerating as we speak. Though we entered a period following the Reagan counterrevolution when the power of oppressed strata seemed to be reversed, it is important that we review this period very carefully.

9

Racial Nationalism and the Multiple Crises
of the U.S. Nation

In 2008, the people of the United States and the world were transfixed as the unexpected trajectory of Barack Hussein Obama led to the attainment of the U.S. presidency by a Black man. Though his mixed-race background somewhat complicated the issue, few born before 1980 thought they would see the election of a person commonly viewed as Black as president of the United States in their lifetimes. What made this event most remarkable is that it seemingly reversed the rising arc of backlash against racial, gender, and social equality that the U.S. public associates with reaction to the civil rights movement (especially its more radical formulations), the women's movement (especially feminists), the labor movement, the grassroots Left, and opposition to the U.S. wars against third-world nations, such as Vietnam. Some scholars and social-justice activists seek to understand the Obama phenomenon within the context of thirty years of a neoliberal onslaught against the gains of lower social strata and sixty years of a cultural counterrevolution against the common good, seeking instead the valorization of the survival of the fittest.

Though neoliberalism seemed a clear political move to undermine the power of the middle and lower social strata within the core states, we were surprised that so many were willing to accept these moves as the expression of a natural economic logic due to what they were now calling "globalization," deemed as a new element in the economic realm that required those of us in the "overdeveloped" world to tighten our belts so that we could compete with lower-cost labor in other parts of the world. Since the struggles of labor, racial and ethnic minorities, and women within the United States and in other cores states upset this natural order, pundits held that the economy naturally adjusted.

We wondered what people thought had happened to the white backlash—

were we out of order for asking such a question? We thought that the Obama phenomenon brilliantly addressed the most pressing problem of our civil society: what to do about the smoldering racial antagonisms borne by racialized lower strata of Blacks, Latinos, and Native Americans and prosecuted by a significant segment of the white population who resented the concessions to those populations that cut into their share of the nation's wealth. William Julius Wilson has duly noted this phenomenon in a way that deemphasizes white culpability in the maintenance of the racial order and calls for a strategy of downplaying race and emphasizing issues that could unite racial minorities with more advantaged populations within the polity with which they shared common interests.

The problem with such a strategy is that opposition to racism was not a common interest between the racially oppressed and those who benefitted from racial privilege. Political realism of the dominant social strata simply did not allow us to address such a question within the context of a national polity able to isolate and insulate itself from the wider world. This, of course, is the province of the very powerful. However, even a hegemonic power cannot isolate itself or insulate itself from outside forces that impinge on it, which was clearly the case during the cold war years, when the United States competed for world imminence against a coalition of powerful states that put themselves forward as the agents of the powerless against the powers of the capitalist world.

However, the pan-European world did not really understand the decolonial work done within the Dark World within its borders and those in its peripheries. This intellectual and epistemological work had an enormous impact on these populations and among whites who made common cause with them and who were thus their comrades.

The Wilson strategy soft-pedals the issue of racism while focusing on common "class" interests. This tactic would not sell on the Black street, but it worked among a significant sector of the white electorate. This success then alerted the Black street to a window of opportunity to work toward coalition, for there was much to lose and gain given that we were entering a historical period of crisis. If the intellectuals did not understand what time it was on the clock of the world, many ordinary people grasped it intuitively. Obama carried out this strategy with great skill.

So though we have to admit that this turn of events did indeed seem unlikely, given the centrality of the institutionalization of the white anti-sixties backlash to the conservative turn, we could not forget the sense of the power of the people that we had felt during the heyday of the revolutionary period. We knew in our hearts that it was not over, that we were living through an interlude in which the powers that be would attempt to reassert their authority. But who could believe such obvious bluster after having lived through the disintegration of hegemonic power from 1965 to 1980? We did not think the Reagan-Thatcher neoliberalism bluff was sustainable and were surprised that so many accepted it as the natural adjustment of the economy to the laws of economic reasoning.

Our skepticism about the triumphalism of the Right and the hegemonic pretensions of the nationalism of empire after 1980 derived from all that we had learned during the 1960s and 1970s, an upsurge that had imbued within us a sense of the power of the people and of possibility that was palpable and seemed indestructible in the long run. Quincy Jones's hymn to the *longue durée* played in our souls in an endless loop.[1] We had absorbed the spirit and wisdom of people at the grassroots level, and we knew that over the long term, this spirit could not be destroyed. We had both grown spiritually as young people in the tutelage of our families and not from any idea about the so-called American Dream. The idea of being our sister's and brother's keeper was the foundation of our value system and gave us a sense of the power of the people that could not be destroyed "for many rains to come" (Jones 1971).

Throughout the Reagan-Bush counterrevolution, we refused to adjust to the "new realities" as some on the Left did. We held firm to what had been so vividly taught and illustrated by Malcolm X—that the geopolitical shift generated by the national liberation movements throughout the Bandung era and the global sixties demonstrated the inability of the white world to impose its will on the Dark World and that we were witnessing a period that historians would later view as the end of white world supremacy. During this same period, Mao Zedong, no doubt remembering his discussions with W.E.B. Du Bois a few years before, formulated his statement indicating the support of the Chinese people for Black liberation in the United States. Mao expressed confidence that the Afro-American people would prevail in their just struggle, concluding, "The evil system of colonialism and imperialism arose and throve with the enslavement of Negroes and the trade in Negroes, and it will surely come to its end with the complete emancipation of the black people" (1964, 4).

Similarly, Malcolm X had articulated the depths of the contradiction of that period when the United States stood poised at the pinnacle of its might and prestige but faced a world in rebellion against white Western hegemony. While the United States attempted to woo the nations of the Dark World as a true friend who itself had fought a war of national liberation against Europeans, in truth it was now in a position of being the police of the historical system dominated by Western capitalism. So while the United States may have been basking in the public relations glow of Martin Luther King Jr.'s testament to the American Dream, it was Malcolm X who had his finger on the pulse of the rebellion of the third world against white Western hegemony and on the pulse of many in the inner cities across the nation.

Melanie Bush (2004 and 2011) argues that racism is so deeply encrusted in the social structures, the superegos, and the institutional and ideological structures of the pan-European world that many racialized practices pass under the radar of the nonracialized populations. They are simply normal, and there is no need to take account of these practices. That is why it is not so readily apparent to the white public that liberal reformism, though frequently well-intended, is simply not adequate in coming to grips with the racialized social structure and ideological system that are so often the elephants in the middle of the room.

While the rearticulation of racial discourse may alter the expression of this pillar of our historical system, it remains as firmly entrenched as ever. However, it is nonetheless true that the twentieth century witnessed the dramatic rise of the Dark World, but not "the end of white world supremacy" that Malcolm X hailed in 1963 (Malcolm X 1971). While Rod Bush (1999) has argued that Malcolm's judgment was premature, he has also argued that it was a sign of the times that we must continue to take seriously, because what Malcolm's observation reflects is the spirit of Bandung, so salient to the times in which he spoke:

> The time is past when the white world can exercise unilateral authority and control over the dark world. The independence and power of the dark world is on the increase; the dark world is rising in wealth, power, prestige, and influence. It is the rise of the dark world that is causing the fall of the white world. As the white man loses his power to oppress and exploit the dark world, the white man's own wealth (power or "world") decreases.... You and I were born at this turning point in history; we are witnessing the fulfillment of prophecy. Our present generation is witnessing the end of colonialism, Europeanism, Westernism, or "White-ism" . . . the end of white supremacy, the end of the evil white man's unjust rule. (1971, 130)

The period during which Malcolm X spoke was the era of decolonization in Africa, a time when the spirit of Bandung was the framework for what Malcolm refers to as a worldwide revolution. For those who accepted the authority of the white world as a given, these were troubled times. Unlike a time when nothing could happen without the approval of the United States, the Soviet Union, or France, the people and nations of the Dark World came together at the Bandung Conference in Indonesia in 1955 and agreed to submerge their differences and present a united front against the common enemy, the colonizing authorities of the European world. It was in the context of this unity of the African-Asian-Arab bloc, Malcolm argues, that African nations were able to obtain independence and join the United Nations. Now the members of the Dark World had a voice, a vote, in the United Nations and were soon able to outvote the white man, who had formerly been their colonial authority. By being able to outvote the colonial powers, they were able to force the people of Europe to "turn loose the Black man in Tanganyika, the Black man in the Congo, and the Black man in what we know today as the former French West African territories" (Malcolm X 1971, 97). While Malcolm is certainly not deceived by the alleged power of the United Nations, he views it as a forum in which international debates and discussions about issues of world power and justice could be aired. For Malcolm, the new arithmetic of the United Nations is an opportunity to exert pressure for more democracy on the hegemonic powers of the white world, which had long exercised unilateral and dictatorial powers over the peoples and nations of the Dark World. The new arithmetic of the United Nations is the handwriting on the wall, and Malcolm X is a master at showcasing this handwriting so that it is plain for all to see. Malcolm will not allow the world to miss the significance of British Prime Minister Harold McMillan's remarks and those of others "crying the blues" because of the passing of the famed British Empire, on which the sun had finally set. Like no one else, Malcolm is able to provide a narrative that explains in the clearest terms the implications of the French defeat in Indochina and the impact of the loss of its colonial possessions there on its economy and, consequently, on its inability to maintain an army sufficient to control its large West African colonies, leading ultimately to the collapse of French colonial power in Algeria under the weight of another fierce war of national liberation. Malcolm turns the spotlight on The Netherlands' loss of Indonesia and the Belgian loss of the Congo. Malcolm taunts the former colonial powers, chiding them to read "The Handwriting on the Wall."

Belgium, he argues, had been a power on this earth as long as it controlled the mineral wealth of the Belgian Congo. However, once it lost control of its central African colony, the economy was so traumatized that the Belgian government collapsed. Malcolm calls out to the Black, Brown, Yellow, and Red victims of Euro–North American hegemony and the residents of the pan-European world themselves to read the handwriting on the wall. He calls on them all to recognize the fundamental fact of that historical moment, in which the rise of the Dark World is the occasion for the decrease in power of the white world over the Dark World. His recognition of this change in the constellation of world power gives Malcolm X remarkable insight and leads him to make the correct call following John F. Kennedy's assassination—that this was a case of the chickens coming home to roost. If King's August 1963 speech represents the most articulate statement of the American Dream and the height of the mature global liberalism that was the signpost of the American Century, then Malcolm most clearly understands and articulates the other side—or the underside—of this phenomenon. Malcolm is a master teacher without peer (see 1971, 81–120, 121–148; Sales 1994). Power in defense of freedom, Malcolm argues, is greater than power on behalf of tyranny and oppression. For Malcolm, the latter inevitably lacks the kind and degree of conviction of the former, because the mentality of most who would implement power on behalf of tyranny and oppression is that of an employee. However, there is a sense in which white supremacy has the capacity to produce a certain derangement and degrading of mentality that can be passionate in a negative and hateful sense. Malcolm clearly believes in the power of a life-affirming passion that can produce uncompromising and hopeful action (see, for example, 1965, 150).

Malcolm X teaches that this was a period of worldwide revolution far beyond the bounds of Mississippi, Alabama, and Harlem. The revolutionary forces coming to the fore were to oppose not simply the U.S., French, or English power structure but an international Western power structure consisting of U.S., French, English, Belgian, and other European interests. These former colonizers of the Dark World had formed an international combine, but Malcolm calls for unity among twenty-two million Black people in the United States and urges them to unite with seven hundred million of their Muslim sisters and brothers in Africa and Asia and with the revolutionary people in Africa, Asia, and the Americas (1992, 106–126).

Malcolm reestablished in the 1960s what other people of African descent had known in the past—that the struggles of Black people in the United States were not just an "American" problem but a world problem. Malcolm restored the sense of internationalism that had long been a part of the imagination of people of African descent—of its leaders and intellectuals and among the common people. Fanon Wilkins (2001) has most effectively navigated the break in this Black internationalism by the "liberal compromise" among segments of the civil rights leadership during the cold-war period of the late 1940s to the late 1960s; he also argues for the continuity of Black internationalism breached by the liberal compromise, which is precisely central to the revolutionary conjuncture of the 1960s.

It is not difficult to understand that Obama's election as the forty-fourth president of the United States has occasioned a quite unexpected discourse in two directions: one arguing that it constitutes the fulfillment of the American Dream, and the other the closing of the American Dream. We have argued in this book that what is actually happening is quite a bit more complex—that we are currently transcending the American Dream.

As the racial colonial subjects of the U.S. empire increasingly become part of the nation's population, the long-mislabeled recession has morphed into a structural crisis of historical capitalism. Arundhati Roy (2002) welcomes the people of the United States to the world that the majority of the world, especially in the Global South, has long inhabited. We do not think that this is just an apt turn of a phrase but a depiction of our current, very urgent moment, what Jack O'Dell and King deemed "the fierce urgency of now" during the opening of the revolutionary era in the mid-1960s. It was not just now but the cumulation of social forces that brought us to the crises of an historical system, a moment of Kairos.

The capitalist world economy that emerged in the sixteenth century consisted of a Western European core and an American periphery. The process of peripheralization of the Americas involved the displacement, dispersion, and destruction of the indigenous people and the formation of a coerced labor force consisting mainly of enslaved Africans. Racism is thus constitutive of our historical social system in providing a pattern of social distinctions between the conquering people and the conquered people naturalized in the notion of race. This pattern of distinction was used to categorize people in the pan-European world as superior and those from the extra-European world as inferior, with Africans and indigenous people at the bottom of the social scale. We insist here on the usefulness of the concept of "white world supremacy/pan-European racism" in stark contrast to the notion of colorblind universalism formulated during the Ronald Reagan years.

At the end of World War II, the United States emerged as the hegemonic power within the capitalist world economy. It had been a peculiar power not known for its colonial history, though it had started as a settler colony on the Eastern Seaboard of the North American continent and had embarked on a process of imperial expansion to obtain its present territorial mass. It had colonized Amerindians, Africans, Mexicans, Cubans, Puerto Ricans, Hawaiians, and Filipinos within its territory, giving it a large proportion of populations who could be said to be internally colonized, or a third world within. It had imported Chinese workers to build the transcontinental railroad but denied them citizenship rights.

But this manner of nation building and its self-conception as a white nation providing freedom and opportunity for all created an increasingly large strata of alienated populations who could be said to be "in but not of" this nation. Neoliberalism emerged as a strategy to restrain the tearing of the social fabric and the increased social power of the oppressed within the nation and of the unruly populations in the periphery of the world-system. The rebellion in Chiapas signaled the beginning of the end of the neoliberal social order, followed by the movement for global democracy in Seattle, the World Social Forum, and the Project for a New American Century, which brandished the specter of preemptive warfare to intimidate any opposition to the United States. As if someone had forgotten the fate of the dream of a Thousand-Year Reich in 1930s Germany, U.S. hegemony was no more, though it took time for many within the United States to recognize this, even on the Left.

The radicalization of the Black freedom struggle after 1965, the movement toward a radical rainbow coalition called by the Black Left, and the rise of a "third world within" during the post-1965 demographic transformation of the United States have provided a setting for a more serious confrontation with the United States as a white nation in which excluded groups—articulating ideas not of revenge but of democracy, justice, and equality for all—will call for a fundamental democratization and liberation of the traditional concept of an "American" nation. Perhaps the November 2008 and 2012 elections of Obama are but signposts of the future to come, including the rejection of the desperate attempts to establish a new American Century by a segment of the ruling class who truly see the handwriting on the wall. We embrace King's contention that the arc of the moral universe is long but bends toward justice, as we are able to glimpse the end of what has been termed "the evil system of imperialism" that arose and throve with the enslavement of the African people.

We often forget that Malcolm X's 1963 declaration that we had arrived at the end of white world supremacy is part of what is more often referred to as the "chickens coming home to roost" speech made in the aftermath of Kennedy's assassination. For this remark, Malcolm was expelled from the Nation of Islam (NOI) for violating Elijah Muhammad's prohibition on speaking out about the assassination. For NOI leadership, this speech was an unforgivable transgression, a ratcheting up of agitation by the national spokesperson that could bring the organization under the scrutiny of the federal, state, and local security forces. Part of this threat to NOI's project stemmed not merely from provocation from ill-considered remarks but, on a much deeper level, from the wider implications of a violation of NOI's prohibition against involvement in the "white devil's" political system. While the members of NOI's inner circles had long been concerned about Malcolm's ventures into the secular arena of world politics, Muhammad had defended Malcolm, since he had been largely responsible for the spectacular growth of the organization since his rise to a top leadership position during the 1950s. Malcolm's stance within the secular arena of world politics had given the organization this standing, but it had also attracted the attention of law enforcement and surveillance authorities. But when Malcolm left NOI and moved toward the philosophies of King and the civil rights movement, the authorities believed that they had to decapitate this movement before its strength defied the ability of the state to bring it to a halt. About this objective, J. Edgar Hoover was very clear. The deafening silence regarding this issue is a clumsy sign of the limits of state power and the authority of the parastate. We are now in a struggle for the soul of a world aborning.

The best-kept secret was that the condition of the working and middle classes had deteriorated substantially as the collapse of what some call the Fordist model of accumulation was replaced by financial wheeling and dealing, creating profit by blowing up economic bubbles that enriched capitalists while the conditions of the working population continued to deteriorate. For some, Obama's emergence as the carrier of the mantle of the civil rights era seemed to promise change. However, his promise faded in the face of snarling, racist, right-wing storm troopers who did the work of capitalists by intimidating all opposition and intensifying the rhetoric of the post-1960s counterrevolution against using public resources for the racialized and gendered undeserving poor. Finally, capital's once-favored children recognized that they were no longer favored, and this moved the focus on the crimes, bad behavior, and bad culture of the usual suspects toward the 1 percent.

The revolution of 1968, which some of us missed, is now back on the agenda, but this time historical capitalism itself has moved far from equilibrium, and our own struggles need to focus on the world beyond capitalism. The concentration of so many within the United States who do not comport with the face of the white nation makes the nationalism of empire that had been the foundation of U.S. power a disintegrating force. We are now called to embark on the project of creating a new world. Not only is a better world possible; the old world is no longer possible, not for long.

We take very seriously Kelvin Santiago-Valles's admonition that we need to draw on and think through subaltern theorizing to pursue theoretically informed historical research as part of contributing to emancipatory struggles. Such theorizing must itself be based in such emancipatory struggles.

Thus we have combined an analysis of the historical processes by which the "American" nation was imagined, looking at not only the conceptualizations of the elites and those who were integrated into the nation as intermediate strata but also the perspectives of those who were problematically integrated as subordinate strata. We have explored the overarching framework within which this nation was inserted into a larger geoculture with a utopian vision as a "city on the hill." We have provided contrast to this notion by focusing on the views and experiences of those who have historically held tentative and marginal status, whose opposition to this oppressive framework articulated ideas of democracy, justice, and equality for all, calling for a fundamental democratization and the liberation of the traditional concept of an "American" nation.

In our analysis of the contradictions of nation through the lived historical reality of the United States, particularly focusing on the second half of the twentieth century and the beginning of the twenty-first century but grounding this focus in the five-hundred-year history of racial capitalism, we believe that we have a sense of the cumulative impact of these social, historical, economic, and political transformations on the lives of ordinary people of all races. As the consciousness of these ordinary people is transformed by their experiences and how they develop a collective discourse to understand that experience on their own terms, we will finally be able to move beyond the discourse of power, the "universalism" of the elite, to a sense of how ordinary people rearticulate the parameters of national belonging and reposition us so that we can truly reexamine the notion of nationhood, justice, equality, human emancipation, and respect for all.

10

Going Forward, with Reflections
on the Revolts of the Past Decade

The rise of the alter-globalization (antiglobalization) movement, or the movement for global democracy, was in part inspired by the rebellion in Chiapas, Mexico, against global neoliberalism. In our view, neoliberalism is not simply a description of the evolution of the natural economy but a counterrevolutionary movement against the increased social power of the working classes of the world and against the increased social power of the peoples of the extra-European world. More specifically within the conjuncture in which it was initiated, it was an attack on the rising social power of the lower social strata worldwide during the post–World War II period. The first counterrevolutionary movement in the postwar period was the attempt to destroy the Left in the 1940s and 1950s.

Popular Front Liberalism—the first counterrevolution of the postwar against the New Deal—gave us the anticommunist liberalism of the Americans for Democratic Action on the one hand and the witch-hunts of Senator Joseph McCarthy and J. Edgar Hoover on the other. But the moral power of the movements of the oppressed inevitably struck a chord among the most sensitive people everywhere. The civil rights movement's embrace of a strategy emphasizing love and nonviolence emphasized the hatefulness of the perpetrators of Jim Crow segregation in the southern United States.

But in the midst of a struggle that President Lyndon Baines Johnson described favorably as a "revolution," the centrist liberal intellectuals who had defected from the Left in the late 1940s and early 1950s began to warn about the dangers of conciliating to the demands of the increasingly influential civil rights movement in the political arena outside the Jim Crow South.

Nathan Glazer and Daniel Patrick Moynihan's *Beyond the Melting Pot: The*

Negroes, Puerto Ricans, Jews, Italians and Irish of New York City is the most notable of the works that reestablish the 1950s rhetoric of the undeserving poor found in Abram Kardiner and Lionel Ovesey's *The Mark of Oppression* and Arthur Schlesinger Jr.'s *The Vital Center*. Norman Podhoretz's 1963 *Commentary* article, "My Negro Problem and Ours," provides an image of young Norman as a child in an inner-city Brooklyn, New York, neighborhood, cowering in fear against Black bullies who were not victims of Jim Crow racism but bitter and angry residents of northern ghettos striking out against poor Jews who were as poor as their Black co-residents. If Norman was able to rise up in the social system, why couldn't the Blacks?

In 1965, Moynihan sought to synthesize these issues with policy prescriptions for government action in his well-known report entitled *The Negro Family: A Case for National Action* (aka "The Moynihan Report"). But social contention within the larger social arena ate into the surplus funds that Moynihan had thought were available to implement his project (notably, the war in Vietnam). Furthermore, the struggle of lower social strata worldwide created a profit squeeze for dominant capital not only across the core economies but especially in the United States, with its historically bifurcated social strata based on class position and on social distinctions between whites and persons of color.

The only solution for these very intense strains was the continuation of the social revolution that Hoover had been so determined to derail, and so Martin Luther King called for the nation to alter its common sense via a revolution of conscience and to get on the right side of history, which included honoring W.E.B. Du Bois, who had taught the nation so much.

The Right Side of History

King's call for a revolution of conscience emboldened many to embrace his stance, but it fell on the deaf ears of Hoover, who incarnated much of the hateful venom of the starkly white supremacist depths of this "evil system." As we have argued, U.S. democracy was always Janus faced: one the face of European conquest, and the other the face of the land of opportunity for European immigrants. However, society's opportunity structure was constrained by its location within an inherently polarizing social system, which defines the capitalist nature of our society. Race, class, and gender polarization were major elements of this social polarization.

The idea of democracy was expressed in the strategies of many social movements, including the abolitionist, feminist, labor, socialist, communist, and minority movements. In the nineteenth century, the abolitionist, feminist, and worker movements were at the forefront of the struggle for equality. In the twentieth century, the New Negro Movement, Popular Front liberals, New Deal liberals, and worker, feminist, and "minority" movements pushed for the expansion of democracy. Though it was once an important element of leftist liberal discourse, this nation of nations consisted in part of conquered people who opposed the nationalism of empire that had been the common sense of the European conquerors. From the Bandung period to the world sixties (Wilson and Connery 2007), the legacies of the New Negro Movement, the Popular Front, and New Deal Liberalism continued to reverberate among the populations, expanding the visas of the postwar civil rights revolution, the incorporation of racialized worker movements, and the radicalization of feminist movements that all projected a collective image of too much largesse and too little strength in a situation when third-world liberation movements allied with the World Left were challenging the authority of the West, which increasingly meant the United States as the power that ensured the stability of the existing world order and the geoculture of pan-European supremacy, though it encouraged formal decolonization to deescalate the radicalism of the anticolonial forces.

The radical sixties had indeed been a social revolution with the racial movement at its core, as Hoover had argued. It was not entirely unprecedented, as we could see with the New Negro Movement of the 1920s and 1930s and the Black Popular Front of the 1930s and 1940s. President Woodrow Wilson's rhetoric about the right to self-determination of nations was nominally anti-imperialist, but his eye was on the threat posed by the radical, left-wing anticolonialism of Vladimir Lenin and the Bolsheviks and its analogue within the borders of the United States itself. Wilson imposed rigid segregation in Washington, D.C., during his years in the White House. He regarded Black soldiers as an especially dangerous group, a fertile conduit for the spread of Bolshevism within the United States. This recalls the pronouncements about the threat of revolutionary internationalist politics and white racial degeneration by Madison Grant and Lothrop Stoddard in 1920s.

What *was* different was the breadth of the conservative counterrevolution and the collapse of the liberal center. The Right ran amok, sweeping everything in its path. There was no alternative, Margaret Thatcher declared, and the Left was alarmed at the loud echo of her approach that they perceived everywhere. The Left was reproached by the liberal center for having gone too far, of having provoked the Right so as to cause a backlash across the breadth of the liberal society.

The neoliberal wrath with the wind at its back sought to undo liberal social democratic possibility for the foreseeable future. However, as the social consequences of neoliberalism spread across the liberal societies of the West and the rising semi-peripheral societies of the South, opposition emerged and grew stronger, as we have indicated.

Wallerstein (2011c) argues that the Arab Spring, the Occupy Movement, and the *indignados* all signify a return to the spirit of 1968, long suppressed by the neoliberalism that was its countercurrent. The revolutionaries of 1968, according to Wallerstein, were protesting against the inherently undemocratic behavior of those in authority. It was a revolt against the use of misuse of authority at all levels in world, national, local, and nongovernmental organizations (from workplaces, to educational structures, to political parties and trade unions).

The revolutionaries of 1968 opposed what we now call vertical, hierarchical decision making and advocated for horizontal decision making that is structured to provide a voice for all involved participants. They were deeply influenced by nonviolent concepts of resistance. The rapid public embrace of this current terrified those in power. The spread of antiauthoritarian logic, and especially its success anywhere, menaced all of them. The governments of the world joined forces to destroy the 1968 current, but without success, as the current spread from Hong Kong to Athens, to Madrid and Santiago, and from Johannesburg to New York. Wallerstein argues that in contrast to the World Left prior to 1968, the world revolution of 1968 focused on the forgotten peoples who had been told that their concerns were secondary and had to be postponed until other primary concerns were resolved. These forgotten peoples included women, minorities, people with "other" sexual preferences and gender identities, people with disabilities, indigenous populations, environmentalists, and pacifists.

As the 1968 current continued to spread, the major geopolitical actors sought to advance their interests in the midst of the turmoil. Though there was not much of a 1968 current in Libya, when Libyan groups began to express discontent in the face of threats from Muammar Gaddafi, the British and the French joined forces to help the rebels and convinced the United States to join them in what they then argued was a North American Trade Organization (NATO) effort to preserve human rights.

If the 1968 current's emerging in Libya had been a possibility, it was undercut by this NATO takeover of the opposition to Gaddafi. The major geopolitical actors then were henceforth sensitive to the necessity to blunt the emergence of the revolutionary current wherever it emerged so that they could not join forces with one another. Thus, they were concerned about the emergence of a 1968 current among the Jewish population in Israel, among the Palestinians, among the Kurds in Turkey, and among multiple factions in the complicated arena of Iranian politics.

In Latin America, the Left has grown remarkably over the past fifteen years or so, moving from being an area considered the U.S. backyard to being an autonomous geopolitical force on the world scene. At the end of 2011, in the midst of adversarial relations on many different fronts with China, Pakistan, Saudi Arabia, Israel, Iran, and Germany, the straw that must have broken the camel's back is that

the Latin American and Caribbean countries met in Venezuela to found a new organization, CELAC—which are Spanish initials for the Community of Latin American and Caribbean States. Every country in the Americas signed on, except for the two that weren't invited—the United States and Canada. CELAC is designed to replace the Organization of American States (OAS), which includes the United States and Canada, and has suspended Cuba.[1] It may take a while for the OAS to disappear and only CELAC remain. Still it's not exactly something they are celebrating in Washington. (Wallerstein 2011d)

Since the abysmal failure of the 2002 U.S.-backed coup to overthrow Venezuela's president, Hugo Chavez, the status of the U.S. superpower has steadily declined. In a series of elections throughout Latin America and the Caribbean, according to Wallerstein, left-of-center candidates won in almost every instance: "It culminated in a 2008 meeting in Brazil to which the United States was not invited and in which Cuba's president, Raúl Castro, was treated as a virtual hero" (Wallerstein 2009c).

In addition to the victory of left-of-center governments in many Latin American countries, members of Latin America's indigenous populations have asserted themselves on an unprecedented scale, demanding the right to organize their political and social lives autonomously. Though most focus on the contradictions between the traditional Left's emphasis on economic growth to enhance their populations' standard of living, Latin American Indigenista movements emphasize coming to terms with Pacha Mama, or Mother Earth. This situation is fertile with the possibility of a new leap in the historical strategy of the antisystemic forces. The Indigenistas seek to expand their use of the earth's resources not to live abundantly but to develop a more sane and balanced use that respects ecological equilibrium. They seek *buen vivir*—a Quechua phrase that means "to live well."

Despite the dramatic changes in relations of force that rapidly dismantled the Washington consensus over the past fifteen years, which had been established by the neoliberal juggernaut, Wallerstein argues that it is not realistic to expect that the countries of the Global South will discover some policy that will turn them into new Denmarks in the next ten, twenty, or thirty years (2004, 11).

Is it credible to hold everything else constant and to assume that, at the very least, everyone else will remain where they are today in terms of standard of living? Where is the surplus value to come from that would permit 50 percent of China's population to consume at the level of 50 percent of Italy's population, while all the rest of the world consumes at a level at least as high as it presently does? Is this all supposed to come from the so-called greater productivity of world (or Chinese) production? It is clear that the skilled workers of Ohio and the Ruhr Valley do not think so. They think they would pay for it, and they are already paying for it via significantly reduced standards of living. Are they really so wrong? Has this not been happening in the past decade (Wallerstein 2004, 3)?

Though the idea of development was popularized by Walt Rostow's *The Stages of Economic Growth: A Non-Communist Manifesto*, it was posed as a technical issue of which all could partake if they could develop the skills that would enable them to succeed, which they would copy from those who had already been successful. So, according to this theory, if poor countries were provided with enough capital to achieve "take-off," or rapid economic growth, they would embrace capitalism and democracy rather than communism.

However, any examination of the capitalist world economy over the five hundred years of its existence shows that the gap between the top and the bottom—what Wallerstein refers to as the core and the periphery—has never gotten smaller, only larger. Though some countries have improved their relative standings in the distribution of wealth in the world-system over time, there has been a constant trimodal distribution of economic activities that Wallerstein describes as the core (wealthy countries of Western Europe, North America, and Japan), the semi-periphery (middle-ranking countries), and the periphery (the least-developed countries in the world-system, long referred to as "the third world"). Though the statistical data are weak, "such comparative studies as we have do show a constant tri-modal distribution of wealth in the world-system, with a few countries moving from one category to another" (Wallerstein 2004).

Wallerstein has also long argued that the ability of accumulators of capital to obtain high levels of profit is based on the extent to which they can obtain a degree of monopolization of given productive activity. So what "we have been calling development for the last fifty years or so is basically the ability of some countries to erect productive enterprises of a type considered to be highly profitable" (Wallerstein 2004). However, to the extent that they are able to gain entry to this locale of high profits, they reduce the degree of monopolization of production in this particular arena and hence its degree of profitability. Wallerstein concludes that this pattern of economic development is evident in the historic pattern of successive so-called leading industries—from textiles to steel and automobiles to electronics to computer technology—that have been successive arenas of high-profit production in the world economy.

Will this phenomenon strengthen and give new life to capitalism? Wallerstein doubts it. He argues that the relative rise of Asia further undermines the system by overloading the number of persons to whom surplus value is distributed. The top end of the capitalist system can never be too large, because it reduces the overall accumulation of capital (Wallerstein 2009a, 10).

Capitalism is an inherently polarizing social system based on the dynamics of the endless accumulation of capital, with the surplus value going disproportionately to the owners of capital. The continuation of historical capitalism is dependent on the ability of capitalists to continue the endless accumulation at what they feel to be adequate levels of profit. As we have seen, this model has been called "development." The most appropriate move for those who are seeking to end the potential disaster of riding a runaway train to potential oblivion is to get off the train. Wallerstein (2004) argues that this is a class struggle, a moral struggle that can best be undertaken by movements, not states.

On this note, let us return to the narrative about the movements that have posed revolutionary challenges to historical capitalism during this period of structural crisis of the system. To contextualize the meaning of what Wallerstein refers to as the 1968 current, we should understand first that he constructs it from the challenge to the liberal geoculture by the world revolution of 1968. We focus on the view from the United States, in which we see the rise of a revolutionary "third world within."

The Revolutionary "Third World Within"

The rebellion of the third world and its echoes among the most marginal groups within the core states (the third world within, youth, and women) shattered the liberal geoculture that had prevailed from 1848 to 1968. As Max Elbaum explains in his important book *Revolution in the Air: Sixties Radicals Turn to Lenin, Mao and Che*:

By early 1971, public opinion polls showed upwards of three million people thought a revolution was necessary in the US. Tens of thousands believed revolution was not only desirable, but possible, and maybe even not too far around the corner.... Between 1968 and 1973, layer after layer of young people went in search of an ideological framework and strategy to bring that revolution about. Inspired by the dynamic liberation movements that threatened to besiege Washington with "two, three, many Vietnams," many decided that a Third World–oriented version of Marxism—sometimes explicitly termed "Third World Marxism" and sometimes not—was the key to building a powerful left here, within the "belly of the beast."

This movement gradually evolved into a more complex amalgam that recognized multiple and interlocking forms of oppression, which is often subsumed under the label of Race, Class, and Gender, which includes more radical formations such as the Third World Women's Alliance, the Third World Within, and the Committee Against Anti-Asian Violence to others which are closer to liberal multiculturalism. (2002, 2)

This is quite a broad front in circumstances that allowed these multiple forms of organization to survive and grow. Though the post-1980s counterrevolution against 1960s' radicalism has maintained its vigor over time, the more moderate conservatives hesitate over some of their more outrageous actions.

On the other hand, our presentation of third-world radicalism as central to the 1960s breaks with the liberal geoculture and may evoke an "I told you this was pretty crazy stuff" reaction from many post-1960s generations who have been attuned to the vicissitudes of a political culture nourished within the womb of a devastating class and culture war against the minority poor. The break with the liberal geoculture had its origins in the continuation of the radical currents passed on from the most emancipatory visions of the American creed, inherited from the greatest generation who gave us, among other ideas, New Deal Liberalism, Popular Front Liberalism, Yiddishkayt, and Social Gospel Christianity (the last shall be first, and so on).

The post-1945 counterrevolution was aimed precisely against what we are calling emancipatory visions that embraced all humanity rather than seeking to construct an iron wall around our national borders that prevented a sense of human solidarity across them and toward cultures thought to be so different from our own.

Within U.S. borders, the heroes of the 1968 revolutionaries included the Student Nonviolent Coordinating Committee (SNCC), the Revolutionary Action

Movement (RAM), the Black Panther Party, the League of Revolutionary Black Workers, the Young Lords Party, the American Indian Movement, and La Raza Unida. Outside the United States, their role models included the anticolonial and socialist revolutionaries in Vietnam, Cuba, China, Algeria, Guinea-Bissau, Angola, and Mozambique. During the 1970s, the line of descent from the civil rights movement seemed clear, and thus the centrality of opposition to racism and imperialism to the grievances of these rebels made perfect sense.

Though there is a clear line of descent from earlier generations, it was manifest more in the transmission of values to the 1960s generation, since the 1945 to 1960 counterrevolutionary interregnum served to erase historical memory by presenting what was called McCarthyism as depoliticized insanity. The rebellions of the 1960s and 1970s were accompanied by a kind of revolutionary euphoria based on the pace of change that they witnessed and thus the anticipation of certain victory. This mood of the radicals of this period clashed with the more cautious approach of the Old Left that had been politically active during the McCarthy period. The more conservative elements among the powerful have sought to reframe the sense of transformative possibility that existed during the 1960s and early 1970s into a time when the young went crazy, a simple narrative of good against evil.

The rise of a revolutionary current in the United States attuned to the influence of third-world radicalism was not new. What was new was the demographic significance of a lower working class composed disproportionately of people of color and women, who have waged courageous struggles for equal rights and for respect for all. In the midst of this massive demographic shift, the policing function of the United States as the hegemonic power of the world-system brought the United States into regular conflict with Marxist-led national liberation movements in the third world whose moral authority often inspired idealistic youth to make common cause with them against the obvious immorality of their own governments. King's continuing call for the nation and the world to focus on that contradiction and to get on the right side of history drew a line in the sand that clarified the dimensions of the "human" struggle in a manner strikingly reminiscent of that of Malcolm X and, even further back, of the internationalist radicals who argued for unity between the rising lower strata within the United States and the rising lower social strata around the world. These internationalists in the socialist, communist, and world federalist movements were loyal to the human race and thus were deemed marginal by the patriots who wanted to use their national borders to not only monopolize privilege but also protect the flow of wealth from other parts of the world to wealthy states, such as the United States, behind their national borders.

Some scholars of the New Left have tended to dismiss the internationalism of the movement as youthful immaturity and rebelliousness. We agree with Elbaum (2002), who contends that such arguments constitute a retreat from a systemic critique of U.S. economic and political structures, misleading its exponents to pose their own "complacency" as maturity. This retreat, he argues, makes it difficult for them to understand the depth of grassroots enthusiasm for revolutionary politics that existed during the period from 1968 to 1973. Periods of intense conflict can alter people's conception of what is possible and desirable, but in more normal times, it may seem out of bounds to take seriously the prospect of building a U.S. radical movement that is antiracist and in solidarity with the third world.

The year 1968 is often used symbolically to mark the end of the 1960s, but in reality it marked a radicalization of world historic proportions in the United States, when seemingly an entire generation attempted to manifest the integrity, courage, and intelligence of their foremost heroes: Ella Baker, Martin Luther King Jr., Malcolm X, and Fannie Lou Hamer. As they struggled for racial justice and against imperialist war, they added another set of heroes that included V. I. Lenin, Mao Zedong, Amilcar Cabral, Frantz Fanon, Fidel Castro, and Che Guevara. This movement shattered the parameters of the social democratic compromise and the liberal geoculture of which it was a part.

The specter of democracy was haunting the United States. By the fall of 1968, one million students saw themselves as part of the Left, and 368,000 people agreed on the need for a mass revolutionary party. Among African Americans, revolutionary sentiments contended not just for influence but for preeminence, especially among those under 30, as more than three hundred rebellions flared up among inner-city Blacks from 1964 to 1968.

While most scholars of the Black freedom struggle clearly connect Malcolm X to the radicalization of the brave youth of SNCC and more broadly to the rise of the radical segment of the Black Power movement, they have only a vague notion of how this process was worked out. Some argue that the combined impact of Malcolm X; Monroe, North Carolina's National Association for the Advancement of Colored People (NAACP) leader, Robert Williams; and the lessons of the struggle gave birth to the radicals among the 1960s Black Power militants.

However, the organic intellectuals who formed the backbone of the Black insurgency of the 1960s were variously associated with the Freedom Now Party, *Liberator Magazine*, and RAM. While RAM forces were much more clandestine than the rest of the movement, it is clear that RAM's spirit pervaded the radical segment of the Black Power movement. During the early and mid-1960s, most of the action was in the South, and people in most of the rest of the country were sympathizers and onlookers. But the revolution spread like an epidemic during the 1967–1968 school year, and tens of thousands of students caught the fever. It was infectious, as was clearly reflected in the activity and theorizing of RAM militants.

The whole world seemed to catch fire at once. Young Black people on and off campus were proclaiming themselves to be revolutionaries. Black student movements emerged everywhere almost simultaneously. The young militants of RAM were feverishly toiling to provide a revolutionary framework and a disciplined infrastructure to support that movement. We did not know the details, but it was often hinted that someone was ensuring that we were preparing our forces to engage the enemy in the final battle for Black liberation. By 1968, Black student unions had emerged on white campuses, demanding a relevant education, more Black professors, and Black representation in other sectors of the universities. At historically Black colleges, students demanded the overturn of the Negro university and the creation of the Black university.

By 1968, the Black Panther Party—and, in some locations, the League of Revolutionary Black Workers—was having some influence on the emerging Black student unions, whereas the earliest influences on the Black student unions had been SNCC and RAM. Although SNCC and the Black Panther Party have captured the lion's share of the scant attention given to the Black Power militants by scholars, RAM was related to mid-1960s radicalism in multiple and complex ways, stemming in part from the necessity of clandestine organizations to work through aboveground organizations. In this sense, RAM might be compared to the most radical manifestation of the post–World War I New Negro Movement, the African Blood Brotherhood (ABB). We hold that the ABB played a decisive role in the radicalization of the Garvey movement and in pushing the Communist Party USA (CPUSA) to take a stand in favor of racial justice to an extent rivaled by no other predominantly white organization. According to Muhammed Ahmad (formerly Max Stanford), RAM was a mobile group that at times operated in its own name and at other times worked within other organizations. Ahmad tells the story of multiple Black Panther Parties noted by a few authors. RAM took the model developed by the Lowndes County Freedom Organization and spread it to other cities; the Oakland Black Panthers distinguished themselves in part because of their skill at revolutionary theater and in part because they opted politically for a public presence rather than a clandestine existence.

The September 1967 *Monthly Review* issue is a key document in making connections between Black radicals and the broader U.S. Left, but a year or so later, after Black inner rebellions had dramatically transformed the relations of force between dominated Blacks and the larger society, a series of exposés in *Life Magazine* and *Esquire* identified RAM as one of the leading extremist groups "plotting a War on Whitey" (Kelley and Esch 1999, 20): "The 'Peking-backed' group was considered not only armed and dangerous but 'impressively well read in revolutionary literature—from Marat and Lenin to Mao, Che Guevara and Frantz Fanon.'"

These highly publicized articles were followed by police raids of the homes of RAM members in Philadelphia and New York City, in which RAM members were charged with conspiracy to instigate a riot, poison police officers with potassium cyanide, and assassinate Roy Wilkins and Whitney Young. By 1969, RAM as an organization had pretty much dissolved, but RAM's significance was much more than its organizational structure—it was its network of members, people in its orbit, allies, and sympathizers. The names mentioned above are but a very short list of individuals associated with RAM; there are many, many more.

This social force saw African Americans in the United States as part of Lin Baio's global countryside. In "Long Live the Victory of People's War!" Baio argues that the world revolution will begin in the global countryside and then spread to surround the global cities. Kwame Nkrumah has also argued that that as the revolutionary third world liberated its territories from the yoke of capitalism and imperialism, revolutionary conditions would come to exist in the capitalist metropole, even in the belly of the beast, the fabled jewel of liberal capitalist civilization, the United States of America. Both these notions still make considerable sense, and, indeed, we see something like this happening now, with increasing resistance emerging around the globe and in the United States itself, although not in such a linear fashion. But the main problem with the notion as propounded in the 1960s and 1970s is that the time frame did not take into consideration the plurality of social times noted by Fernand Braudel, and with the subsiding of the mass mobilizations during this revolutionary period, the cadres drew conclusions that their expectations and their tactics had been excessive and that their practices were characterized by a form of revolutionary romanticism that had led them to make mistakes when estimating what was possible.

By 1970, this network of revolutionary-minded youth and other segments wielded an oppositional spirit similar in density to that of the revolutionaries of the 1930s, but more intense in its projection. Richard Nixon's brutal invasion of Cambodia in May 1970 led to the largest explosion of protests on U.S. college campuses in our history. By then, four out of ten college students—nearly three million people—thought that a revolution was necessary in the United States. An article in *Business Week* laments, "The invasion of Cambodia and the senseless shooting of four students at Kent State University in Ohio have consolidated the academic community against the war, against business, and against government. This is a dangerous situation. It threatens the whole economic and social structure of the nation" (qtd. in Elbaum 2002, 18–19).

In search of a more adequate ideology, the New Left turned to third-world Marxism, as Students for a Democratic Society (SDS) split into more radical forces, such as Weathermen and the Revolutionary Youth Movement (RYM) II. Within the Puerto Rican Left, the Young Lords, El Comite, and the Puerto Rican Socialist Party lured tens of thousands to revolutionary politics in the 1970s (Elbaum 2002, 78), making Leninism the dominant perspective on the Puerto Rican Left. While third-world liberation movements had a powerful influence on all Left-leaning youth, for those with powerful communist movements in their homelands, community formation itself was linked to the deepening of a radical sensibility. The third-world strikes at San Francisco State and Berkeley were crucial in the evolution of Asian American radicalism. While cultural nationalism was a strong feature of Chicano organizations, such as the Brown Berets, Marxism was the dominant perspective within CASA: Centro de Accion Social Autonomo, Comite Nacional Hermandad de Trabajadores, which did not distinguish between Mexicans born north of the border and those born south of the border. Marxist ideas also were established within the Native American movement. Of course, the story of Black radicals is by now familiar, as most people know some of the histories of the Black Panther Party, the League of Revolutionary Black Workers, and SNCC.

Left organizations composed primarily of persons of color included the Communist League (later the Communist Labor Party, and now the League of Revolutionaries for a New America), I Wor Kuen, the August Twenty-Ninth Movement, and the Revolutionary Communist League (formerly the Congress of African People), which all eventually merged to form the U.S. League of Revolutionary Struggle. The Black Workers Congress split into a number of smaller groups. The Revolutionary Workers League, which stemmed from the merger of People's College, Malcolm X Liberation University, and the Youth Organization for Black Unity, would later establish powerful links with the Young Lords Party offshoot the Puerto Rican Revolutionary Workers Organization to form the short-lived Revolutionary Wing. The Workers Viewpoint Organization, which stemmed from the Asian Study Group, became the Communist Workers Party, which incorporated a significant number of cadre from the Revolutionary Workers League. The Union of Democratic Filipinos united with members of the Third World Women's Alliance and the Northern California Alliance to form Line of March.

Not an End—a New Beginning

While a much longer story must be told about this period, we want to be clear that though the 1968 Left is distinct from the Old Left for the reasons that we argue above, it is crucial that we understand it as a continuation of the historical strategy of the U.S. Left. The collapse of the organizations associated with what Wallerstein refers to as the 1968 current during the 1980s and early 1990s was part of the larger crisis of the *strategy* of the World Left. The individuals who were involved in that movement, as were the authors, could no more step back from the consciousness that they had gained than they could disassociate themselves from their networks of family, friends, and comrades who infused them with their sense of human possibility. Indeed, tensions in the American Dream have been building since the formation of the U.S. nation and its rise to power in the twentieth century. Movements have in turn been resisting and responding from the very beginning. In the voices of the people we spoke with, we heard that these tensions have become increasingly evident in the minds of people of all backgrounds in the United States. The momentum is gaining, even, or perhaps particularly, as circumstances are becoming increasingly difficult for people in the United States overall—perhaps not as difficult as they have been for people around the globe, but more challenging all the same. One of the frequent criticisms of the 1968 generation is that its reliance on voluntarist notions of social transformation underlined its disillusionment. The voluntarist spirit that pervaded the movement followed logically from the pace of events during that period. And while the militants may have profoundly wrongly assessed how ripe capitalism was for defeat in the United States, this type of wrong assessment is

less an anomaly than most think. After all, in 1848, Karl Marx and Friedrich
Engels thought the specter of communism haunted Europe. Lenin talked about
moribund capitalism during World War I. Interestingly, it was Mao who argued
that revolution was not an event but a process that covered a long historical period
of transition from capitalism to communism, including the socialist states that
were still creatures of the capitalist world. In addition, the Chinese revolutionaries were operating in a state in which a socialist movement had captured state
power and was under attack from imperialism from every direction. They could
be forgiven for making every effort to defend what they had built. However, we see
very little resignation or disillusion in our comrades from the 1968 movement.

The Fire This Time

> God gave Noah the rainbow sign. No more water,
> the fire next time.
> —JAMES BALDWIN, THE FIRE NEXT TIME

As we have argued throughout, the framework for the current crisis in the world-
system is the crisis of neoliberal globalization, which itself was an attempt to
discipline the working classes of the world through arguing that the natural adjustment of the economy was a response of the hubris of some who believed that
they could force the economic system to respond to their needs without regard
for the needs of the accumulators of capital who were the job creators and thus
must be given priority in economic adjustments. The global liberalism of the
post-1945 world-system led to the elaboration of social compacts between capital
and labor and the populations of the third world that required such adjustments.

Neoliberal globalization challenged the social compacts that had been established in the core zones of the world economy dominated by social democracies and in the peripheral zones dominated by national liberation movements
in power (Wallerstein 2009a). The successful implementation of the neoliberal
counterrevolution led initially to widespread disillusion among the cadres of the
surging popular classes, to the dismay of their remaining cadres, and therefore
to a dismayingly widespread sense of defeat almost everywhere, which led to the
collapse of the radical Left that had been a product of those times. However, the
dogmatic rigidity of the neoliberal overlords had none of the give and flexibility
of the global liberalism of the period of U.S. hegemony, or what some in the
United States have referred to as the American Century.

The famous Egyptian economist Samir Amin thus argues that we should
situate these rearrangements in the political culture of capitalism in Lenin's ear-
ly-twentieth-century analysis of imperialism as moribund capitalism (actually,
Amin uses the term "putrefied"). The implication for Amin and for Wallerstein
is that the imperialist system "is transformed into the collective imperialism of
the Triad" (Amin 2011b, 10).

Wallerstein (2011b) focuses his analysis of the world revolutionary outbreak on what he views as the continuation of "the 1968 current." The Arab Spring is held to be composed of "two quite different currents" that are "going in radically different directions," but this idea has not been fully analyzed. Understanding this division is key to negotiating a sustainable resistance.

Wallerstein (2011b) identifies one of these currents as "the 1968 current," or the "second Arab revolt," which aims to "achieve the global autonomy of the Arab world" that was prevented by Franco-British measure during the "first Arab revolt." Arguing that the Arab Spring is the heir of the "world revolution of 1968," Wallerstein points out that both movements are rooted in anti-authoritarianism and rejection of corrupt power systems. He writes that, like the rebels in the Arab world, the revolutionaries of 1968 were protesting against the inherently undemocratic behavior of those in authority. This was a revolt against such use (or misuse) of authority at all levels, including at the level of the world-system as a whole, the level of the national and local governments, and the level of the multiple nongovernmental institutions in which people take part or to which they are subordinated (from workplaces to educational structures to political parties and trade unions).

The Arab Spring has become simply one part of what is now very clearly worldwide unrest: Oxi in Greece, *Indignados* in Spain, students in Chile, the Occupy movements that spread to eight hundred cities in North America and elsewhere, strikes in China and demonstrations in Hong Kong, and multiple happenings across Africa.

Wallerstein (2011b) leaves those who believe that world unrest is simply a "passing moment" with a warning: The "1968 current" will no longer be so easily contained. We now briefly speak to a few of the very many movements of this moment.

The Roots and Trajectory of the Arab Spring

Amin (2012) argues that during the Bandung and Non-Alignment period from 1955 to 1970, the Arab countries were in the forefront of the struggles of the peoples and nations of the Global South for social and economic equality within the world-system. He mentions the Algerian National Liberation Front (FLN), Gamal Abdel Nasser's Egypt, the Arab Socialist Baa'th Parties of Iraq, the South Yemen Republic, and Syria. Though they were not democratic regimes, they were viewed as legitimate by their people because they provided mass education, health, and other public services; industrialization and guarantees of employment; and upward social mobility associated with independent initiatives and anti-imperialist postures. They faced the unmitigated hostility of the Western powers and ran out of steam, according to Amin, because of their internal contradictions and the demise of the Soviet camp and the world order of which it was a part. Though there were contradictions between the Soviet Union and the Arab-Islamic world, as in the Sultan Galiev affair, Amin does not go into detail and thus presents a silence that is not helpful to analysis. We would argue that the demise of the European world of communism altered the relations of force between Western capitalism and the countries of the Global South, though there were strong countries in the South, such as China, that represented the heart of the Bandung project.

But the demise of the Soviet bloc itself represented the heart of the neoliberal attack on the social power of the global lower strata, regardless of the ideological conflicts within the World Left.

Nonetheless, Amin (2012) argues that the economic deterioration caused by the neoliberal project produced a proliferation in the activities of the informal sector in economic and social life, an important source of income for about 60 percent of the Egyptian population:

> The Brotherhood's organizations have real ability to work in these circumstances, so that the success of the Brotherhood in these areas in turn has produced more inflation in these activities and thus ensured its reproduction on a larger scale. The political culture offered by the Brotherhood is known for its great simplicity. As this culture is content with only conferring Islamic "legitimacy" to the principle of private property and the "free" market relations, without considering the nature of the activities concerned, which are rudimentary ("Bazaar") activities that are unable to push forward the national economy and lead to its development.

The Gulf States have provided funds in the form of small loans or grants that have essentially undermined the productive capacity of the development of Egypt, so it operates on what Andre Gunder Frank deems a form of lumpen development. For Amin (2012), this form of lumpen development[2] undermines the strength of Egypt's economy in such a way that Egypt could not challenge the domination of the Gulf States and, of course, the domination of the United States in the region.

For Amin, the kind of "Bazaar economy" that hides behind "political Islam" makes the countries of the Arab world subject to impoverishment and thus vulnerable to the domination of the West. Amin (2012) holds that the other country that has occupied a prominent position during the first wave of awakening of the South is Algeria. Because French colonialism had so degraded Algerian "traditional" society in independent Algeria, the demand for equality was a distinguishing feature of the behavior and attitudes of its citizens to a degree unparalleled in all other Arabic countries. In contrast to Algeria, Egypt's traditional society was dominated by the demand for modernization, so modern Egypt became a project of the aristocratic bourgeoisie.

Amin (2012) continues to hammer out one of his main theses, which suggests that the strategy of contemporary imperialism in the Middle East is not the establishment of democracy but the weakening of the states of the area by supporting so-called Islamic regimes, which he argues guarantee the continuation of a form of lumpen development, a process of continuous pauperization that allows for the Western plunder of these societies:

> The final real target of contemporary imperialism is "containment and then after rolling back" by preemptive war the most dangerous emerging countries (China first). Add here Russia, which, if it succeeds in modernising its army, can put an end to the exclusive military power of the US. . . .
>
> That implies the total subordination of all other countries of the South with a view to ensuring exclusive access to the natural resources of the whole planet to the benefit of the societies of the triad (US, Europe and Japan), their plunder and waste. It implies therefore more of lumpen development, more of pauperisation and more of terrorist regimes. Contemporary capitalism has nothing else to offer.

Per-capita real-income growth within the Arab countries in the 1970s and 1980s was zero, according to the World Bank, and remained the lowest in the world from the 1990s to the present. This includes the economic performance of such oil-rich countries as Iraq, Algeria, Libya, and even Gulf countries, such as Saudi Arabia and the Emirates. Of course, it also created the social disaster that led to the Arab revolt (Shukrallah 2013).

For Amin, the stakes of this struggle are profound: If this struggle is the inception of a second "awakening" of the Arab world, the forward movement of the Arab world would become a part of the movement to go beyond imperialist capitalism on a world scale. Failure would keep the Arab world in its current status as a submissive periphery, "prohibiting its elevation to the rank of an active participant in shaping the world" (2011a).

Egypt had been the first country in the periphery of the capitalist world-system that tried to "emerge," at the start of the nineteenth century, well before China and Japan. Viceroy Mohammed Ali had initiated a process of renovation for Egypt and its neighbors in eastern North Africa that spanned two-thirds of the century before being brutally crushed by Britain, then the hegemonic power of the world-system, but nearing the end of its reign. However, it sought to ensure that a modern Egypt could not emerge. But despite the nineteenth-century defeat and the refashioning of its institutions to serve the needs of capitalist/imperialist accumulation, the people of Egypt would not surrender. A second wave of rising movements emerged from 1919 to 1967, whose first moment was the formation of the Wafd in 1919, which embarked on the path to political modernization through the adoption of a constitutional democracy in 1923. The form of democracy envisioned by the Wafd allowed progressive secularization. The British Embassy and royal palace, with the full support of Egypt's monarchy, great landlords, and rich peasants, used their full power to dismantle the democratic reforms made by the Wafdist leadership. In the 1930s, the dictatorship of Sedki Parsha abolished the constitution and clashed with the student movement, which spearheaded the democratic, anti-imperialist movement. It was against this threat, according to Amin, that the British supported the formation of the Muslim Brotherhood in 1927.

Though the increasing democratization of Egyptian society was interrupted by World War II, following the war the struggles resumed, marked in particular by the February 21, 1946, formation of the worker-student bloc, reinforced in its radicalization by the entry of communists and the workers' movement onto the stage of Egyptian society. Once again, Amin (2011a) argues, the bloc of wealthy conservatives with British support responded with violence and mobilized the Muslim Brotherhood behind a second dictatorship of Pasha. But this dictatorship could not silence the protest movement, and elections were allowed in 1950, resulting in the return of the Wafd to power, but its repudiation of the Anglo-Egyptian Treaty of 1936 and the inception of guerilla warfare in the Suez Canal Zone were defeated only by setting fire to Cairo in January 1952, an action in which the Muslim Brotherhood was deeply involved.

Amin (2011a) then argues that the "first coup d'état in 1952 by the 'Free Officers,' and above all a second coup in 1954 by which Nasser took control, was taken by some to 'crown' the continual flow of struggles and by others to put it to an end." Nasserism put forth an ideological discourse that wiped out the whole history of the years from 1919 to 1952 to push the start of the "Egyptian Revolution" to July 1952.

After the Bandung Conference of 1955, Nasserism increasingly took an anti-imperialist stance, emphasizing support for both pan-Arab and pan-African movements. Despite the radicalism of his anti-imperialism, he did not offer the masses the right to organize. Instead, Nasser focused on industrialization as a way out of the colonial division of labor that consigned Egypt to the role of an exporter of cotton. His policies maintained a division of incomes that favored the expanding middle classes without impoverishing the popular masses (Amin 2011a).

In ten years, according to Amin (2011a), the Nasser regime had used up its progressive potential. The 1967 defeat by Israel marked the end of the second wave, when Nasser moved to the Right against a radical student movement.

Anwar Sadat and Hosni Mubarak dismantled Egypt's productive system, replacing it with an incoherent system based on the profitability of firms that were mostly subcontractors for imperialist monopolies. This system led to an incredible increase in inequality and unemployment that affected the majority of the country's youth. It was an explosive situation, which indeed exploded.

The apparent stability of the system was based on a "monstrous police apparatus" counting 1.2 million men, compared to only 500,000 in the army. Though the Western powers claimed that the police force was built to protect Egyptian society from Islamism, Amin (2011a) argues that the regime had already integrated political Islam (on the Wahhabite model of the Gulf States) by giving them control of education, the courts, and the major media. Amin holds that the de facto power of political Islam destroyed the capacity for Egyptian society to confront the challenges of the "modern world," bringing about a catastrophic decline in education and research.

Amin argues that this Egyptian component of the Arab Spring allowed for the emergence of a democratic movement staunchly opposed to the neoliberal regime imposed on the Egyptian people. The coalition was composed of youth, the radical Left, and the democratic middle classes, with the youth at the forefront, though a group of young bloggers from the wealthy classes called for a U.S.-style democracy and distanced the movement from their aim of progressive social transformation. The Muslim Brotherhood had originally called for a boycott of the movement but joined it once fifteen million demonstrators went into the streets:

> Conspicuous progress in constructing the united front of workers and democratic forces is happening in Egypt. In April 2011 five socialist-oriented parties (the Egyptian Socialist Party, the Popular Democratic Alliance—made up of a majority of the membership of the former "loyal-left" Tagammu party, the Democratic Labor Party, the trotskyist Socialist Revolutionary Party, and the Egyptian Communist Party—which had been a component of Tagammu) established an Alliance of Socialist Forces through which they committed themselves to carry out their struggles in common. In parallel, a National Council (*Maglis Watany*) was established by all the active political and social forces of the movement (the socialist-oriented parties, the diverse democratic parties, the independent unions, the peasant organizations, the networks of young people, numerous social associations). The Council has about 150 members, the Muslim Brotherhood and the right-wing parties refusing to participate and thus reaffirming their well-known opposition to continuation of the revolutionary movement. (Amin 2011a, 6)

Though Amin was criticized by some for his December 2007 *Monthly Review* article "Political Islam in the Service of Imperialism," he seems to have responded to Dyab Abou Jahjah's critique, which challenged him to specify "which Political Islam."[3] In an interview with Aijaz Ahmad, he focuses on the intent of the Western powers to destroy potential opponents of neoliberalism that emerge in the region. He claims they are destroying societies just as they did Libya. They destroyed Iraq; next they will seek to destroy Syria and then Iran; then they will seek to contain and possibly rollback the major emerging countries: China and Russia and India (if she is "naughty"). The "destruction" of these societies would allow the continuation of lumpen development.

He then argues that the Muslim Brotherhood's support for this effort in Egypt has nothing to do with their being advocates of Political Islam. Amin can only laugh at the farce of the emir of Qatar and the king of Saudi Arabia standing with Westerners Barack Obama, Nicolas Sarkozy, and David Cameron as leaders of the struggle for democracy. However, their hegemony in the region "in the name of Islam" is what they have in common. There are different understandings of Islam. Their project is a comprador project that will allow Western domination of a neoliberal social order.

That the Muslim Brotherhood supports these policies shows, according to Amin (2012), that we should look at the Muslim Brotherhood not as an "Islamic Party, but as an reactionary party using Islam as a front." This, Amin concludes, is the global picture of the strategic targets of Western imperialism and their internal allies, reactionary forces within the societies of the Middle East.

On June 30, 2013, the largest revolutionary popular mobilization in Egyptian history saw up to seventeen million people take to the streets to demand the resignation of the Muslim Brotherhood government of Mohammed Morsi. Lebanese Marxist Gilbert Achcar has concluded that the Arab uprising is just beginning (K. Anderson 2013).

Two years after the start of what we are calling the Arab Spring, Achcar (2013) argues that we are in the beginning of a long-term revolutionary process, which is not simply an issue of regime change of but dealing with what he refers to as the social-economic problem, the main manifestation of which is high levels of unemployment, which have been a prominent feature of the economies of the entire region for several decades.

Tunisia experienced regime change but no change in the orientation of social-economic problems. Libya saw a more radical overthrow of the state, but the overthrow of such a strong state led to a degree of chaos, which should have been expected with the destruction of a state that had lasted for forty-four years and was not replaced by an occupying army, which the Libyans rejected. In Yemen, the revolution has been aborted by a compromise dictated by the Gulf countries and the United States. In Bahrain, the movement has been somewhat repressed by the intervention of Gulf countries but continues to be an active force in the country. Syria is in the midst of a civil war.

Achcar (2013, 1) tells us that the formula "the people want" reveals "the emergence of the people as a collective will on the public stage, the people as a political subject." People who have lived for decades under conditions that Achcar characterizes as despotism are now entering into a revolutionary era, which, he is very careful to point out, is just in its infancy, the early stages of a long-term revolutionary process. In Syria, Achcar argues that Western powers hesitate to intervene because of Russia's and Iran's support for the regime of Bashar al-Assad. This support has enabled the regime to massacre quietly for two years, with estimates of up to seventy thousand dead.

Eventually, this long-term process may break the bounds of the structural constraints that bind it to the social economic status quo with the "emergence of leaderships based on the workers' and popular movement, with a program of a progressive nature, centered on the satisfactions of social needs and able to engage the countries of the region on the path of development, taking into account the multiple dimensions that this term has acquired" (Achcar 2013, 128). Key here, Achcar argues, is that the state plays a central role, contrary to neoliberal dogma that dominates throughout the capitalist world. Achcar also argues that synergies can be established with the crisis that is shaking Europe and the radicalization that is under way in such countries as Greece and Spain.

Amin argues along similar lines but with longer organizational history in Egypt than Achcar. In an interview with Wang Hui and Lau Kin Chi on February 26, 2011, he suggested that if elections were held immediately, many people would vote for the Muslim Brotherhood because it is well organized and has the media on its side. On the other hand, if they would allow a year of real freedom, the Left and the youth could organize themselves. In contrast to the strong transition with an election that the army wanted, the movement wanted a slow transition in order to allow for the new political, democratic forces to organize themselves; to elaborate their programs and projects; and to have access to public opinion before the elections (Amin 2011b, 2).

Amin argues that the conception of a long struggle demanded by the movement is based on Egypt's history as a country of long revolutions, from 1920 to 1952. In the long run, the youth and the Left are in the majority of those with a capacity for action. But the Muslim Brotherhood has been a stealth figure in the movement, which opened the prisons and released seventeen thousand criminals; gave them pro-Mubarack badges, arms, and money; and guaranteed that they would not be returned to prison.

The opposition consists of four components: the youth, the radical Left, middle-class Democrats, and the Muslim Brotherhood. The movement was started by the youth, numbering more than one million in its organizational ranks, who oppose the social economic system but have not fully developed their ideas about capitalism. They are nationalist and anti-imperialist in the sense that they are opposed to domination by the United States. Though they initially numbered one million, they rapidly drew about fifteen million into the ranks of the movement on the ground all around Egypt.

The radical Left, which came out of the communist tradition, immediately joined the youth in the movement. The youth are not anti-communist but do not wish to be placed in the box with chiefs and take orders. But the relationship between the youth and the communists is a coming together, according to Amin (2011b, 3), not of leadership and followership but of interaction. The middle-class Democrats joined the movement on the second day.

The Muslim Brotherhood boycotted the movement during the first four days of its existence because it thought that it would be defeated by the police. However, when it saw that the movement could not be defeated, it joined the protests (Amin 2011b, 4).

From the Arab Spring to Occupy Wall Street

As we have argued throughout this book, the framework for the current crisis in the world-system is the crisis of neoliberal globalization, which itself was an attempt to discipline the working classes of the world through arguing that the natural adjustment of the economy was a response to the hubris of some who believed that they could force the economic system to respond to their needs without regard for the needs of the accumulators of capital, who were the job creators and thus must be given priority in economic adjustments.

As we have discussed in these pages, the revolts of the last decade include rebellions against misuse of authority at all levels, including at the world-system as a whole, national and local governments, and multiple nongovernmental institutions in which people take part or to which they are subordinated (from workplaces to educational structures to political parties and trade unions).

It is not only the revolt against corrupt power structures but also the modes of organizing that Wallerstein recognizes from 1968. These two factors, combined with the influence of nonviolent resistance inherited from Gandhi, Martin Luther King, and Thoreau and the empowering image of "forgotten peoples" previously marginalized from political activity, prompt Wallerstein to argue that the "1968 current" can be seen at work in Egypt, Tunisia, and beyond. It is this, he suggests, that has unsettled the powerful everywhere:

> The rapid public embrace of this current . . . terrified those in power—
> the rulers of every Arab state without exception, the governments of
> the "outside" states who were an active presence in the geopolitics of the
> Arab world, even the governments of very distant states. (2011b)

However, Wallerstein is quick to point out that challenging corrupt power structures is never simple. "Make no mistake about it," he writes, "all regimes want, above all, to stay in power" (2011b). It is this fact that has created the second current at work in the Arab Spring, a current that involves all important geopolitical actors in an attempt to "divert collective activity in the Arab world" through "repression, concessions and diversion" in order to secure their own interests (2011b). This current expresses itself through a variety of tactics.

One way to stay in power is for some of those who are in power to join the uprising, casting overboard a personage who happens to be the president or ruler in favor of the pseudo-neutral armed forces. This is exactly what happened in Egypt, leading those who are today reoccupying Tahrir Square in Egypt to complain as they seek to reinvigorate the "1968 current" (2011b). It is not only in Arab states that this second reactionary current has found expression; Wallerstein also sees its influence in the actions of France, Great Britain, and the United States in Libya. France and Great Britain—the fading former colonial powers— were both badly caught with their pants down in Tunisia and Egypt when it was discovered that their leaders had been personally profiting from the two dictatorships. They did not merely support them against the uprising but also actively counseled them on how to repress it. Despite the degree to which these two countries (and others) had engaged in profitable business in Libya for at least a decade, they suddenly "realized" that Gaddafi was a terrible dictator, which no doubt he was, and set out to redeem themselves by offering open military support for the Libyan rebels. Wallerstein concludes his analysis on a hopeful note, arguing, "The '1968 current' is expanding—despite repression, despite concessions, despite co-option" (2011b). While the leaders of the powerful nations have been involved in geopolitical "juggling" over their response to the Arab Spring, rebellion has spread worldwide.

On December 17, 2010, in Tunisia, vegetable peddler Mohammed Bouazizi set himself ablaze in the town of Sidi Bouzid after his cart was confiscated by a policewoman who slapped him and spit in his face. This incident became the single spark that started a prairie fire, as the general anger over the greed of the political elite spilled over into protests, which were brutally subdued. Bouazizi died, and after nearly a month of protests, with public anger mounting over the increasingly violent response of the security forces and after senior generals told President Zine El Abiding Ben Ali that they had lost confidence in his ability to continue as president, the president fled the country on January 14, 2011. In the meantime, the spark spread to Egypt, where Mubarack was forced from office on January 14, 2011, and then to Libya, where protests against Gaddafi's regime in February 2011 led to the occupation of Benghazi and eventually to his ouster in August 2011. On March 14, 2011, Saudi Arabia and the Gulf States sent troops into Bahrain to defend the Suni Al Khalifa monarchy. On March 18, 2011, the Syrian government of President al-Assad killed five protesters in the southern city of Deraa, sparking an uprising across the country that, by October, had led to the deaths of three thousand people.

The manifesto of the Occupy Wall Street movement clearly acknowledges the inspiration that it received from the occupation of Tahrir Square and its impact on what the movement terms "a worldwide shift in revolutionary tactics." The spirit of this fresh tactic, a fusion of Tahrir with the *Indignados* of Spain, is captured in this quote:

> The anti-globalization movement was the first step on the road. Back then our model was to attack the system like a pack of wolves. There was an alpha male, a wolf who led the pack, and those who followed behind. Now the model has evolved. Today we are one big swarm of people. (Raimundo Viejo, Pompeu Fabra University, Barcelona, Spain)

Its members argue that the time has come to deploy this emerging stratagem against the greatest corrupter of our democracy: "Wall Street, the financial Gomorrah of America."

This approach offers a renewal of the tactics of direct democracy, which had been the coin in trade of the New Left that emerged during the 1960s on a world scale, or what Wallerstein refers to as the 1968 current. The movement's members herald the beauty of that approach to be its pragmatic simplicity: They talk to each other in various physical gatherings, focus on a strategic demand, and then "go out and seize a square of singular symbolic significance and put our asses on the line to make it happen."

The Occupy Wall Street manifesto argues that Tahrir succeeded in large part because the people of Egypt made a straightforward ultimatum—that Mubarak must go—over and over again until they won. Following this model, it puts forward an equally uncomplicated demand: "We demand that Barack Obama ordain a Presidential Commission tasked with ending the influence money has over our representatives in Washington. It's time for DEMOCRACY NOT CORPORATOCRACY, we're doomed without it."[4]

Adbusters and the Origins of Occupy Wall Street

David Graeber (2011b) argues that in a generation or so, capitalism will no longer exist, but this concept is beyond the imagination of so many that one has to really think about why:

> The last 30 years have seen the construction of a vast bureaucratic apparatus for the creation and maintenance of hopelessness, a giant machine designed, first and foremost, to destroy any sense of possible alternative futures. At its root is a veritable obsession on the part of the rulers of the world—in response to the upheavals of the 1960s and 1970s—with ensuring that social movements cannot be seen to grow, flourish or propose alternatives; that those who challenge existing power arrangements can never, under any circumstances, be perceived to win. To do so requires creating a vast apparatus of armies, prisons, police; various forms of private security firms and police and military intelligence apparatus, and propaganda engines of every conceivable variety, most of which do not attack alternatives directly so much as create a pervasive climate of fear, jingoistic conformity and simple despair that renders any thought of changing the world, an idle fantasy.

This state of affairs is not a reflection of the death of imagination but of a system of thought control about which we are simply afraid to speak, less we be thought to be wild-eyed romantics, out of touch with the real world. Kenneth Boulding (2011), a former president of the American Economic Association and author of the authoritative textbook of neoclassical-Keynesian economic synthesis, has pointed out that "anyone who believes exponential growth can go on forever in a finite world is either a madman or an economist" and that "mathematics brought rigor to economics. Unfortunately it also brought mortis."

The editors of *Adbusters* argue that the biggest impediment to revolution is our own deep-seated feelings of cynicism and impotence. Because we are so much a part of the social world that we contemplate, it is hard to see that the social system is simply one stage of a never-ending cycle that sooner or later will fall and be replaced by another social system. They do not think that a million activists are needed but an influential minority "that smells the blood, seizes the moment and pulls off a set of well-coordinated strategic moves" in the midst of a certain level of collective disillusionment from the very clear disastrous missteps of the corporate and political elites in their handling of a crisis like global warming, a stock market crash, or a nuclear standoff in the Middle East.[5]

Graeber (2013, xvi) points out that nothing scares the rulers of America more than the prospect of democracy breaking out. Thus, a Democracy Project would dramatically broaden the sense of possibility of all those who participate in the movement and would also affect the sense of possibility among the general public who are paying attention to the activities of the movement on the stage of societal interaction.

Participation in horizontal decision making and action transforms one's sense of possibility overnight. And once people's sense of possibility is expanded, the change is permanent (Graeber 2013, xix). This process brings about the revival of the radical imagination that conventional wisdom has long declared dead. But with this change in consciousness arises a new kind of wisdom that recognizes that creating a democratic culture is a long-term process, a profound moral transformation (xx).

When Graeber returned to his native New York from London, his old friend Marissa Holmes from the New York anarchist scene introduced him to Ahmed Maher and Waleed Rashed, two of the founders of the Egyptian April 6 Movement[6] that had played a key role in the Egyptian revolution. These founding members had been invited to speak at New York City's landmark Left institution, the Brecht Forum (Graeber 2013, 8). In discussing the plan for Occupy Wall Street with the Egyptian revolutionaries, Graeber (2011b) explains what the speech revealed to him about the need to use direct democracy as the tactical and strategic center of the approach of the Occupy Wall Street movement:

> "The funny thing is," my Egyptian friend told me, "you've been doing this so long, you kind of forget that you can win. All these years, we've been organizing marches, rallies. . . . And if only 45 people show up, you're depressed. If you get 300, you're happy. Then one day, you get 500,000. And you're incredulous: on some level, you'd given up thinking that could even happen."

Then Graeber (2011b) attempts to think through the difference between the circumstances of the Egyptian movement and the U.S. movement:

> Mubarak's Egypt was one of the most repressive societies on Earth—the entire apparatus of state was effectively organized around ensuring that what ended up happening could never happen. And yet it did.
>
> Military regimes like Egypt live on fear. Their leadership assume that most of the populace despise them, but people are aware that any attempt at mass opposition will be met instantly by torture and death. For most of those who live under these regimes, "political life" is a matter of continual, barely suppressed rage. The real question is whether people

detect an opportunity, a crack in the façade. That is why when soldiers refused to fire on protesters in Tunisia, uprisings in Egypt, Yemen, and Libya followed almost instantly. In modern democracies like the UK, in contrast, political life is organized more around cynicism and despair. You not only have to reveal the system as vulnerable—which the students began to do—and overcome the endless divisions that politicians and media have created between students, trade unionists, immigrants, and the unemployed; you also have to convince people that a social order based on human solidarity and mutual aid would even be possible.

There is only one known way to do that, and that is for people to experience it. This is why, emboldened by the students, grassroots organizations across the UK are planning to respond to the attacks by a wave of occupations, turning every shut-down youth center, hospital or library into an experiment in real democratic self-management. Will it work? Will the bulk of the British working class, battered by 30 years of defeat, finally rally to take back what is theirs? No one knows. But everywhere there are signs, some angry, some whimsical, most small, that this time something really might be different.

When Joseph Stiglitz published an article in the May 2011 issue of *Vanity Fair* entitled "Of the 1%, by the 1%, for the 1%," Graeber noticed that there was a great deal of commentary in newspapers about how the top 1 to 2 percent of the population had come to increasingly monopolize the lion's share of the nation's wealth. Graeber (2013, 38–39) is struck by Stiglitz's argument that members of the 1 percent were the ones creating the rules about how the political system works and had turned it into one based on legalized bribery.

With assistance from two members of the Spanish *Indignados*, members of the General Assembly decided that they wanted to achieve something similar to what had already been accomplished in Athens, Barcelona, and Madrid, where ordinary citizens who were not seasoned activists occupied public squares in opposition to the trajectories that each of their countries had taken under the direction of the top 1 percent against the interest of the 99 percent. The Wall Street action was considered to be a stepping stone toward the creation of a network of such assemblies throughout the United States and beyond (Graeber 2013, 42–43).

On September 17, 2011, the Arab Spring was to become the new American Fall, with twenty thousand revolutionaries in a tent city, plus solidarity occupations in major financial centers worldwide, all ready for a long siege, all vowing not to leave until they got their one simple demand: They stood against the greed and corruption of the 1 percent and wanted to get the corrupting influence of money out of the political process, the greatest corrupter of our democracy.

Though we have discussed the influence of the Arab Spring on the Occupy Wall Street movement, it should be noted that this movement's organizers took greater inspiration for their organizing tactics from movements in similarly configured societies, such as the encampments of central squares in Spain, at

Madrid's Puerta del Sol on May 15, 2011, and subsequently at Barcelona's Plaça Catalunya. Michael Hardt and Antonio Negri (2011) argue that the Spanish protests brought together a wide array of social and economic grievances regarding debt, housing, and education, but their "indignation" was clearly directed at the political system that they deemed incapable of addressing these issues.

The Spanish *Indignados*

The editors of a special issue of the journal *Social Justice* attempt to situate the crisis in Spain within a process of dispossession that they argue takes place at the intersection of the crisis of debt, the crisis of management, and the crisis of the European project itself (Coma et al. 2013, 62). They perceive a disaffection from representational politics of parties and unions and a movement to reimagine political activism from scratch. At the beginning of the crisis, many voices were raised across the political spectrum, calling for the recondition of capitalism to move away from financial speculation back to productive capitalism. Financial powers, however, took advantage of the crisis to reorganize the system in their interests (63). Bailouts of creditors at the expense of local economies are said to have shifted the cost of the crisis onto society. The social and political rights gained over the past decades are also said to be under attack.

As the economic crisis in Spain deepened, a group of activists sought to unify the country's disparate progressive activists into a movement they called *Democracia Real YA* (Real Democracy Now), calling for a day of action on May 15, 2011. In opposition to the government, which claimed the Spanish people were living beyond their means, the movement argued that the unemployment rate in Spain was twice that of any other European country. It has also been acknowledged that the "recession" that has ravaged Spain and much of southern Europe has disproportionately affected youth, with unemployment rates of more than 40 percent for ages 20 to 24—about twice the national average, and the highest rate in the European Union (Daley 2011). The encampment lasted from May 15 to August 2, 2011, when the national police evicted the protesters and closed the central plaza to the public. During the evictions, a number of activists and members of the press were victims of unprovoked police violence. But these evictions inspired more fury from the public, who demanded that these spaces be returned to the public for their use. The authorities relented after several days of demonstrations.

But the encampment itself was not restored, and the movement joined forces with the *Platforma Afectados por la Hipoteca*, a group that had been founded in early 2009 to promote solidarity among people who could not pay their mortgages. They began to mobilize to stop evictions in November 2010, and by May 15, 2011, they had successfully stopped some twenty evictions (Gimbel 2012). By the time of the *Real News* interview, they had stopped 116 evictions.[7]

The movement got another burst of energy as it spread around the world with the October 15 call to action that came to be known as Occupy Everywhere.

This mobilization called out 500,000 people into the streets of Madrid and another 250,000 into the streets of Barcelona. The target of these mobilizations was not public squares, but abandoned hotels. The Spanish constitution specifically requires the state to provide dignified housing to all citizens, so in the absence of access to dignified housing, citizens are justified in their occupation of hotels. The preface to the Declaration of Human Rights specifically guarantees the right of rebellion to citizens.

And so, the appropriation of unused and abandoned buildings has a precedent in Spain. An example in one neighborhood is the conversion of a former tobacco factory into a self-sustaining popular space for art, music, gardening, social gatherings, and political assemblies. Other occupied spaces exist outside the law. Some seek to provide housing for victims of evictions, and others provide radical spaces where people are able to provide alternatives to dominant social norms. Though journalists are generally denied access to such occupied spaces, they do provide examples of forms of resistance to neoliberal corporatism for the movement's international counterparts (Gimbel 2012).

Democracia Real YA and the 15-M (May 15) movement are seeking to expand beyond Spain to partners in the United States; Sidney, Australia; New Zealand; different European countries; and wherever conferences are held that can provide audiences who might be interested in the work that they have done. They view themselves as obligated to help generate a critical spirit in society to eliminate the conformity that prevails so that people can bring about change.

They caution against attempting to impose solutions on others but emphasize the art of listening so as to learn the perspectives of others that might lead to an enrichment that benefits all. The importance of such connections is that we enlarge our collective presence from a small one to a larger one. In the end, they argue, we all grow stronger from our ability to work together and to share the information and strategies that we have.

But 15-M has affirmed the reappropriation of politics as a radical collective act that not only advanced the peoples' movements but also disrupted the interpretative framework established by the Democratic Transition in Spain since the late 1970s (Coma et al. 2013, 69) and that we all know as the period of establishing the neoliberal framework around the world as a means of constraining the bargaining power of the world's working classes and the people of the Global South.

Mauro Castro Coma, Joan M. Gaul Bergas, Francesco Salvini, and Alto Tinoco i Girona argue that the crisis that the people of Spain are living in is a lie. Rather "it is a process of exploitation and dispossession led by the morbid will to power of financial capitalism" (2013, 74). In response, the social movements that have emerged in this period are seeking to create a new kind of social insurrection based on the power of a productive and hierarchical-free body whose desires are taken into consideration. Therefore, the movements are not based on representation but on active listening and real cooperation, which will enable them to create a new horizon for politics (74).

Chilean Youth

On December 1, 2011, in support of Chile's ongoing student protests and voicing their own demands, thousands of people took to the streets in more than a dozen cities in Latin America to call for quality public education. The Latin American March for Education was organized by the Chilean students' confederation, and demonstrations were held in Argentina, Brazil, Chile, Colombia, Costa Rica, Ecuador, Guatemala, Honduras, Mexico, Paraguay, Peru, Uruguay, and Venezuela (Sepulveda 2011). In Chile itself, some ten thousand protesters are said to have marched through the streets of Santiago to demand reforms of the educational system.

Most young people have a negative view of Augusto Pinochet and have taken a robust aim at the economic policies that brought him into power. While Pinochet used the military prowess of the Chilean armed forces to oust his predecessor, Salvador Allende, he clung to power by maintaining close ties with the rich landowners and urban industrialists of the country. He succeeded in this by scrapping welfare programs for the poor in favor of fiscal prudence, deregulating the economy, and delegalizing trade unions. The result was a dramatic rise in inequality that still persists today: The top 10 percent owns 40 percent of the wealth, and the bottom 10 percent owns 1 percent (Marotta 2013).

In contemporary Latin America more than any place, the dictatorships of the 1970s and 1980s are remembered as brutally repressive, free-market regimes that institutionalized inequality across the Southern Cone. But given the Honduran coup of 2009, it is evident that the specter of military authoritarianism persists across Latin America (Merrota 2013). The Chilean students are undertaking an important task in calling out that hideous legacy, forcing others to recall it for what it was. Henry Kissinger bragged to Christopher Hitchens, who questioned his role in Allende's overthrow and murder, that the writer did not have the "character" to preside over and carry out such an operation. And to think that such a man still holds a position of honor in U.S. society. How can we possibly go forward without fully acknowledging the role of our government and characterizing the act for what it was?

According to documents revealed by Peter Kornbluh (2013), in 1970, the CIA's deputy director of plans wrote in a secret memo: "It is firm and continuing policy that Allende be overthrown by a coup. . . . It is imperative that these actions be implemented clandestinely and securely so that the USG [the U.S. government] and American hand be well hidden." That same year, President Nixon ordered the CIA to "make the economy scream" in Chile to "prevent Allende from coming to power or to unseat him."

President Nixon, speaking in a March 1972 phone call, acknowledged that he had given instructions to "do anything short of a Dominican-type action" to keep Allende, the elected president of Chile, from assuming office. The phone conversation was captured by his secret Oval Office taping system. In this clip, President Nixon tells his press secretary, Ron Ziegler, that he has given orders to undermine Chilean democracy to the U.S. ambassador, but "he just failed."[8]

Kornbluh (2013) tells us:

> Richard Nixon and Henry Kissinger launched a preemptive strike against Salvador Allende. They decided to stop him from being inaugurated as president of Chile. He hadn't even set foot in the Moneda Palace, when Nixon and Kissinger just simply decided to change the fate of Chile. Nixon instructed the CIA to make the Chilean economy scream, to use as many men as possible. The first plan was to actually keep Allende from being inaugurated as president. And then, when that plan failed, after the assassination of the Chilean commander-in-chief that the United States was behind, General René Schneider, Kissinger then went to Nixon and said, "Allende is now president. The State Department thinks we can coexist with him, but I want you to make sure you tell everybody in the U.S. government that we cannot, that we cannot let him succeed, because he has legitimacy. He is democratically elected. And suppose other governments decide to follow in his footstep, like a government like Italy? What are we going to do then? What are we going to say when other countries start to democratically elect other Salvador Allendes? We will—the world balance of power will change," he wrote to Nixon in a secret document, "and our interests in it will be changed fundamentally."

To our disgrace, the long hand of the United States delivered Chile into the hands of tyrants—and we have done absolutely nothing about it. Just another *fait accompli*. We should thank the Chilean students for their bravery on this front. This is ultimately the best way to commemorate those who died under Pinochet's reign: to continue our fight for a better society, regardless of what adversity may lie ahead.

In 2011, Chilean students took to the streets in large numbers more than forty times to denounce a system that funnels state subsidies to private institutions while public schools in poor areas struggle. It is said that on September 12, 2013, tens of thousands of students marched in Santiago, Chile, to demand an end to the educational system inherited from General Pinochet. This is particularly significant, because Chile is preparing to mark the fortieth anniversary of the coup that brought him to power.

Similar protests took place in other Chilean cities as part of a nationwide mobilization convened by groups representing high school and college students and the educators' professional association. Andres Fielbaum, leader of the University of Chile Students Federation, told reporters that it was important to frame these actions within the context of dreadful history from which it stemmed and to erase the legacy for which it stands, saying, "Forty years ago, education became a product. And it continues to be that way to this day." Pinochet, who led the bloody September 11, 1973, coup that removed the elected President Allende, pursued free-market fundamentalism and privatization during his repressive seventeen-year rule. He went on to reshape Chile's education system, slashing government support for public schools and giving municipalities control over how to spend the reduced amounts coming from Santiago. Privatization, as we have seen throughout the reign of the neoliberal regime, has remained the name of the game. In Chile, private schools mushroomed under the military regime, but the trend continued even after democracy was restored in 1990.[9]

The privatization of what had been public services, of course, is a central component of the neoliberal social order, and it maintains a hold wherever it can, though the winds of change are blowing everywhere. The Chilean students are organizing broadly among other sectors of the population, so this radical-ization will likely have a significant effect on Chilean society. On April 11, 2013, more than one hundred thousand (some say two hundred thousand) marched all around Chile to demonstrate the resurgence of the student movement. Members of this cohort in Chilean society were born between 1988 and 1995 and are often referred to "as the generation with no fear" (Leon 2013).

Given the winds that are blowing in Latin America, Spain, Greece, and the Arab world, and elsewhere around the globe, do we dare say that the emergence of this particular cohort of the Chilean Student Movement is a continuation of the 1968 current, with its sophisticated organizing strategy and its analysis of Chilean society?

Puerto Rican Student Strike at the University of Puerto Rico

Though the 2010–2011 Puerto Rican student protest movement at the University of Puerto Rico (UPR) was a reaction to the elimination of tuition waivers and an $800 tuition increase, some have sought to make a more critical examination of the UPR student protests to discern a complex and interconnected political, social, and economic dilemma facing the island and citizens of Puerto Rico. There is a broader concern reflected in the student protests—that social-class stratification of the island will increase if the island's historical vehicle of upward social mobility is made less accessible to those with less ability to pay higher tuition coasts.

Gabriel Barela holds that the tuition increase and simultaneous budget cuts also embody neoliberal ideology, which continues to influence the political agenda set forth by UPR administration, Puerto Rico government officials, and U.S. corporate interests.

In February 2011, José Ramón de la Torre, head of the sixty-thousand-student system, resigned after a series of violent clashes between students and riot police throughout 2010. Some two hundred people were arrested and scores of students injured, prompting professors and university workers to walk out for two days in sympathy with the students. Conservative Governor Luis Fortuño

finally relented and pulled back the hundreds of riot police who had been occupying the system's eleven campuses for weeks.

It was the first police occupation of the university in more than thirty years.
More than ten thousand protesters at one point engaged in a civil disobedience
sit-in, periodically shutting down a highway, in solidarity with more than 150
students who had been arrested for such acts weeks earlier. The march drew
members from seventy-two civic and political organizations, and seen participating were professors from the College of Natural Sciences, notables from the
arts, seniors, community groups from housing projects, clergy, Vieques activists,
and even members of the Fortuño administration.

Overall, some of the most astute Puerto Rican observers note that struggle
for power and influence during the UPR student strikes of 2010 and 2011 was
determined in part by Puerto Rico's colonial condition and "influenced the ideological construction of the country's colonial conflict" (Atiles-Osoria 2013, 105).
As we have seen throughout the social revolts of this period, the strikes themselves were caused by the economic crisis and the austerity measures and budget
cuts used almost everywhere to undercut the bargaining power of the workers,
and therefore the cost of labor.

The university used the austerity measures to justify its cutbacks, and the
students used the law to justify the reduction in their life chances by the university. At the same time, the criminalization and state terrorism employed in
response to the strikes were the same strategies traditionally used against Puerto
Rican independence movements. The neoliberal counterrevolution here, as elsewhere, served as a space of encounter in the colonial conflict and in the class
struggle and social struggles within the larger social system.

The Puerto Rican people have been under colonial rule for almost 520 years,
with the past 114 years spent under the control of the United States (Atiles-
Osoria 2013, 106). This situation, as almost always happens, intensifies the po-
liticization of the people and the social polarization within their society.

In the course of its 108-year-history, UPR has faced ten large-scale strikes
and hundreds of protests. These struggles have represented opposition to the
power relations between a colonial regime and society in constant struggle for
the recognition of its right to self-determination and the eradication of economic, social, racial, and gender inequalities (Atiles-Osoria 2013, 107). The administration sought to create a criminalized collective to justify the use of extreme
repression against them. Hundreds of students were prosecuted for participating
in demonstrations at the UPR, though these cases were most often dismissed in
court because of lack of evidence (Atiles-Osoria 2013, 111).

Overall, the social struggles at UPR led to the administration's elaboration
of a new conception of social security that calls for the sacrifice of individual
and collective freedom. But it also gave rise to "radical democracy" as a con-
tingency strategy, using new means of struggle, such as cyberactivism (Atiles-
Osoria 2013, 114).

This, of course, reflects an arena of struggle in which the forces of the status quo are inventing new means of control, and the forces of resistance to domination are growing in their determination and social power.

The Dream of Human Possibility and Human Solidarity

The dream of human possibility and human solidarity is at the root of what many people of the United States refer to as the American Dream. It was the dream of a people of a relatively young nation still emerging but paradoxically contending for global hegemony in the worldwide social system that some refer to as historical capitalism. In many ways, this young nation was different from the world-dominating countries of old Europe, whose conquest of the extra-European world included the establishment of a number of settler colonies, of which the United States was the most successful.

Though the young nation fought a war of liberation against the British and presented itself as different from the colonial powers of old Europe, it was formed by the European conquest of the extra-European world, was indeed a part of the same social system, and came to be the dominant power in that social system by the twentieth century. But it, too, contained the logic of domination and liberation that characterizes the life of an inherently polarizing social system, such as the capitalist world-system in which we have lived for the past five hundred years. Furthermore, the process of nation building; emerging and internal social class, gender, and racial conflict; and the consequent internalization of geopolitical and geocultural conflict gave the United States the aura of a "nation of nations," which was thought to make it particularly fit for the position of world leadership but which also undermined the logic of pan-European racism that was the social glue of pan-European world domination and the hierarchical structure of the capitalist world economy.

When Malcolm X, Martin Luther King Jr., Angela Davis, Gloria Anzaldua, Elizabeth Martinez, and Ella Baker called for us to get on the right side of history, they dramatized the need for more humility among the people of the United States and showed that we could not grow if we did not reach out to learn from others and join with them in the creation of a liberated world, one in which we live in peace with all people and with Mother Earth.

The emergence of the world liberation struggle against global neoliberalism, during a period when world capitalism has entered into a structural crisis, means that now human agency is decisive, unlike during the long period of relative stability of our historical social system, historical capitalism. Now we must engage in discussion of our collective dreams (for humanity, and not just "America" or a small part of the nation's citizens). We must organize and build communities that transcend the old paradigms that we see everywhere in the social struggles now being engaged. We must put aside sectarian bickering about which organizations should lead and establish a system of community building based on the highest principles of inclusion, representation, self-determination, democracy, and respect. We must dismantle the existing social hierarchies in our practice.

We must do more than embrace this human dream: We must get on the right side of history by not only protesting but also building community on the basis of a collective human dream, which is not simply about the redistribution of wealth but also about our collective responsibility for each other and for Mother Earth. That struggle begins with each and every act and exchange, each and every day, and extends to putting a stop to the violence that results from differential valuation of human life based on race, gender, religion, sexuality, nation, class, and all forms of exploitation and domination. The time on the clock of the world is way past due.

> . . . And so they are won for the people.
> And so the infinite example is born.
> Not because they fought a part of their lives
>
> But because they fought all the days of all their lives.
> . . . And so they are, distant fires,
> Living, creating the heart
> Of example.[10]

Acknowledgments

First and foremost, we thank Sarafina for your patience as we conducted our research, your wisdom as we excitedly shared our observations, and your production assistance in the last stages of the manuscript; Malik for your ever-present optimism and depth of thought; Thembi for your cheery disposition and determination that tomorrow will be even better; and Soji (Sojourner Truth) for her eternal inspiration. We thank our grandchildren for your energy, spirit, creativity, humor, and intelligence—Tajalia, Angelo, Orlando, Jedidiah, Isabella, and Wisdom—and our in-law children, Jamal and Donna. You have all educated us over the years about honesty, integrity, and faith and have shown us that being life learners is a gift, not a weakness. We are humbled by your example and your patience with our long hours and routine silliness.

We are indebted to Rozzie for your compassion, thoughtfulness, and fun company during our many adventures in the course of this research and writing, and to Stanley, Momma, and Aunt Honey, whose grounding and voices centered us throughout this project as believers, fighters, and critical thinkers.

To the many other members of our family and the dear friends who were there for us through the many challenges we faced during the process of conducting research, doing the analysis, and writing this book, we are truly grateful: Andree, James, Pete, Renzie, Shug, Ken and Freda, Funke and Muoyo, Loretta, Leonher, Millicent, Dave and Val, Matt, Donna, Muriel, Hanna, Perry, Deb, Maggie, Stephanie, Janice, Gina, Della, Traci, Diana, Devin, Charlie, Maggie, Marsha, Godfrey, Cappy, Betita, Laura, Joseph, Dawn, Bill, Natalie, Gia, Letycia, Harlie, Mattie, Sandy, Lou, Pat, Yuan, Edward, Chris, Roseann, Billy, Gina, Dave, Luda, Miguel, Kizie, Tyrone, Isaac and crew, Yusuf, Ethan and family, Pat F., Raymond, Scott, Stephanie and everyone at Atria Tanglewood, and many others, too. There are so many people whose kind, patient, and supportive gestures and words made this project possible. Please know that we appreciate all the ways that each of you has been there for us and see your name represented here. Of course, we thank Athena, Zeus, and Mozz for always being there for us when we need you. To our family and friends in Brooklyn, Florida, Rochester, Kansas City, and the Bay Area, we express our utmost appreciation for always, collectively, being our anchor and for your love and support.

We have been blessed with deep friendships and connections to many communities and offer thanks to the wide circle of comrades who are fighting for a better world and who continuously inspire us. To our co-workers and colleagues at St. John's University and Adelphi University and our extraordinary students (you have always rocked our world!) and to our many colleagues, friends, and acquaintances who have given us strength and a reason to believe that we can live firmly centered in love, collaboration, and community, we extend our heartfelt gratitude. We hope you feel you are represented in this story.

Our professional friends and collaborators also have our deep appreciation—we cherish all that we have learned from you: Immanuel Wallerstein, Rose Brewer, Bob Newby, Steve Steinberg, Walda Katz Fishman, Jerome Scott, Bill Sales, Abdul Alkalimut, Komozi Woodard, Bill Martin, Frances Fox Piven, Grace Lee Boggs, Robin D. G. Kelley—all those referenced here and so many more.

We are grateful to all those who shared your thoughts so generously—unquestionably, this book would not be here without your insights, wisdom, and the hope represented in your reflections, even through the evident despair.

To Micah Kleit and the team at Temple University Press, we extend great thanks for your patience and guidance throughout this process.

And most importantly, we are grateful to all those who have fought and continue to fight today, holding onto the vision of a new day regardless of the challenges we face individually and together. We call out each and every one of your names here, to give tribute to the shining light that you provide in the spirit and toward the future of a just and loving world.

We are so very grateful, and we reside in the firm belief that a new day is coming.

For now and until then, we offer our eternal love, admiration, and appreciation.

—Melanie and Rod

Notes

PREFACE

1. Also known as the cheerleading squad.

2. The Harrisons had been veterans of the Greenwood Movement of the Student Non-violent Coordinating Committee (SNCC) in Greenwood, Mississippi, in 1964.

3. Scott-Heron 2000. Copyright © 2000 Gil Scott-Heron. Reprinted with permission of the publisher, Canongate.

4. Eleanor Bumpers was a Black woman who was shot and killed in 1984 by officers in the New York Police Department (NYPD) after she had refused to open the door when they arrived at her apartment to evict her for overdue rent. Yusef Hawkins was a 16-year-old Black man who was killed in Bensonhurst, Queens, in 1989 after being attacked by a crowd of white youth. Michael Griffith was a 23-year-old Black man who was killed after a group of white youth chased him onto the parkway in Howard Beach, Queens, in 1986. Abner Louima was a 30-year-old Haitian man who was sodomized by NYC police officers in 1997 in Flatbush, Brooklyn.

5. Amadou Diallo was a 23-year-old immigrant from Guinea who was shot and killed outside his residence in the Soundview section of the Bronx on February 4, 1999, by four plainclothes NYPD officers, who fired a combined total of forty-one shots, nineteen of which struck Diallo. The four officers were acquitted at their trial in Albany, New York. Diallo was unarmed at the time of the shooting.

6. Using Du Bois's terminology, particularly for the uprising of African peoples against colonialism and white supremacy.

7. King 1963.

CHAPTER 1

1. Many people reject the United States' arrogant appropriation of the term "America" to refer solely to the United States rather than to the Americas (North, South, and Central). See, for example, Martinez 2003.

2. By the 1960s and 1970s, some scholars began to refer to these groups as a "Third World Within," thus complicating the concept of "nation" as it applied to the United States (Allen 1967; Blauner 1972; Newton 1968; Schurmann 1974; Wallerstein 1979).

3. G. Bush 2001.

4. See National Archives 2013 and SOA Watch, n.d.

5. See www.census.gov/how/infographics/foreign_born.html. The foreign-born population is relatively small in absolute terms (40.1 million in 2010), representing 12.5 percent of the U.S. population. It is growing far more rapidly than the native-born population; in 1970, the foreign-born population was 4.7 percent of the total U.S. population.

6. In a discussion entitled "Citizenship Destabilized," Saskia Sassen explores these questions and others, such as whether current changes in the sociopolitics of today's world may signal an "emerging political subjectivity that partly lodges itself outside the national, but also changes the meaning of the national." She asserts that the functionality of citizenship relates to such issues as budget allocation but that our current system needs reformulation, in the direction of partial denationalization (2003, 14–21).

CHAPTER 2

1. See the documentary *Slavery by Another Name,* about the forced labor of Africans that continued well into the twentieth century, and the many well-documented reports about the extraordinary expansion of the prison industrial complex and mass incarceration of Black and brown men that has provided an extremely cheap labor force (e.g., www .theguardian.com/commentisfree/2012/jul/06/prison-labor-pads-corporate-profits-tax-payers-expense).

2. In the late nineteenth century, Black scholars began to write the real history of Black people to counter the mythical history presented by pan-European scholars and journalists, who often were constructors of the national myths that justified slavery and conquest. In 1882, George Washington Williams published his two-volume, 1,100-page work, *A History of the Negro Race in America from 1619 to 1880.*

CHAPTER 3

1. The word "geoculture" emphasizes that culture is not an abstraction but exists within a social world and is affected by the social relations of that world.

2. Senator Herschel V. Johnson of Georgia, quoted in Weinberg 1963, 178–179.

3. Elizabeth Martinez speaks of origin narratives that every society creates "to explain that society to itself and the world with a set of mythologized stories and symbols." She explores the "American" origin narrative in detail (1996) and attributes this labeling to Roxanne Dunbar Ortiz.

4. This material draws from M. Bush 2011.

5. The House Un-American Activities Committee (HUAC) functioned from 1938 to 1975 as a committee of the House of Representatives.

6. For a thorough exploration, see California Newsreel 2003a.

7. The Fourteenth Amendment "enshrined in the Constitution the ideas of birthright citizenship and equal rights for all Americans" (Foner [1990] 1998, 105).

8. During the last decade of the twentieth century, 7.6 million people immigrated to the United States: 17.4 percent from Europe, 38.9 percent from Asia, 33.4 percent from North America, 33.4 percent from South America, 4 percent from Africa, and 0.7 percent from Oceania (Kraly and Miyares 2001, 49).

9. Quijano and Wallerstein 1992.

10. Here, we mean the conquest of all of North and South America, not just the area that would become the United States.

11. The "long sixteenth century" is a concept used by world-system theorists to describe the extended development of the capitalist world-system.

12. For an explanation of the research methodology, see the online appendix at http://bit.ly/1uVN4rR.

CHAPTER 4

1. King 1965.

2. Roughly translated as "evil spirits," per the respondent.

3. In 2011, the average income for the middle 60 percent of households stood at $53,042 (Breslow and Wexler 2013).

4. See California Newsreel 2003a.

CHAPTER 5

1. The policy of "There Is No Alternative" (TINA) was brought into the public discourse particularly by British Prime Minister Margaret Thatcher. She and others argued that the current historical moment offered no options other than to pursue a course of neoliberalism to preserve capitalism, a presumed good.

2. McGruder 2007, 154.

3. See www.cnn.com/2012/11/07/politics/5-things-election-night.

4. See www.people-press.org/2012/11/26/young-voters-supported-obama-less-but-may-have-mattered-more/.

5. Katz 1992, 33.

CHAPTER 6

1. Roosevelt 1936.

2. See www.udel.edu/History/suisman/206_08-Fall/Online-readings/dubois.pdf.

3. Quoted in Dalfiume 1969a, 1969b, 305.

4. This is an important and underexplored issue in Malcolm's life, which needs more attention, especially his relationship to the Black Popular Front.

5. Quoted in Sitkoff 1971, 662.

6. See www.americanprogress.org/issues/2009/03/political_ideology.html.

7. See www.salon.com/2013/07/16/goodbye_to_my_american_dream/.

8. In this usage, the *paleros* were the ones leading the group.

9. See Center for the Study of the American Dream 2011.

10. See Pew Charitable Trusts 2011.

11. See Pew Charitable Trusts 2009, 11.

12. Ibid., 9.

CHAPTER 7

1. See http://dictionary.reference.com/browse/reverie.

2. In fact, the Americas as a whole receive 27 percent of the world's migrants, equal to Asia (28 percent), less than Europe (33 percent), and more than Africa (9 percent) and Oceania (3 percent). See www.migrationinformation.org/DataHub/wmm.cfm.

3. "One love" is a Rastafarian notion of their relationship with their God. Marcus Garvey ended most of his speeches with the phrase "one love."

4. See www.people-press.org/2011/12/28/little-change-in-publics-response-to-capi talism-socialism/.

5. See www.gallup.com/poll/158978/democrats-republicans-diverge-capitalism-fed eral-gov.aspx.

6. See www.gallup.com/poll/161927/majority-wealth-evenly-distributed.aspx ?utm_source=alert&utm_medium=email&utm_campaign=syndication& utm_content =morelink&utm_term=All%20Gallup%20Headlines.

CHAPTER 8

1. See https://web.archive.org/web/20050205041635/http://www.newamericancen tury.org/statementofprinciples.htm.

2. A group of economists who studied with Milton Friedman at the University of Chicago.

3. Initiated at the Bandung Conference in 1955, this represented the coming together of newly formed African and Asian states opposing colonialism and neocolonialism and seeking mutual economic and political cooperation.

CHAPTER 9

1. Though the theme to *Roots*, "Many Rains Ago (Oluwa)," speaks poignantly to the *longue durée* of African people captured and enslaved in America, it applies as well to the history of all people in our imagination and hearts.

CHAPTER 10

1. In January 1962, at the meeting of the Organization of American States (OAS), the United States proposed that Cuba be suspended from membership. The U.S. proposal was supported by fourteen of twenty-one members, the bare two-thirds needed to pass it. Cuba voted no, and six Latin American countries abstained. The principal ground for the suspension was the fact that Cuba had announced its adherence to Marxism-Leninism, which was deemed incompatible with membership. The United States, in addition, launched a total embargo on trade relations with Cuba and sought to get acquiescence in this boycott from its NATO allies in Western Europe and from Latin American states.

2. Of course, the term "lumpen development" recalls the Marxist use of the terminology of the *lumpenproletariat*, which refers to the same social strata that Amin refers to in Egypt. Marx and Engels (1998, 27) write that "'the dangerous class,' [*lumpenproletariat*] the social scum, that passively rotting mass thrown off by the lowest layers of the old society, may, here and there, be swept into the movement by a proletarian revolution; its conditions of life, however, prepare it far more for the part of a bribed tool of reactionary intrigue."

3. For access to articles from the Arab and Middle Eastern press, see Dyab Abou Jah-jah, "Samir Amin Frustrated: Which Political Islam Is Allied with Imperialism?" *Ouraim Archive,* posted by Sukant Chandan.

4. See www.adbusters.org/blogs/adbusters-blog/occupywallstreet.html.

5. See www.adbusters.org/about/adbusters.

6. The April 6 Movement had been influenced by the Serbian student group Optor,

which had played an important role in organizing the mass protests and various forms of nonviolent resistance that had overturned the regime of Slobodan Milosevic in 2000 and had used some of the tactics of the Global Justice Movement, whose members were included among the people gathered at the Brecht Forum that night to hear them speak.

7. See www.therealnews.com/t2/index.php?option=com_content&task=view&id=31&Itemid=74&jumival=7825.

8. See www.democracynow.org/2013/9/10/40_years_after_chiles_9_11.

9. See www.globalpost.com/dispatch/news/agencia-efe/130905/chilean-students-demand-end-pinochet-education-model.

10. Castillo 1965, 28. Reprinted with permission from Juan Castillo.

References

Achcar, Gilbert. 2013. *The People Want: A Radical Exploration of the Arab Uprising.* Berkeley: University of California Press.

Acuna, Rodolfo. 2003. *Occupied America: A History of Chicanos.* 5th ed. New York: Pearson Longman.

Adams, James Truslow. 1931. *The Epic of America.* New York: Blue Ribbon Books.

Ahmad, Muhammad. 1986. "Revolutionary Action Movement (RAM): A Case Study of an Urban Revolutionary Movement in Western Capitalist Society." M.A. thesis, Atlanta University.

_____. 2007. *We Will Return in the Whirlwind: Black Radical Organizations 1960–1975.* Chicago: Charles H. Kerr.

Alba, Richard D. 1990. *Ethnic Identity: The Transformation of White America.* New Haven, CT: Yale University Press.

Ali, Tariq. 2002. *The Clash of Fundamentalisms: Crusades, Jihads and Modernity.* New York: Verso.

Allen, Richard. 1967. *Democracy and Communism: Theory and Action.* Princeton, NJ: Van Nostrand for the Institute of Fiscal and Political Education.

Allen, Robert. 2005. "Reassessing the Internal Colonialism Theory." *Black Scholar* 35, no. 1 (Spring): 2–11.

Amin, Samir. 1974. *Unequal Development: An Essay on the Social Formations of Peripheral Capitalism.* New York: Monthly Review Press.

_____. 2004. *The Liberal Virus: Permanent War and the Americanization of the World.* New York: Monthly Review Press.

_____. 2006. *Beyond U.S. Hegemony? Assessing the Prospects for a Multipolar World.* New York: Monthly Review Press.

_____. 2011a. "An Arab Springtime." *Monthly Review* 63 (October). Available at http://monthlyreview.org/commentary/2011-an-arab-springtime/.

_____. 2011b. "The Trajectory of Historical Capitalism and Marxism's Tricontinental Vocation." *Monthly Review* 62 (February). Available at http://monthlyreview

.org/2011/02/01/the-trajectory-of-historical-capitalism-and-marxisms-tricontinen
tal-vocation/.

_____. 2012. "The Arab Revolutions: A Year Later." *Pambazuka News* 576 (March 14).
Available at http://pambazuka.org/en/category/features/80745.

Amin, Samir, and Ali El Kenz. 2005. *Europe and the Arab World: Patterns and Prospects
for the New Relationship.* London: Zed Books.

Anderson, Benedict. 2000. *Imagined Communities: Reflections on the Origin and Spread
of Nationalism.* London: Verso.

Anderson, Kevin. 2013. "Islamists Out, Military In, Arab Spring Just Beginning in Egypt."
Popular Resistance, July 28. Available at www.popularresistance.org/islamists-out-
military-in-arabspring/.

Anzaldua, Gloria. 1987. *Borderlands/La Frontera: The New Mestiza.* San Francisco: Aunt
Lute Books.

Arrighi, Giovanni. 2003. *The Resurgence of East Asia (Asia's Transformations).* New York:
Routledge.

Arrighi, Giovanni, Terrence K. Hopkins, and Immanuel Wallerstein. 1992. "1989, the
Continuation of 1968." *Review* 15, no. 2 (Spring): 221–242.

Arrighi, Giovanni, and Beverly J. Silver. 1999. *Chaos and Governance in the Modern World
System.* Minneapolis: University of Minnesota Press.

Atiles-Osoria, José M. 2013. "Neoliberalism, Law, and Strikes: Law as an Instrument of
Repression at the University of Puerto Rico, 2010–2011." *Latin American Perspectives*
40 (September): 105–117.

Babb, Valerie, 1998. *Whiteness Visible: The Meaning of Whiteness in American Literature
and Culture.* New York: New York University Press.

Baker, Lee. 1998. *From Savage to Negro: Anthropology and the Construction of Race, 1896–
1954.* Berkeley: University of California Press.

Baldwin, James. 1963. *The Fire Next Time.* New York: Vintage Press.

Baldwin, Kate A. 2002. *Beyond the Color Line and the Iron Curtain: Reading Encounters
Between Black and Red, 1922–1963.* Durham, NC: Duke University Press.

Balibar, Etienne, and Immanuel Wallerstein. 1991. *Ambiguous Identities.* New York: Verso.

Barrett, David, George Kurian, and Todd Johnson. 2001. *World Christian Encyclopedia.*
2nd ed. New York: Oxford University Press.

Barry, Dan. 1999. "Giuliani Says Diallo Shooting Coverage Skewed Poll." *New York Times,*
March 17. Available at www.nytimes.com/1999/03/17/nyregion/giuliani-says-diallo-
shooting-coverage-skewed-poll.html.

Barstow, David, and Diana B. Henriques. 2001. "Gifts to Rescuers Divide Survivors." *New
York Times,* December 2.

Bartels, Larry M. 2006. "What's the Matter with *What's the Matter with Kansas?*" *Quarterly
Journal of Political Science* 1:201–226. Available at www.princeton.edu/~bartels/kan
sasqjps06.pdf.

Bashi, Vilna. 1999. "Review of *Crosscurrents: West Indian Immigrants and Race* by Milton
Vickerman." *American Journal of Sociology* 105, no. 3 (November): 890–892.

Bell, Derrick. 1993. *Faces at the Bottom of the Well: The Permanence of Racism.* New York:
Basic Books.

Bennett, Lerone. 1993. *Before the Mayflower: A History of Black America.* New York:
Penguin Books.

Biao, Lin. 1966. *Long Live the Victory of People's War! In Commemoration of the 20th
Anniversary of Victory in the Chinese People's War of Resistance against Japan.* Beijing:
Foreign Languages Press.

Biondi, Martha. 2003. *To Stand and Fight: The Struggle for Civil Rights in Postwar New York City*. Cambridge, MA: Harvard University Press.

Blackhurst, Chris. 2001. "Anthrax Attacks Now Being Linked to U.S. Right-Wing Cranks." *The Independent*, October 21. Available at http://news.independent.Co.uk/world/ Americas/story.jsp?story=100635.

Blassingame, John, ed. 1982. *The Frederick Douglass Papers*. New Haven, CT: Yale University Press.

Blauner, Bob. 1972. *Racial Oppression in America*. New York: Harper and Row.

Bloom, Allen. 1987. *The Closing of the American Mind*. New York: Simon and Schuster.

Bobb, Vilna Bashi. 2001. "Neither Ignorance nor Bliss: Race, Racism and the West Indian Immigrant Experience." In *Migration, Transnationalization and Race in a Changing New York,* edited by Hector R. Cordero-Guzman, Robert C. Smith, and Ramon Grosfoguel, 212–238. Philadelphia: Temple University Press.

Bobo, Lawrence D. 2000. "Reclaiming a Du Boisian Perspective on Racial Attitudes." *Annals of the American Academy of Political and Social Science* 568, no. 1 (March): 186–202.

Boggs, Grace Lee. 1998. *Living for Change: An Autobiography*. Minneapolis: University of Minnesota.

_____. 2004. "Think Globally, Act Locally: Towards a New Concept of City-zenship." Community Cultural Development Leadership Summit, Intermedia Arts, Minneapolis, June 24.

_____. 2006. "Revolution as a New Beginning (Part 2 of 2): An Interview with Grace Lee Boggs." *Upping the Anti,* no. 2 (February). Available at http://uppingtheanti.org/jour nal /article/02-revolution-as-a-new-beginning/.

Boggs, Grace Lee, and Boggs, James. 1974. *Revolution and Evolution in the Twentieth Century*. New York: Monthly Review Press.

Boggs, James. 1970. *Racism and the Class Struggle: Further Pages from a Black Worker's Notebook*. New York: Monthly Review Press.

Bogues, Anthony. 2010. *Empire of Liberty: Power, Desire, and Freedom*. Hanover, NH: Dartmouth College Press.

Boulding, Kenneth. 2011. "Thought Control in Economics." *Adbusters,* February 14.

Braudel, Fernand. 1982. *On History*. Chicago: University of Chicago Press.

_____. 1992. *Civilization and Capitalism, 15th–18th Century*. Vol. I: The Structure of Everyday Life. Berkeley: University of California Press.

Braverman, Harry. 1974. *Labor and Monopoly Capital: The Degradation of Work in the Twentieth Century*. New York: Monthly Review Press.

Breslow, Jason M., and Evan Wexler. 2013. "The State of America's Middle Class in Eight Charts." *Frontline,* July 9. Available at www.pbs.org/wgbh/pages/frontline/business-economy-financial-crisis/two-american-families/the-state-of-americas-middle-class-in-eight-charts/.

Brown, Wendy. 2011. "Occupy Wall Street: Return of a Repressed Res-Publica." *Theory and Event* 14:4.

Buhle, Paul. 1997. "Spies Everywhere." *Radical History Review* 67:187–198.

_____. 2000. "The (Jewish) Liberals and the Cold War." *TIKKUN,* May.

Bush, George W. 2001. "Address to a Joint Session of Congress and the American People." Washington, DC, September 20. Available at http://georgewbush-whitehouse.archives .gov/news/releases/2001/09/20010920-8.html.

Bush, Melanie E. L. 2003. "American Identity and the Mechanisms of Everyday Whiteness." *Socialism and Democracy* 17 (1): 209–226.

_____. 2004. *Breaking the Code of Good Intentions: Everyday Forms of Whiteness.* Lanham, MD: Rowman and Littlefield.

_____. 2011. *Everyday Forms of Whiteness: Understanding Race in a "Post-Racial" World.* Lanham, MD: Rowman and Littlefield.

Bush, Melanie E. L., and Roderick D. Bush. 2008. "United States Nationalism and Nationalism Post-World War II." In *Nations and Nationalisms in Global Perspective: An Encyclopedia of Origins, Development, and Contemporary Transitions,* edited by David H. Kaplan and Guntram H. Herb, 1299–1312. Oxford, UK: ABC-CLIO.

Bush, Roderick D. 1999. *We Are Not What We Seem: Black Nationalism and Class Struggle in the American Century.* New York: New York University Press.

_____. 2001. "The Domestic Costs of the War on Vietnam: The Great Society and the Civil Rights Movement." Paper presented as part of a seminar entitled "The Human Costs of War," October 24, St. John's University, Jamaica Queens, New York.

_____. 2009. *The End of White World Supremacy: Black Internationalism and the Problem of the Color Line.* Philadelphia: Temple University Press.

California Newsreel. 2003a. "Episode 2: The Stories We Tell." In *Race: The Power of an Illusion.* Available at www.newsreel.org/nav/title.asp?tc=CN0149.

_____. 2003b. "Episode 3: The House We Live In." In *Race: The Power of an Illusion.* Available at www.newsreel.org/nav/title.asp?tc=CN0149.

Castillo, Otto Rene. 1965. "Satisfaction." *Let's Go! Vamonos Patria a Caminar.* Cape Goliard Press.

Center for the Study of the American Dream. 2011. "Second Annual State of the American Dream Survey." March. Available at www.xavier.edu/americandream/documents/Second-Annual-American-Dream-Survey.pdf.

Césaire, Aimé. 2010a. "Culture and Colonization." *Social Text* 103 (Summer): 127–144.

_____. 2010b. *A Season in the Congo.* London: Seagull Books.

Chittister, Sister Joan. 2003. "I Give Up: What Is Americanism?" *National Catholic Reporter* 1, no. 16 (July 15). Available at http://nationalcatholicreporter.org/fwis/pc071503.htm.

Churchill, Ward, and Jim Vander Wall. 1988. *Agents of Repression: The FBI's Secret Wars against the Black Panther Party and the American Indian Movement.* Boston: South End Press.

Cloward, Richard A., and Frances Fox Piven. 1991. "Race and the Democrats." *The Nation* 253, no. 20 (December 9): 737–740.

Cohen, Adam. 2006. "According to Webster: One Man's Attempt to Define 'America.'" Editorial Observer. *New York Times,* February 12. Available at http://www.nytimes.com/2006/02/12/opinion/12sun3.html.

Cohen, Joshua, and Martha Nussbaum, eds. 1996. *For Love of Country: Debating the Limits of Patriotism.* Boston: Beacon Press.

Collins, Patricia Hill. 1989. "A Comparison of Two Works on Black Family Life." *Signs: Journal of Women in Culture and Society* 14 (4): 875–884.

_____. [1991] 1998. *Black Feminist Thought: Knowledge, Consciousness, and the Politics of Empowerment.* New York: Routledge.

_____. 2006. *From Black Power to Hip Hop: Racism, Nationalism, and Feminism.* Philadelphia: Temple University Press.

Coma, Mauro Castro, Joan M. Gaul Bergas, Francesco Salvini, and Alto Tinoco i Girona. 2013. "For a Democratic Revolution: Notes from the Universidad Nomada." *Social Justice* 39:62–75.

Cook, Blanche Wiesen. 1995. "The Rosenbergs and the Crimes of a Century." In *Secret Agents: The Rosenberg Case, McCarthyism, and Fifties America,* edited by Marjorie Garber and Rebecca Walkowitz, 23–30. New York: Routledge.

Cox, Oliver Cromwell. 1948. *Caste, Class and Race: A Study in Social Dynamics.* New York: Monthly Review Press.

Crispell, Diane. 1994. "We Don't Need Much to Have It All." *Wall Street Journal,* October 21.

Cruse, Harold. 1968. *Rebellion or Revolution?* New York: Morrow.

Cullen, Jim. 2003. *The American Dream: A Short History of an Idea That Shaped a Nation.* Oxford: Oxford University Press.

Daley, Suzanne. 2011. "An Awakening That Keeps Them Up All Night." *New York Times,* June 6.

Dalfiume, Richard. 1969a. *American Politics since 1945.* Chicago: Quadrangle Books.

_____. 1969b. "The Forgotten Years of the Negro Revolution." In *The Negro in Depression and War: Prelude to Revolution 1930–1945,* edited by Bernard Sternsher, 298–316. Chicago: Quadrangle Books.

Davis, Leneice T. 2005. "Stranger in Mine Own House: Double-Consciousness and American Citizenship." *National Political Science Review* 10 (February): 149–157.

Degler, Carl N. 1984. *Out of Our Past: The Forces That Shaped Modern America.* 3rd ed. New York: Harper and Row.

Delgado Wise, Raul. 2013. "The Migration and Labor Question Today: Imperialism, Unequal Development, and Forced Migration." *Monthly Review* 64, no. 9 (February): 25–38. Dickinson, Tim. 2005. "The Return of the Draft." *Rolling Stone,* January 27. Available at http://www.rollingstone.com/politics/news/the-return-of-the-draft-20060823.

DiLeonardo, Micaela. 1999. "'Why Can't They Be Like Our Grandparents?' and Other Racial Fairy Tales." In *Without Justice for All: The New Liberalism and Our Retreat from Racial Equality,* edited by Adolph Reed Jr, 29–64. Boulder, CO: Westview Press.

"Do Immigrants Block African American Progress? A Debate." 2006. *New Labor Forum,* Spring.

Donate, Gaston Alonso, Corey Robin, Roberta Satow, and Alex Vitale. 2002. *People, Power and Politics.* Boston: Pearson Custom Publishing.

Douglass, Frederick. [1855] 1970. *My Bondage and My Freedom.* Chicago: Johnson Publishing.

Drake, St. Clair. 1970. *The Redemption of Africa and Black Religion.* Chicago: Third World Press.

_____. 1987. *Black Folk Here and There: An Essay in History and Anthropology.* Vol. 1. Los Angeles: University of California Center for African American Studies.

Dreier, Peter. 2013. "Martin Luther King, Jr., Was a Radical Not a Saint." *Huffington Post,* January 20. Available at http://www.huffingtonpost.com/peter-dreier/martin-luther-king-was-a-_b_2516915.html.

Du Bois, W. E. Burghardt. [1903] 1986. "The Souls of Black Folk." In *W.E.B. Du Bois: Writings,* edited by Nathan Huggins, 358–547. New York: Library of America.

_____. 1928. *Dark Princess: A Romance.* New York: Harcourt, Brace.

_____. [1933] 1971. "Marxism and the Negro Problem." *Crisis,* May, p. 103.

_____. [1935] 1979. *Black Reconstruction in America: 1860–1880.* West Hanover, MA: Atheneum.

_____. [1940] 1970. *Dusk of Dawn: An Essay Toward and Autobiography of a Race Concept.* New York: Schocken Books.

_____. [1953] 1961. *The Souls of Black Folk: Essays and Sketches*. Greenwich, CT: Fawcett Premier.

_____. 1970. *The Redemption of Africa and Black Religion*. Chicago: Third World Press.

_____. 1999. *Darkwater: Voices from within the Veil*. New York: Kraus-Thomson Organization.

Dudziak, Mary L. 2000. *Cold War Civil Rights: Race and the Image of American Democracy*. Princeton, NJ: Princeton University Press.

Edsall, Thomas Byrne, and Mary Edsall. 1992. *Chain Reaction: The Impact of Race, Rights, and Taxes on American Politics*. New York: Norton.

Ehrenreich, Barbara. 2002. "Hobo Heaven." Review of *Down and Out, On the Road*, by Kenneth L. Kusmer. *New York Times Book Review*, January 20.

Eitzen, D. Stanley, and Maxine Baca Zinn. 2001. *In Conflict and Order: Understanding Society*. Boston: Allyn and Bacon.

Elbaum, Max. 2002. *Revolution in the Air: Sixties Radicals Turn to Lenin, Mao, and Che*. New York: Verso.

Farkas, Steve, Ann Duffett, and Jean Johnson, with Leslie Moye and Jackie Vine. 2003. "Now That I'm Here: What America's Immigrants Have to Say about Life in the U.S. Today." *American Educator* (Summer): 28–36.

Fisher, John R. 1968. "The Rebellion of Tupac Amaru, 1780." *History Today*, August 1, pp. 562–569.

Foley, Barbara. 2010. *Wrestling with the Left: The Making of Ralph Ellison's* Invisible Man. Durham, NC: Duke University Press.

Foner, Eric. [1990] 1998. *The Story of American Freedom*. New York: Norton.

_____. 2003. "Rethinking American History in a Post-9/11 World." *Liberal Education* 89, no. 2 (Spring): 30–37.

Foner, Philip, ed. 1970. W.E.B. Du Bois Speaks: Speeches and Addresses 1920–1963. New York: Pathfinder Press.

Franken, Al. 2003. *Lies: And the Lying Liars Who Tell Them*. New York: Penguin.

Freeman, Joanne B. 2001. *Affairs of Honor: National Politics in the New Republic*. New Haven, CT: Yale University Press.

Galbo, Joseph. 2004. "From the Lonely Crowd to the Cultural Contradictions of Capitalism and Beyond: The Shifting Ground of Liberal Narratives." *Journal of the History of the Behavioral Sciences* 40:47–76.

Gallicchio, Marc. 2000. *The African American Encounter with Japan and China: Black Internationalism in Asia, 1895–1945*. Chapel Hill: University of North Carolina Press.

Galston, William A. 2001. "Can Patriotism Be Turned into Civic Engagement?" *Chronicle of Higher Education*, November 16.

Gilmore, Brian. 2002. "Stand by the Man: Black America and the Dilemma of Patriotism." *The Progressive* 66, no. 1 (January): 24–27.

Gimbel, Noah. 2012. "Spain's 'Indignados' and the Globalization of Dissent." *The Real News*, January 20. Available at http://therealnews.com/t2/index.php?option=com_content&task=view&id=31&Itemid=74&jumival=7825.

Glazer, Nathan. 1983. *Ethnic Dilemmas 1964–1982*. Cambridge, MA: Harvard University Press.

Glazer, Nathan, and Daniel Patrick Moynihan. 1963. *Beyond the Melting Pot: The Negroes, Puerto Ricans, Jews, Italians and Irish of New York City*. Cambridge: Massachusetts Institute of Technology.

_____. 1975. *Ethnicity: Theory and Experience*. Cambridge, MA: Harvard University Press.

Gonzalez, Juan. 2000. *Harvest of Empire: A History of Latinos in America.* New York: Penguin.

Graeber, David. 2011a. "Awaiting the Magical Spark." *Adbusters* 96 (July/August). Available at https://www.adbusters.org/magazine/96/david-graeber.html.

_____. 2011b. "Bursting Capitalism's Bubble." *Adbusters,* August 24. Available at https://www.adbusters.org/magazine/97/capitalism-eating-itself.html.

_____. 2013. *The Democracy Project: A History, a Crisis, a Movement.* New York: Spiegel and Grau.

Grant, Madison. 1920. *The Passing of the Great Race or the Racial Basis of European History.* New York: Scribner.

Griffler, Keith, 1993. "The Black Radical Intellectual and the Black Worker: The Emergence of a Program for Black Labor, 1918–1938." Ph.D. diss., Ohio State University.

Grosfoguel, Ramon. 1999. Introduction. "'Cultural Racism' and Colonial Caribbean Migrants in the Core Zones of the Capitalist World-Economy." *Review* 22 (4): 409–434.

Grosfoguel, Ramon, and Ana Margarita Cervantes-Rodriguez. 2002. "Unthinking Twentieth-Century Eurocentric Mythologies: Universalist Knowledges, Decolonization, and Developmentalism." In *The Modern/Colonial/Capitalist World-System in the Twentieth Century: Global Processes, Anti-systemic Movements, and the Geopolitics of Knowledge,* edited by Ramon Grosfoguel and Ana Margarita Cervantes-Rodriguez, xi–xxix. Westport, CT: Praeger.

Grosfoguel, Ramón, and Nelson Maldonado Torres, eds. 2006. *Latino/as in the World-System: Decolonization Struggles in the 21st Century U.S. Empire.* Boulder, CO: Paradigm.

Grossman, Zoltan. 2001. "A Century of U.S. Military Interventions: From Wounded Knee to Afghanistan." *Znet,* September 20. Available at www.zmag.org/crisescurevts/interventions.htm.

Haley, Alex, and Malcolm X. 1965. *The Autobiography of Malcolm X.* New York: Ballantine Books.

Hanson, Sandra L., and John Kenneth White. 2011. *The American Dream in the 21st Century.* Philadelphia: Temple University Press.

Hardt, Michael, and Antonio Negri. 2011. "The Fight for 'Real Democracy' at the Heart of Occupy Wall Street." *Foreign Affairs,* October 11. Available at http://www.foreignaffairs.com/articles/136399/michael-hardt-and-antonio-negri/the-fight-for-real-democracy-at-the-heart-of-occupy-wall-street.

Harewood, Adrian, and Tom Keefer. 2005. "Revolution as a New Beginning (Part 1 of 2): An Interview with Grace Lee Boggs." *Upping the Anti,* no. 1 (April). Available at http://uppingtheanti.org/journal/article/01-revolution-as-a-new-beginning.

Harrison, Faye. 1998. "Introduction: Expanding the Discourse on 'Race.'" *American Anthropologist* 100, no. 3 (September): 609–631.

Harrison, Hubert Henry. 1997. *When Africa Awakes.* Baltimore, MD: Black Classics Press.

Hawkins, Clifton C. 2000. "'Race First versus Class First': An Intellectual History of Afro-American Radicalism, 1911–1928." Ph.D. diss., University of California, Davis.

Hayduk, Ron. 2006. "Response to Stephen Steinberg." *New Politics* X-4, no 40 (Winter). Available at http://newpol.org/fromthearchives?nid=233.

Herbert, Bob. 2007. "Righting Reagan's Wrongs?" Op-Ed column, *New York Times,* November 13.

Herndon, Angelo, and Ralph Ellison. 1942. Editorial Comment. *Negro Quarterly* 1, no. 2 (Summer): i–v.

Herold, Marc W. 2001. "A Dossier on Civilian Victims of United States' Aerial Bombing of Afghanistan: A Comprehensive Accounting." Available at www.cursor.org/stories/ civilian_deaths.htm.

Hewitt, Cynthia Lucas. 2002. "Racial Accumulation on a World-Scale: Racial Inequality and Employment." *Review* 25 (2): 137–171.

Hill, Robert. 1987. *The Crusader.* Vols. 1–3. Los Angeles: University of California Press.

Hitchens, Christopher. 2001. "The Case against Henry Kissinger: The Making of a War Criminal, Part One." *Harper's Magazine,* March. Available at http://harpers.org/ archive/2001/02/the-case-against-henry-kissinger-2/.

Ho, Fred, Carolyn Antonio, Diane Fujino, and Steve Yip, eds. 2000. *Legacy to Liberation: Politics and Culture of Revolutionary Asian Pacific America.* San Francisco: AK Press.

Hobsbawm, Eric. 2003. "Only in America." *Chronicle of Higher Education,* July 4.

Hochschild, Jennifer L. 1995. *Facing Up to the American Dream: Race, Class and the Soul of the Nation.* Princeton, NJ: Princeton University Press.

Honig, Bonnie. 2001. *Democracy and the Foreigner.* Princeton, NJ: Princeton University Press.

Horne, Gerald. 1986. *Black and Red: W.E.B. Du Bois and the Afro-American Response to the Cold War, 1944–1963.* Albany: State University of New York Press.

_____. 2004a. *Black and Brown: African Americans and the Mexican Revolution, 1910–1920.* New York: New York University Press.

_____. 2004b. *Race War! White Supremacy and the Japanese Attack on the British Empire.* New York: New York University Press.

Hui, Wang, and Lau Kin Chi. 2011. "Samir Amin on Egypt." February 26. Available at http://futurefastforward.com/images/stories/featurearticles/samir-amin-on-egypt .pdf.

Huntington, Samuel. 2004a. "The Hispanic Challenge." *Foreign Policy,* March/April, pp. 30–45.

_____. 2004b. *Who Are We? The Challenges to America's National Identity.* New York: Simon and Schuster.

Ignatiev, Noel, and John Garvey, eds. 1996. *Race Traitor.* New York: Routledge.

Isserman, Maurice, and Michael Kazin. 2000. *America Divided: The Civil War of the 1960s.* New York: Oxford University Press.

Jacobs, Harriet. 1861. *Incidents in the Life of a Slave Girl.* Boston: Self-Published.

James, C.L.R. 1993. *World Revolution 1917–1936: The Rise and Fall of the Communist International.* Atlantic Highlands, NJ: Humanities Press.

James, Winston. 1998. *Holding Aloft the Banner of Ethiopia: Caribbean Radicalism in Early Twentieth-Century America.* New York: Verso.

Jensen, Robert. 2011. "The Painful Collapse of Empire: How the 'American Dream' and American Exceptionalism Wreck Havoc on the World." *Alternet.* Available at www.alternet.org/economy/151433/the_painful_collapse_of_empire:_how_ the_%22american_dream%22_and_american_exceptionalism_wreck_havoc_on_ the_world/.

Johnson, Lyndon Baines. 1965. Commencement Address at Howard University: "To Fulfill These Rights." Lyndon B. Johnson's Presidential Library. Available at www .lbjlib.utexas.edu/johnson/archives.hom/speeches.hom/650604.asp.

Jones, Quincy. 1977. "Many Rains Ago (Oluwa)." Theme to *Roots: Saga of an American Family.* (African Theme: English Version).

Jordan, Winthrop D. 1974. *The White Man's Burden: Historical Origins of Racism in the United States.* New York: Oxford University Press.

"The Journey to 2000." 1999. Editorial. *New York Times,* December 31.

Kandel, William A. 2011. "The U.S. Foreign-Born Population: Trends and Selected Characteristics," January 18. Available at www.fas.org/sgp/crs/misc/R41592.pdf.

Kaplan, Amy. 2002. *The Anarchy of Empire in the Making of U.S. Culture.* Cambridge, MA: Harvard University Press.

Katz, Jon. 1992. "White Men Can't Rule: A Melting Pot Revolt." *Rolling Stone,* August 6, pp. 33–36.

Kelley, Robin D. G. 1990. *Hammer and Hoe: Alabama Communists during the Great Depression.* Chapel Hill: University of North Carolina Press.

Kelley, Robin D. G., and Betsy Esch. 1999. "Black Like Mao: Red China and Black Revolution." *Souls* 1 (4): 6–41.

King, Martin L. 1963. "Letter from a Birmingham Jail." Available at www.thekingcenter .org/prog/non/Letter.pdf.

———. 1965. "Remaining Awake through a Great Revolution." Commencement Address for Oberlin College, Oberlin, Ohio, June.

———. 2013. "Our God Is Marching On." *Michigan Citizen,* July 3.

Kochiyama, Yuri. 2004. *Passing It On: A Memoir.* Los Angeles: University of California, Los Angeles, Asian American Studies Center Press.

Kolko, Gabriel. 2006. *The Age of War: The United States Confronts the World.* New York: Lynne Reiner.

Kornbluh, Peter. 2013. "Make the Economy Scream: Secret Documents Show Nixon Kissinger Role Backing 1973 Chile Coup." *Democracy Now.* Available at http://www .democracynow.org/2013/9/10/40_years_after_chiles_9_11.

Kornweibel, Theodore. 1998. *Federal Injustice: Campaigns against Black Militancy during the First Red Scare.* Bloomington: Indiana University Press.

———. 2002. *Investigate Everything: Federal Efforts to Compel Black Loyalty during World War I.* Bloomington: Indiana University Press.

Koshiro, Yukiko. 1992. "Trans-Pacific Racism: The U.S. Occupation of Japan." Ph.D. diss., Columbia University.

Kousser, J. Morgan, 1999. *Colorblind Injustice: Minority Voting Rights and the Undoing of the Second Reconstruction.* Chapel Hill: University of North Carolina Press.

Kraly, Ellen Percy, and Ines Miyares. 2001. "Immigration to New York: Policy, Population and Patterns." In *New Immigrants in New York,* edited by Nancy Foner, 33–80. New York: Columbia University Press.

Krauthammer, Charles. 1990. "The Black Rejectionists." *Time Magazine* 136, no. 4 (July 23): 80–81.

Kristol, William, and Robert Kagan. 1996. "Toward a Neo-Reaganite Foreign Policy." *Foreign Affairs,* July/August. Available at www.foreignaffairs.com/articles/52239/ william-kristol-and-robert-kagan/toward-a-neo-reaganite-foreign-policy.

Langdon, Jennifer E. 2009. *Caught in the Crossfire: Adrian Scott and the Politics of Americanism in 1940s Hollywood.* New York: Columbia University Press. Available at www.gutenberg-e.org/langdon/chapter2.html.

Lao-Montes, Agustin. 2007. "Decolonial Moves—Trans-locating African Diaspora Spaces." *Cultural Studies* 21:309–338.

Lavin, David E., Richard D. Alba, and Richard A. Silberstein. 1979. "Ethnic Groups in the City University of New York." *Harvard Educational Review* 49, no. 1 (February): 53–92.

Lemert, Charles, and Esme Bhan. 1998. *The Voice of Anna Julia Cooper.* New York: Rowman and Littlefield.

Leon, Oscar. 2013. "'Generation without Fear,' Demands Free Education in Chile." *Real News Network,* May 1. Available at http://therealnews.com/t2/index.php?option=com_content&task=view&id=31&Itemid=74&jumival=10159.

Lerner, Gerda. 1997. *Why History Matters: Life and Thought.* New York: Oxford University Press.

Lester, Toby. 2002. "Oh, Gods!" *Atlantic Monthly,* February, pp. 37–45.

Lewis, David Levering. 1993. *W.E.B. Du Bois: Biography of a Race, 1868–1919.* New York: Holt.

———. 1995. *W.E.B. Du Bois: A Reader.* New York: Holt.

Lewis, Oscar. 1961. *The Children of Sanchez: Autobiography of a Mexican Family.* New York: Random House.

———. 1969. "Author's Response to Culture and Poverty: Critique and Counter-Proposals." *Current Anthropology* 10, nos. 2–3 (April/June): 189–192.

Livingston, Andrea, John Wirt, Susan Choy, Stephen Provasnik, Patrick Rooney, Anindita Sen, and Richard Tobin. 2003. "The Condition of Education 2003." National Center for Education Statistics, U.S. Department of Education, Institute of Education Sciences NCES 2003-067.

Lopez, Ian F. Haney. 2003. *Racism on Trial: The Chicano Fight for Justice.* Cambridge, MA: Harvard University Press.

Magubane, Bernard. 1984. "The Political Economy of the Black World—Origins of the Present Crisis." In *The Next Decade: Theoretical and Research Issues in Africana Studies,* edited by James Turner, 281–298. Ithaca, NY: Africana Studies and Research Center, Cornell University.

Makalani, Minkah. 2004. "For the Liberation of Black People Everywhere: The African Blood Brotherhood, Black Radicalism, and Pan-African Liberation in the New Negro Movement, 1917–1936." Ph.D. diss., University of Illinois at Urbana-Champaign.

———. 2011. *In the Cause of Freedom: Radical Black Internationalism from Harlem to London, 1917–1939.* Chapel Hill: University of North Carolina Press.

Malcolm X. 1965. *The Autobiography of Malcolm X.* New York: Grove Press.

———. 1971. *The End of White World Supremacy: Four Speeches.* New York: Merlin House.

Mao, Zedong. 1964. *Statement Calling on the People of the World to Unite to Oppose Racial Discrimination by U.S. Imperialism: And Support the American Negroes in Their Struggle against Racial Discrimination.* Peking: Foreign Languages Press.

Marable, Manning. [1985] 1991. *Race, Reform, and Rebellion: The Second Reconstruction in Black America, 1945–1990.* Jackson: University Press of Mississippi.

———. 1986a. *Race, Reform and Rebellion: The Second Reconstruction in Black America, 1945–1982.* Jackson: University Press of Mississippi.

———. 1986b. *W.E.B. DuBois, Black Radical Democrat.* Boston: Twayne.

———. 2001. "The Economic Crisis and Globalization." *Left Turn,* June, pp. 44–45.

Markowitz, Norman D. 1973. *The Rise and Fall of the People's Century: Henry A. Wallace and American Liberalism, 1941–1948.* New York: Free Press.

Marotta, Adriano Mérola. 2013. "Chilean Students Defy Pinochets Legacy." *New Internationalist,* September 12. Available at http://newint.org/blog/2013/09/12/chilean-students-defy-pinochets-legacy/.

Marshall, T. H. 1963. *Sociology at the Crossroads, and Other Essays.* London: Heinemann.

———. 1964. *Class, Citizenship, and Social Development.* Garden City, NY: Doubleday.

Martinez, Elizabeth. 1996. "Reinventing 'America.'" *Z Magazine,* December, pp. 20–25.

———. 1998. *De Colores Means All of Us: Latina Views of a Multi-colored Century.* Boston: South End Press.

_____. 2003. "Don't Call This Country 'America': How the Name Was Hijacked and Why It Matters Today More Than Ever." *Z Magazine,* July/August, pp. 69–72. Available at www.zcommunications.org/dont-call-this-country-and-quot-america-and-quot-by-elizabeth-martinez.html.

_____. 2006. "Open Letter to African Americans from Latinos." *Black Scholar* 36:40.

Marx, Anthony. 1998. *Making Race and Nation: A Comparison of South Africa, the United States and Brazil.* New York: Cambridge University Press.

Massey, Douglas, and Nancy Denton. 1993. *American Apartheid: Segregation and the Making of the Underclass.* Cambridge, MA: Harvard University Press.

Maxwell, Anne. 1999. *Colonial Photography and Exhibitions: Representations of the "Native" and the Making of European Identities.* London: Leicester University Press.

McGruder, Aaron. 2007. *All the Rage: The Boondocks Past and Present.* New York: Three Rivers Press.

Mignolo, Walter. 2000. *Local Histories/Global Designs: Coloniality, Subaltern Knowledges, and Border Thinking.* Princeton, NJ: Princeton University Press.

_____. 2002. "The Geopolitics of Knowledge and the Colonial Difference." *South Atlantic Quarterly* 101, no. 1 (Winter): 57–96.

_____. 2009. *Globalization and the Decolonial Option.* London: Routledge.

Mitchell, Kirsten B. 2003. "Members of Congress with Children in Iraq." *Footnote Fahrenheit.* Media General News Service. November 16. Available at www.newsaic.com/f911chap7-8.html.

Mollenkopf, John, John Kasinitz, and Mary Waters. 2001. "Chutes and Ladders: Educational Attainment among Young Second Generation and Native New Yorkers." Paper presented at the ICMEC Conference on New Immigrants in New York City. Center for Urban Research: City University of New York Graduate Center, November.

Montagu, Ashley M. F. 1945. *Man's Most Dangerous Myth: The Fallacy of Race.* New York: Columbia University Press.

Morgan, Edward S. 1975. *American Slavery, American Freedom: The Ordeal of Colonial Virginia.* New York: Norton.

Morin, Richard. 2001. "Misperceptions Cloud Whites' View of Blacks." *Washington Post,* July 11, final edition.

_____. 2012. "Rising Share of Americans See Conflict between Rich and Poor." Pew Research Center. Available at www.pewsocialtrends.org/2012/01/11/rising-share-of-americans-see-conflict-between-rich-and-poor/.

Morrison, Toni. 1992. *Playing in the Dark: Whiteness and the Literary Imagination.* New York: Vintage Books.

Moses, Wilson Jeremiah. 1978. *The Golden Age of Black Nationalism: 1850–1925.* New York: Oxford University Press.

_____. 1998. *Afrotopia: The Roots of African American Popular History.* New York: Cambridge University Press.

Moyers, Bill. 2006. "Restoring the Public Trust." *TomPaine.com,* February 24. Available at http://www.caclean.org/problem/tompaine_2006-02-24.php.

Moynihan, Daniel Patrick. 1965. *The Negro Family: The Case for National Action.* Washington, DC: U.S. Department of Labor.

_____. 1967. "The Negro Family: A Case for National Action." In *The Moynihan Report and the Politics of Controversy,* edited by Lee Rainwater and W. L. Yancey, 39–124. Cambridge, MA: Massachusetts Institute of Technology Press.

_____, ed. 1968. "The Professors and the Poor." In *On Understanding Poverty: Perspectives from the Social Sciences,* 3–35. New York: Basic Books.

Mullen, Bill. 2004. *Afro-Orientalism*. Minneapolis: University of Minnesota Press.

Mullings, Leith. 1978. "Ethnicity and Stratification in the Urban United States." *Annals of the New York Academy of Sciences*, no. 318, pp. 10–22.

Muto, Ichiyo. 1993. "For an Alliance of Hope." In *Global Visions: Beyond the New World Order*, edited by Jeremy Brecher, John Brown Childs, and Jill Cutler, 147–162. Boston: South End Press.

———. 1998. "Alliance of Hope and Challenges of Global Democracy." In *Trajectories: Inter-Asia Cultural Studies*, edited by Kuan-Hsing Chen and Ang Ien, 312–324. New York: Routledge.

———. 2002. "Neo-liberal Globalization and People's Alliance." Paper presented at the People's Plan 21 General Assembly, Rajabhat Institute, Bangkok, June 22–23.

Myrdal, Gunnar. [1944] 1964. *An American Dilemma*. Vols. 1 and 2. New York: McGraw-Hill.

National Archives. 2013. "Teaching with Documents: The Treaty of Guadalupe Hidalgo." Available at www.archives.gov/education/lessons/guadalupe-hidalgo/.

National Urban League. 2013. "2013 Equality Index." Available at http://iamempowered .com/soba/2013/about-book.

Ndlovu, Abednigo. 2006. Personal conversation with author, Johannesburg, South Africa, January 20.

Newton, Huey. 1968. *Huey Newton Talks to the Movement about the Black Panther Party, Cultural Nationalism, SNCC, Liberals, and White Revolutionaries*. Boston: New England Free Press.

———. 1972. *To Die for the People*. New York: Random House.

Norton, Michael, and Dan Ariely. 2011. "Building a Better America—One Wealth Quintile at a Time." *Perspectives on Psychological Science* 6:9–12.

Nussbaum, Martha. 1996. "Reply." In *For Love of Country: Debating the Limits of Patriotism*, edited by Martha Nussbaum and Joshua Cohen, 131–144. Boston: Beacon Press.

———. 2001. "Can Patriotism Be Compassionate?" *The Nation*, December 17, p. 11.

O'Leary, Cecilia Elizabeth. 1999. *To Die For: The Paradox of American Patriotism*. Princeton, NJ: Princeton University Press.

Olsen, Joel. 2001. "The Democratic Problem of the White Citizen." *Constellations* 8:163–183.

Omi, Michael, and Howard Winant. 1994. *Racial Formation in the United States*. New York: Routledge.

Ong, Paul, Edna Bonacich, and Lucie Cheng. 1994. *The New Asia Immigration in Los Angeles and Global Restructuring*. Philadelphia: Temple University Press.

O'Reilly, Kenneth. 1989. *Racial Matters: The FBI's Secret File on Black America, 1960–1972*. New York: Free Press.

———. 1994. *Black Americans: The FBI files*. New York: Carroll and Graf.

Orleck, Annelise. 2001. "Soviet Jews: The City's Newest Immigrants." In *New Immigrants in New York*, edited by Nancy Foner, 111–140. New York: Columbia University Press.

Padmore, George. 1972. *PanAfricanism or Communism*. Garden City, NY: Doubleday.

Parini, Jay. 2012. "The American Mythos." *Dædalus, the Journal of the American Academy of Arts and Sciences* 141, no. 1 (Winter): 52–60.

Perry, Jeffrey. 2001. *A Hubert Harrison Reader*. Middletown, CT: Wesleyan University Press.

Pew Charitable Trusts. 2009. "Opinion Poll on Economic Mobility and the American Dream." Available at http://www.pewtrusts.org/en/research-and-analysis/analy sis/2009/03/12/opinion-poll-on-economic-mobility-and-the-american-dream.

_____ 2011. "Economic Mobility and the American Dream: Where Do We Stand in the Wake of the Great Recession." Available at www.pewtrusts.org/en/research-and-anal ysis/reports/2011/05/19/economic-mobility-and-the-american-dream-where-do-we-stand-in-the-wake-of-the-great-recession1.

Piven, Frances Fox, and Richard A. Cloward. 1997. *The Breaking of the American Social Compact*. New York: New Press.

Plummer, Brenda G. 1996. *Rising Wind: Black Americans and U.S. Foreign Affairs, 1935–1960*. Chapel Hill: University of North Carolina Press.

Ponce, Albert. 2013. "War against Migrants, Racial Violence in the United States: A Critical Ethnography of Mexican and Latino Day Labor." Ph.D. diss., University of California: Los Angeles. Electronic Theses and Dissertations.

Postel, Danny. 2001. "Outsiders in America." *Chronicle of Higher Education*, December 7.

Prashad, Vijay. 2000. *The Karma of Brown Folk*. Minneapolis: University of Minnesota Press.

Pulido, Laura. 2006. *Black, Brown, Yellow, and Left: Radical Activism in Los Angeles*. Berkeley: University of California Press.

Quadagno, Jill. 1994. *The Color of Welfare: How Racism Undermined the War on Poverty*. New York: Oxford University Press.

Quijano, Anibal. 1998. "La Colonialidad del Poder y la clasificacion social." Unpublished manuscript.

_____. 2000. "Coloniality of Power, Eurocentrism, and Latin America." *Nepantla: Views from South* 1 (3): 533–580.

Quijano, Anibal, and Immanuel Wallerstein. 1992. "Americanity as a Concept, or the Americas in the Modern World-System." *Social Science Journal* 44 (4): 549–557.

Reich, Robert. 2011. *On Occupy Wall Street: "You Can't Stop This Once It's Started."* *MoveOn.org* video. November 11.

Renique, Gerardo. 2005. "Introduction, Latin America Today: The Revolt against Neoliberalism." *Socialism and Democracy* 19:1–11.

Rhea, Joseph Tilden. 1997. *Race Pride and the American Identity*. Cambridge, MA: Harvard University Press.

Rieder, Jonathan. 1985. *Canarsie: The Jews and Italians of Brooklyn against Liberalism*. Cambridge, MA: Harvard University Press.

Robinson, Cedric. 1983. *Black Marxism: The Making of the Black Radical Tradition*. London: Zed Press.

Rodney, Walter. 1982. *How Europe Underdeveloped Africa*. Washington, DC: Howard University Press.

Roediger, David R. [1991] 1999. *The Wages of Whiteness: Race and the Making of the American Working Class*. New York: Verso.

_____. 1994. *Toward the Abolition of Whiteness: Essays on Race, Politics and Working Class History*. New York: Verso.

_____. 1998. *Black on White: Black Writers on What It Means to Be White*. New York: Schocken Books.

Roosevelt, F. D. 1936. "1936 Acceptance Speech." Democratic National Convention, Philadelphia, June 27. Available at www.presidency.ucsb.edu/ws/index.php?pid =15314#axzz1r0YmOkn5.

Roper Organization. 1938. iPOLL from Roper/Fortune Survey [November] based on personal interviews with a national adult sample of 5,171. Data provided by the Roper Center for Public Opinion Research, University of Connecticut. USROPER.38-003.RC4A and RC4B. Available at http://www.ropercenter.uconn.edu/data_access/ipoll/ipoll.html.

Roper Survey Organization. 1993. "How We Classify Ourselves." *American Enterprise,* May/June, p. 87.

Rosenthal, A. M. 1995. "On My Mind; Naming the Enemy." *New York Times,* May 9. Available at www.nytimes.com/1995/05/09/opinion/on-my-mind-naming-the-ene my.html.

Ross, Andrew. 1987. "Dimensions of Militarization in the Third World." *Armed Forces and Society* 13 (Summer): 561–578.

Roy, Arundhati. 2002. Transcription of Arundhati Roy reading and Ms. Roy and How-ard Zinn in conversation. Lensic Performing Arts Center, Santa Fe, New Mexico, September 18. Available at www.lannan.org/images/events/arundhati-roy-020918-trans-read.pdf.

Ryan, Joseph. 1973. *White Ethnics: Their Life in Working Class America.* Englewood Cliffs, NJ: Prentice-Hall.

Sack, Kevin, and Janet Elder. 2000. "Poll Finds Optimistic Outlook but Enduring Racial Division." *New York Times,* July 11.

Sales, William W., Jr. 1994. *From Civil Rights to Black Liberation: Malcolm X and the Organization of AfroAmerican Unity.* Boston: South End Press.

San Juan, E., Jr. 2002. *Racism and Cultural Studies.* Durham, NC: Duke University Press.

_____. 2003. "US Imperial Terror, Cultural Studies, and the National Liberation Struggle in the Philippines." *Inter-Asia Cultural Studies* 4 (3): 516–522.

Santiago-Valles, Kelvin. 2003a. "'Race,' Labor, 'Women's Proper Place,' and the Birth of Nations: Some Notes on Historicizing the Coloniality of Power." *New Centennial Review* 3, no. 3 (Fall): 47–69.

_____. 2003b. "Some Notes on 'Race,' Coloniality, and the Question of History among Puerto Ricans." In *Decolonizing the Academy: Diaspora Theory and African-New World Studies,* edited by Carole Boyce-Davies, 217–234. Trenton, NJ: Africa World Press.

_____. 2005. "Racially Subordinate Labour within Global Contexts: Robinson and Hopkins Re-examined." *Race Class* 47:54–70.

Sassen, Saskia. 2003. "Citizenship Destabilized." *Liberal Education* 89, no. 2 (Spring). Available at www.aacu.org/liberaleducation/le-sp03/le-sp03feature2.cfm.

Schaefer, Richard T. 1995. *Race and Ethnicity in the United States.* New York: Harper-Collins College Publishers.

Schneider, Nathan. 2013. *Thank You, Anarchy: Notes from the Occupy Apocalypse.* Berkeley: University of California Press.

Schouten, P. 2008. "Theory Talk #13: Immanuel Wallerstein on World-Systems, the Imminent End of Capitalism and Unifying Social Science." Available at www.sinsys .business.t-online.de/wallerstein_theorytalk13.pdf.

Schurmann, Franz. 1974. *The Logic of World Power: An Inquiry into the Origins, Currents, and Contradictions of World Politics.* New York: Pantheon Press.

Schwartz, Barry, Hazel Rose Markus, and Alana Conner Snibbe. 2006. "Is Freedom Just Another Word for Many Things to Buy? That Depends on Your Class Status." *New York Times Magazine,* February 26, pp. 14–15.

Scott, Janny. 2003. "The Changing Face of Patriotism." *New York Times Week in Review,* July 6, p. 1.

Scott-Heron, Gil. 2000. "'B' Movie—The Poem." In *Now and Then: The Poems of Gil Scott-Heron,* by Gil Scott-Heron, 10–12. Edinburgh: Canongate Books Ltd.

Shapiro, Michael. 1997. *Violent Cartographies: Mapping Cultures of War.* Minneapolis: University of Minnesota Press.

Shukrallah, Salma. 2013. "Contextualising the 'Arab Spring.'" Interview with Samir Amin. *Ahram Online.* Available at http://english.ahram.org.eg/NewsContent/1/64/68431/ Egypt/Politics-/Samir-Amin-talks-to-Ahram-Online-on-future-of-Egyp.aspx.

Silver, Beverly, and Eric Slater. 1999. "The Social Origins of World Hegemony." In *Chaos and Governance in the Modern World System,* edited by Giovanni Arrighi and Beverly J. Silver, 131–206. Minneapolis: University of Minnesota Press.

Singh, Nikhil Pal. 1998. "Culture/Wars: Recoding Empire in an Age of Democracy." *American Quarterly* 50:471–522.

_____. 2004. *Black Is a Country: Race and the Unfinished Struggle for Democracy.* Cambridge, MA: Harvard University Press.

Sites, William, and Virginia Parks. 2011. "What Do We Really Know about Racial Inequality? Labor Markets, Politics, and the Historical Basis of Black Economic Fortunes." *Politics and Society* 39 (March): 40–73.

Sitkoff, Harvard. 1971. "Racial Militancy and Interracial Violence in the Second World War." *Journal of American History* 58, no. 3 (December): 661–681.

Sklar, Holly. 2003. "Imagine a Country." *Z Magazine,* May, pp. 53–59.

Sleeper, Jim. 1991. *The Closest of Strangers: Liberalism and the Politics of Race in New York.* New York: Norton.

Smedley, Audrey. 1993. *Race in North America.* San Francisco: Westview.

_____. 1998. "'Race' and Construction of Human Identity." *American Anthropologist* 100, no. 3 (September): 690–702.

Smith, Robert C., and Richard Seltzer. 2000. *Contemporary Controversies and the American Racial Divide.* Oxford, UK: Rowman and Littlefield.

Smith, Rogers. 1993. "Beyond Tocqueville, Myrdal, and Hartz: The Multiple Traditions in America." *American Political Science Review* 87 (September): 549–566.

_____. 1997. *Civic Ideals: Conflicting Visions of Citizenship in U.S. History.* New Haven, CT: Yale University Press.

Soanes, Catherine, and Angus Stevenson, eds. 2004. *The Concise Oxford English Dictionary.* Oxford: Oxford University Press. Available at www.oxfordreference.com.

SOA Watch. n.d. "What Is White Supremacy?" Available at http://soaw.org/index .php?option=com_content&view=article&id=482.

Solomon, Mark. 1998. *The Cry Was Unity: Communists and African Americans, 1917–36.* Jackson: University Press of Mississippi.

Staples, Robert. 1993. "The Illusion of Racial Equality." In *Lure and Loathing: Essays on Race, Identity and the Ambivalence of Assimilation,* edited by Gerald Early, 481–490. New York: Penguin Books.

Steinberg, Stephen. 1995. *Turning Back: The Retreat from Racial Justice in American Thought and Policy.* Boston: Beacon Press.

_____. 1999. "Occupational Apartheid in America: Race, Labor Market Segmentation and Affirmative Action." In *Without Justice for All: The New Liberalism and Our Retreat from Racial Equality,* edited by Adolph Reed Jr., 215–234. Boulder, CO: Westview Press.

_____. 2001. *The Ethnic Myth: Race, Ethnicity and Class in America.* Boston: Beacon Press.

_____. 2006. "Immigration, African Americans, and Race Discourse." *New Politics,* Winter. Available at http://newpol.org/content/immigration-african-americans-and-race-discourse.

Stephens, Michelle. 1998. "Black Transnationalism and the Politics of National Identity: West Indian Intellectuals in Harlem in the Age of War and Revolution." *American Quarterly* 50 (3): 592–608.

_____. 1999. "Black Empire: The Making of Black Transnationalism by West Indians in the United States." Ph.D. diss., Yale University.

Stoddard, Lothrop. 1921. *The Rising Tide of Color against White World-Supremacy.* New York: Scribner.

Street, Paul. 2001. "The White Fairness Understanding Gap." *Z Magazine,* October, pp. 9–11.

_____. 2003a. "Behind the Smoking Gun: Notes from Chicago on Racism's Persistent Significance." *Znet,* May 7. Available at www.zmag.org/Znet.htm.

_____. 2003b. "The Repair of Broken Societies Begins at Home," *Znet,* July 18. Available at http://www.zmag.org/content/showarticle.cfm?SectionID=40&ItemID=3928.

Takaki, Ronald. 1979. *Iron Cages: Race and Culture in 19th-Century America.* New York: Oxford University Press.

_____. 1993. *A Different Mirror: A History of Multicultural America.* Boston: Little, Brown.

Tanenbaum. 2011. "Religion and Diversity in Schools." Available at www.tanenbaum .org/sites/default/files/Religion%20and%20Diversity%20in%20Schools%20Fact%20 Sheet%20FORMATTED.pdf.

Tell, Shawgi. 1999. E-mail to the Mult-cul@ubvm.cc.buffalo.edu list, July.

Tolentino, Cynthia. 2000. "The Road Out of the Black Belt: Sociology's Fictions and Black Subjectivity in Native Son." *Novel* 33, no. 3 (Summer): 377–405.

Tolerance.org. 2001. "Hate in the News." Hate Goes to School. Available at www.tolerance .org/news/article_hate.jsp?id=312.

Torres, Rodolfo, and George Kastiaficas, eds. 1999. *Latino Social Movements: Historical and Theoretical Perspectives.* New York: Routledge.

Tuan, Mia. 1998. *Forever Foreigners or Honorary Whites? The Asian Ethnic Experience Today.* New Brunswick, NJ: Rutgers University Press.

United States Election Project. 2004. "Voting-Age and Voting-Eligible Population Estimates and Voter Turnout." Available at http://elections.gmu.edu/Voter_Turnout_2004.htm.

Vigil, Ernesto B. 1999. *The Crusade for Justice: Chicano Militancy and the Government's War on Dissent.* Madison: University of Wisconsin Press.

Von Eschen, Penny. 1997. *Race against Empire: Black Americans and Anti-colonialism, 1937–1957.* Ithaca, NY: Cornell University Press.

Waas, Murray. 1986. "The Soul of a New Machine Politician." *New Republic,* March 10, pp. 19–25.

Waldinger, Roger. 1996. *Still the Promised City: African-Americans and New Immigrants in Postindustrial New York.* Cambridge, MA: Harvard University Press.

_____. 2001. "Rethinking 'Race.'" *Ethnicities* 1 (1): 19–21.

Wallerstein, Immanuel. 1974. *The Modern World System: Capitalist Agriculture and the Origins of the European World Economy in the Sixteenth Century.* New York: Academic Press.

_____. 1979. *The Capitalist WorldEconomy.* Boston: Cambridge University Press.

_____. 1989. *The Modern World-System, III: The Second Great Expansion of the Capitalist World-Economy, 1730-1840's.* San Diego: Academic Press.

_____. 1992. "1989, The Continuation of 1968." *Review* 15, no. 2 (Spring). Available at http://www.jstor.org/discover/10.2307/40241219?uid=3739256&uid=2&uid=4&s id=21104969833963.

_____. 1995. *Historical Capitalism and Capitalist Civilization.* New York: Verso.

_____. 1999. *The End of the World as We Know It: Social Science for the Twenty-First Century.* Minneapolis: University of Minnesota Press.

_____. 2000a. "Cultures in Conflict? Who Are We? Who Are the Others?" Y. K. Pao

Distinguished Chair Lecture, Center for Cultural Studies, Hong Kong University of Science and Technology, September 20.

_____. 2000b. "The Racist Albatross: Social Science, Jorg Haider, and Widerstand." *Eurozine.* Available at www.eurozine.com/articles/2000-09-13-wallerstein-en.html.

_____. 2001. "America and the World: The Twin Towers as Metaphor." Presentation at the Charles R. Lawrence II Memorial Lecture, Brooklyn College, December 5. Available at www.binghamton.edu/fbc/iwbkln02.htm.

_____. 2003a. "Citizens All? Citizens Some! The Making of the Citizen." *Comparative Studies in Society and History* 45:650–679.

_____. 2003b. *The Decline of American Power: The U.S. in a Chaotic World.* New York: New Press.

_____. 2004. "After Developmentalism and Globalization, What?" Keynote address at the Development Challenges for the 21st Century Conference, Cornell University, October 1.

_____. 2006a. "The Curve of American Power." *New Left Review* 40 (July/August): 77–94.

_____. 2006b. *European Universalism: The Rhetoric of Power.* New York: New Press.

_____. 2008. "Theory Talk #13: Immanuel Wallerstein on World-Systems, the Imminent End of Capitalism and Unifying Social Science." *Theory Talks,* April 8. Available at www.theorytalks. org/2008/08/theory-talk-13.html.

_____. 2009a. "Crisis of the Capitalist System: Where Do We Go from Here?" Harold Wolpe Lecture, University of KwaZulu-Natal, November 5. Published in *Monthly Review Zine,* December 11. Available at http://mrzine.monthlyreview.org/2009/wallerstein121109.html.

_____. 2009b. "Cuba and the United States: The Slow Thaw." *Wallerstein Commentary* 256 (May 1). Available at www.binghamton.edu/fbc/archive/256en.htm.

_____. 2009c. "Obama, Bush, and Latin American Coups." *Wallerstein Commentary* 269 (November 15). Available at www.binghamton.edu/fbc/archive/269en.htm.

_____. 2011a. "Contradictions in the Latin American Left (Thinking Politically)." *Synthesis/Regeneration,* January 1. Available at http://www.highbeam.com/doc/1G1-245473363.html.

_____. 2011b. "The Contradictions of the Arab Spring." *Al Jazeera,* November 14.

_____. 2011c. "The 1968 Current: From the Arab Spring to Occupy Wall Street." *Al Jazeera,* November 14.

_____. 2011d. "The United States versus Everybody." *Wallerstein Commentary* 319 (December 15). Available at http://www.iwallerstein.com/united-states/.

_____. 2011e. "The World Social Forum, Egypt, and Transformation." *Wallerstein Commentary* 299 (February 15).Available at http://www.iwallerstein.com/the-world-social-forum-egypt-and-transformation/.

_____. 2012. "The World Left after 2011." *Wallerstein Commentary* 320 (January 1). Available at http://www.iwallerstein.com/world-left-2011/.

Wallerstein, Immanuel, and Terence K. Hopkins, 1997. *The Age of Transition: Trajectory of the World System, 1945–2025.* London: Zed Press.

Ward, Stephen M., ed. 2011. *Pages from a Black Radical's Notebook: A James Boggs Reader.* Detroit, MI: Wayne State University Press.

Weinberg, Albert Katz. 1963. Manifest Destiny: *A Study of Nationalist Expansionism in American History.* Chicago: Quadrangle Books.

West, Michael O., William G. Martin, and Fanon Che Wilkins. 2009. *From Toussaint to Tupac: The Black International since the Age of Revolution.* Chapel Hill: University of North Carolina Press.

White, John Kenneth, and Sandra L. Hanson. 2011. "The Making and Persistence of the American Dream." In *The American Dream in the 21st Century,* edited by John Kenneth White and Sandra L. Hanson, 1–16. Philadelphia: Temple University Press.

Wilkins, Fanon Che. 2001. "'In the Belly of the Beast': Black Power, Anti-imperialism, and the African Liberation Solidarity Movement, 1968–1975." Ph.D. diss., New York University.

Williams, Patricia J. 2001. "Disorder in the Court." *The Nation,* December 10, p. 11.

Wilson, Rob, and Christopher L. Connery. 2007. *The Worlding Project: Doing Cultural Studies in the Era of Globalization.* Berkeley: North Atlantic Press.

Wiltse, Charles M. 1965. *David Walker's Appeal.* New York: Hill and Wang.

Winant, Howard. 2001. *The World Is a Ghetto: Race and Democracy since World War II.* New York: Basic Books.

Wright, Quincy. 1955. *The Study of International Relations.* New York: Appleton-Century-Crofts.

Wright, Richard. [1955] 1995. *Black Power: A Record of Reactions in a Land of Pathos.* New York: Harper and Row.

_____. 1956. *The Colour Curtain, a Report on the Bandung Conference.* London: D. Dobson.

Wynter, Sylvia. 2003. "Unsettling the Coloniality of Being/Power/Truth/Freedom: Towards the Human, after Man, Its Overrepresentation—an Argument." *New Centennial Review* 3, no. 3 (Fall): 257–337.

Zia, Helen. 2000. *Asian American Dreams: The Emergence of an American People.* New York: Farrar, Straus, and Giroux.

Zinn, Howard. 1980. *A People's History of the United States.* New York: Harper and Row.

_____. 1995. *A People's History of the United States 1492–Present.* New York: Harper Perennial.

_____. 2005. "The Scourge of Nationalism." *Common Dreams,* May 20. Available at www.commondreams.org/views05/0516-29.htm.

Index

Page numbers followed by the letter *t* refer to tables.

Achcar, Gilbert, 196–197
Adbusters, 200
Africa, 13–14, 19, 42, 67, 73, 102, 158, 172, 174, 191, 214n6 (chap. 1), 214n1 (chap. 2), 214n8
African Americans, xvii, 7, 12, 63, 83, 87, 151, 159–160, 186–187.
African Blood Brotherhood (ABB), 12, 187
Algeria, 69, 185, 192–193
American Century, xvi, 71, 92, 153, 158, 173, 190
American identity, xvii, 21, 40t
American Indian Movement, 159, 185
American Legislative Exchange Council (ALEC), 70
Amin, Samir, 14, 190–197, 216n2 (chap. 10)
Antisystemic movements, 165, 168
Arab Spring, 180, 191, 195–196, 198–199, 202
Arab World, 161, 191, 193, 198, 207
Asia, 174, 183, 214n8, 215n2 (chap. 7)

Baker, Ella, 186, 209
Bandung world, 159
Belonging, xvii, 3–5, 15, 18–19, 31, 41, 45, 152
Berkeley, 188
Black freedom struggle, xiv–xvi, 93, 161–162, 175, 186–188
Black Internationalism, 174
Black Liberation, 171, 187
Black Panther Party, 159, 185, 187, 189
Black Popular Front, 180, 215n4 (chap. 6)

Black street, 170
Boggs, Grace Lee, 162
Boggs, James, 161–163
Borders, national, 4, 184–185
Brooklyn, 44, 47–48, 52, 213n4

Capitalism, 18–19, 23, 26, 64–66, 131, 144–148, 145t, 153–154, 156, 163, 165–167, 182–183, 188, 190, 197, 200; capitalist system, 4, 13, 161, 163, 183; capitalist world economy, 13, 24–26, 92, 174, 182, 209; global, 154–155, 168; structural crisis of, 5, 90, 94, 151, 156, 167, 174, 176, 183, 209; world capitalist system, xvii, 5, 11–13, 25, 156, 163, 170, 190, 195, 197, 209
Chile, 181, 191, 205–207; Chilean students, 205–207
China, 46, 56, 59, 69, 78, 102, 107–108, 114, 133, 181, 185, 191–193, 195
Citizenship, xvii, 4–5, 7–11, 15, 18–19, 45, 214n6 (chap. 1), 214n7; rights, 8–10, 175
Civil rights, xiii, xv, xvii, 8–10, 97, 115, 153
Civil rights movement, 74, 99, 106, 169, 176, 178, 185
Civil War, 8
Class struggle, 183, 208
Colonialism, 66, 147, 165–166, 171–172, 213n6, 216n2 (chap. 8)
Coloniality, 165–166
Communist Party USA (CPUSA), 12, 187

Community, xii–xiv, 9–11, 32–33, 35, 41, 43, 47, 64, 72, 101–102, 108, 113, 131, 143–144; political, 8, 10–11, 13–14, 165
Community of Latin American and Caribbean States (CELAC), 181
Control, social, 83, 130, 132
Cuba, 24, 34, 69, 155, 185, 216n1 (chap. 10)
Culture, 16, 18, 23, 41, 47, 49–50, 53, 61, 66, 88–89, 129, 134, 153, 157, 164–165

Decolonization, 165, 172
Democracy, 3, 5, 16, 18, 43, 46, 59–61, 175, 177, 179, 192–193, 195, 199–202, 207, 209
Discrimination, 50, 52, 57, 63t, 68, 74, 94, 111, 115, 120, 145t, 148
Domination, 7, 14, 18–20, 24, 26, 127, 128, 162, 166, 192, 197, 208–210
Du Bois, W.E.B., xvi, 7, 11–12, 20–21, 23, 93–94, 157, 163, 165, 171, 179

Education, 34, 72, 88, 95, 98, 104, 108, 114, 118, 120, 142, 144, 194–195, 203, 205–206
Egypt, 192–195, 197–202, 216n2 (chap. 10)
Elections, 69, 82, 84, 86t, 90, 129, 139, 155, 169, 175, 182, 194, 197
Empire, xvii, 4, 17, 25, 91, 94, 112, 148, 151, 164, 171, 174, 176, 180
Europe, 14, 19, 22, 26, 33, 41–42, 110–111, 159, 162, 165, 172, 193, 203–204, 209, 214n2 (chap. 2), 214n8, 215n2 (chap. 7); pan-European world, 10, 12, 14, 153–154, 159, 166, 170–171, 173–174, 209
Europeans, 20, 33–34, 42, 58, 66–67, 95, 111, 160, 171; immigrants, 18–19, 23, 156, 158, 179

Freedom, xv, 18, 21, 32, 35, 59–60, 91, 101, 104, 111–112, 114, 132–133, 152, 173, 175
Freedom of speech, 10, 36, 60, 73

Gender, xii, 5, 18, 31, 48, 54, 103, 128, 159, 169, 184, 209
Geoculture, liberal, 15, 183–184, 186
Global Dream, 130, 139–140
Globalization, 169

Hegemony, 3, 12, 33, 69–71, 90–91, 94, 152–154, 170–172, 174–175, 185, 190, 193, 195
Hoover, J. Edgar, 83
Howard University, xiv
Human dream, 129, 134, 209
Immigrants, 19, 22–24, 32, 39–43, 50, 80–81, 115, 118–119, 120–121, 125–126, 128, 142, 148, 159–161, 166–167

Immigration, 22, 42, 111, 117, 159–161, 166–167
India, 33, 69, 78, 121, 126, 134
Indians, 42, 63, 66, 116
Inequality, xii, xiv, xvi, 5, 8–12, 16, 24–25, 43, 57t, 63t, 67, 69, 87, 128, 145t, 148, 194, 205
Internationalism, 44, 174, 185

Jim Crow, xii

King, Martin Luther, Jr., xvii, 85, 132, 173–174, 176, 179, 185

Labor movement, 75, 167, 169
Latin America, xv, 43, 154–155, 158, 161, 167, 181–182, 205, 207, 216n1 (chap. 10)
Latinos, 16, 34, 37, 48, 60–61, 63, 95, 122, 142, 164
League of Revolutionary Black Workers, 185, 187, 189
Left, 74, 154, 157–158, 160, 162, 167, 169, 171, 175, 178, 180–181, 186–187, 189, 197
Lenin, Vladimir, 82, 157, 186–187, 190
Liberation, xiv, 8, 12, 16, 103, 148, 151, 164–165, 175, 177, 209
Libya, 181, 193, 195–196, 198–199, 202

Malcolm X, xvi–xvii, 93, 139, 157, 171–176, 185–186, 209
Martinez, Elizabeth, 7, 154, 209, 214n3 (chap. 3)
Meritocracy, 16–17, 46, 75, 121, 168
Mexicans, 21, 34, 49–50, 175, 188
Movement for Afro-American Unity (MAAU), xiv
Muslim Brotherhood, 194–197

NAACP (National Association for the Advancement of Colored People), 12, 93, 159, 186
Nation, imperial, 16–17, 25, 159
National identity, 14, 18, 20, 23, 26, 39–40, 40t, 64, 94
Nationalism, 3–5, 14, 31–34, 38, 41, 73, 121, 133, 151, 156, 158, 161, 165, 188; of empire, 25, 94, 151, 171, 176, 180; nationalistic worldview, 14
National liberation movements, 153–154, 158, 171, 173, 185, 190
National myths, 11, 214n2 (chap. 2)
National origins, 8, 23
Nationhood, 26, 177
Nation of immigrants, 4, 23–24, 42–43
Nation of Islam (NOI), xiii, xv, 159, 175–176
Nations, nation of, 24, 180, 209
Native Americans, 17, 60, 100, 115, 170, 188

Neoliberalism, 70–71, 75, 153, 155, 169, 175, 178, 180, 195, 215n1 (chap. 5)
New American Century, 70–71, 94, 175
New Deal, xv, 152, 159, 178–179
New Negro Movement, 12, 158, 179–180, 187
Nineteenth century, 8–10, 14, 18–19, 21–22, 161, 163, 165, 179, 193
North American Trade Organization (NATO), 181

Obama, Barack, 40, 53, 54, 67, 81–87, 106, 109, 167, 170, 175, 200; Black president, 74, 83–86, 143; election of, 81, 83, 85, 86t, 86–88, 174
Occupy Wall Street, 199–202
Organization for Afro-American Unity (OAAU), 159
Organization of American States (OAS), 181, 216n1 (chap. 10)

Patriotic Americans, 33–38, 40t, 40–41, 74, 146; unpatriotic Americans, 35–36
Patriotism, xiii, 3–4, 11, 18, 31, 33–38, 40t, 40–41, 73–74, 77, 86, 88, 185
Political Islam, 154, 192, 194–195
Poor Law, 8–9
Popular Front, 158, 179–180
Project for the New American Century (PNAC), 153
Puerto Rico, 105, 135, 207–208; Puerto Ricans, 39, 50, 52, 135, 175, 179, 208

Racial Nationalism, 169, 171, 173, 175, 177
Racism, xii, xiv–xv, 5, 8, 11–14, 20, 88, 93–94, 103, 106, 156, 160, 162, 164, 170–171
Radicalism, third-world, 184–185
Rebellion, 154–155, 159, 162, 171, 175, 178, 184–185, 198–199, 204
Republicans, 47–48, 85, 145–146; Republican Party, 85
Revolution, 13, 70, 73–74, 82–83, 152, 156–157, 161–162, 176, 178–180, 184, 186, 188, 190, 194, 196; worldwide, 172–173, 181, 183, 188
Revolutionaries, 25, 51, 158, 161–162, 180–181, 183–186, 188–189, 191, 202
Revolutionary Action Movement (RAM), 157, 159, 185–187
Revolutionary Workers League (RWL), xiv, 189
Revolutionary Youth Movement (RYM), 188
Russia, 49–50, 70–71, 105, 193, 195–196; Russians, 49
Socialism, xv–xvi, 82, 144–146, 145t
Spain, 191, 197, 199, 202–204, 207

Steinberg, Stephen, 23, 160–161, 163–164, 166–167
Stereotypes, 49, 166
Student Nonviolent Coordinating Committee (SNCC), xiii, 159, 184, 186–187, 189, 213n2
Students for a Democratic Society (SDS), xiv–xv, 188

Tensions, 4–6, 11, 15, 17, 19, 21, 23, 25–27, 32, 38, 128, 136, 143, 148–149, 189
Third world, 34, 65, 69–70, 153, 159, 171, 175, 184–186, 188, 190, 214n2 (chap. 1); third world within, 24, 89–90, 156, 158–159, 175, 183
Third World Women's Alliance, 184, 189
Tunisia, 196, 198–199, 202

United Nations, 13, 172
University of Puerto Rico (UPR), 207–208
Upward mobility, 5, 15, 19, 23, 32, 41–42, 50, 95, 104, 108, 120, 121, 127, 142, 146
U.S. exceptionalism, 4, 16, 26, 32, 151

Vietnam, xiii, 56, 69, 153, 169, 179, 184–185

Wallerstein, Immanuel, xii, xvi, 5, 13–14, 70–71, 89–90, 153, 166–168, 180–183, 189–191, 198–199
Wall Street, 78, 80–81, 199–200
Wealth, 7–8, 18, 20, 43, 57t, 62, 64–66, 95, 105–107, 114, 119, 127, 132–133, 172, 183, 185
White nation, 12, 175–176
Whiteness, xvii, 15, 20–21, 23, 40, 116, 157
White world supremacy, xii–xiii, xvii, 5, 17–20, 24, 90, 95, 154, 164, 171–173, 175, 213n6
Workers, 13, 23, 59, 98, 159, 161, 163, 179, 194–196, 208
Working classes, xiii, xv–xvi, 10, 25, 55, 65, 75, 161, 163, 178, 190, 197, 204
World, one, 133
World economy, 25, 69, 75, 89, 163, 166, 183, 190
World Left, 94, 180–181, 189, 192
World power, 3, 71, 133, 172–173
World Social Forum, 175
World-system, 5, 13, 15–16, 24–26, 69, 152–154, 156, 159, 167–168, 171–172, 174–175, 183, 190–191, 193, 197–198; modern world-system, 24, 166
World War I, 93, 160, 190
World War II, 37, 56, 93, 158, 174, 194

Youth, 146–147, 184, 195, 197, 203
Youth Organization for Black Unity, xiv, 189

Melanie E. L. Bush is an Associate Professor in the Department of Anthropology and Sociology at Adelphi University and the author of *Everyday Forms of Whiteness: Understanding Race in a "Post-Racial" World* (the second edition of *Breaking the Code of Good Intentions: Everyday Forms of Whiteness*).

Roderick D. Bush (1945–2013) was a Professor in the Department of Sociology and Anthropology at St. John's University and the author of *The End of White World Supremacy: Black Internationalism and the Problem of the Color Line* (Temple), which won the Paul Sweezy Marxist Sociology Book Award from the American Sociological Association. Visit his website at http://rodbush.org/.